The Archaeology of American Capitalism

The American Experience in Archaeological Perspective

UNIVERSITY PRESS OF FLORIDA

Florida A&M University, Tallahassee
Florida Atlantic University, Boca Raton
Florida Gulf Coast University, Ft. Myers
Florida International University, Miami
Florida State University, Tallahassee
New College of Florida, Sarasota
University of Central Florida, Orlando
University of Florida, Gainesville
University of North Florida, Jacksonville
University of South Florida, Tampa
University of West Florida, Pensacola

The Archaeology of American Capitalism

Christopher N. Matthews

Foreword by Michael S. Nassaney

University Press of Florida
Gainesville/Tallahassee/Tampa/Boca Raton
Pensacola/Orlando/Miami/Jacksonville/Ft. Myers/Sarasota

Copyright 2010 by Christopher N. Matthews
All rights reserved
Published in the United States of America

First cloth printing, 2010
First paperback printing, 2012

30 29 28 27 26 25   7 6 5 4 3 2

Library of Congress Cataloging-in-Publication Data
Matthews, Christopher N., 1965–
The archaeology of American capitalism / Christopher N. Matthews ; foreword by Michael S. Nassaney.
p. cm.—(The American experience in archaeological perspective)
Includes bibliographical references and index.
ISBN 978-0-8130-3524-6 (cloth)
ISBN 978-0-8130-4416-3 (pbk.)
1. Archaeology and history—United States. 2. Social archaeology—United States. 3. Archaeology—Moral and ethical aspects—United States. 4. Capitalism
—Social aspects—United States—History. 5. Self—United States—History.
6. Community life—United States—History. 7. Success—United States—History. 8. Material culture—United States—History. 9. Landscapes—United States—History. 10. United States—Antiquities. I. Title.
E159.5.M295 2010
973—dc22   2010016591

The University Press of Florida is the scholarly publishing agency for the State University System of Florida, comprising Florida A&M University, Florida Atlantic University, Florida Gulf Coast University, Florida International University, Florida State University, New College of Florida, University of Central Florida, University of Florida, University of North Florida, University of South Florida, and University of West Florida.

University Press of Florida
2046 NE Waldo Road
Suite 2100
Gainesville, FL 32609
http://upress.ufl.edu

Contents

List of Illustrations	vii
Foreword	ix
Acknowledgments	xiii
Introduction	1
1. Freedom, Culture, and the Authentic Self in Capitalism	9
2. The Expansion of Capitalism and the Inventions of America	27
3. Georgian Practice: Defining Nature in Colonial America	57
4. The Capitalist Metropolis	85
5. Translating Survival into Success: The Archaeology of Victorious Capitalism	116
6. Communities Outside Capitalism: Archaeologies of Resistance	149
7. The Archaeology of Race and African American Resistance	177
8. Archaeology and Ethics within and against Capitalism	195
Conclusion: The Materialization of Capitalism	227
Bibliography	231
Index	251

Illustrations

Figure 2.1. Plan of burials at Narragansett Cemetery   33

Figure 2.2. Prestige artifacts from Mohawk Indian Castle site   53

Figure 3.1. Westover, a Georgian manor house   60

Figure 3.2. Floor plan of Fairbanks House in Dedham, Massachusetts   63

Figure 3.3. Bordley-Randall House in Annapolis, Maryland   66

Figure 3.4. Mott farmhouse in Portsmouth, Rhode Island   68

Figure 3.5. Matched set of Creamware plates   74

Figure 3.6. Common decorated ceramics from late eighteenth and early nineteenth century   75

Figure 3.7. Chase-Lloyd House in Annapolis, Maryland   81

Figure 4.1. Map of New York City in 1833   92

Figure 4.2. Midsummer in the Five Points, 1873   93

Figure 4.3. White granite tea and tableware forms in the popular Gothic pattern   97

Figure 4.4. Trinity Church at the west end of Wall Street in New York, 1847   98

Figure 4.5. Features at Lot 6 in Five Points, New York City   103

Figure 4.6. Personal artifacts from Five Points site, New York City   107

Figure 5.1. An 1876 bird's-eye view of Lowell Manufacturing District   126

Figure 5.2. Diverse housing plans for mill employees at Lowell   127

Figure 5.3. Layout of Alabama Gates labor camp   137

Figure 5.4. Reinhart Ranch, Paradise, Nevada   144

Figure 6.1. An 1884 Sanborn insurance map of the John Russell Cutlery Factory   154

Figure 6.2. Wasters and knife blades from Russell Cutlery site 155

Figure 6.3. Teacups from Greenwich Village, New York City. 160

Figure 6.4. Plans for a "Christian House" and "a rational kitchen" from Beecher and Stowe's *The American Woman's Home*, 1869 165

Figure 6.5. An 1857 landscape at Canterbury Village, New Hampshire 170

Figure 6.6. Archaeological survey map of Canterbury Shaker Village 171

Figure 6.7. Fragments of redware tobacco pipes from Canterbury Shaker Village 174

Figure 7.1. Colonoware copy in the style of the delft English-made vessel 181

Figure 7.2. Incised colonoware bowl 184

Figure 7.3. Artifacts constituting a *minkisi* bundle 186

Figure 7.4. *An evening thought*, a poem by Jupiter Hammon 190

Figure 8.1. Bird's-eye view of Central Park in New York City, 1863 204

Figure 8.2. Luxor Casino, Las Vegas, Nevada 210

Figure 8.3. Ground Zero memorials 219

Figure 8.4. Design for the New York African Burial Ground Memorial 223

Table 1. RI-1000 Burials 38

Foreword

In their pursuit of the science of humankind, anthropologists have sought to distinguish the cultural and natural elements of human experience. Paradoxically, culture—as an extrasomatic means of human adaptation—creates the illusion whereby the constructed, artificial, arbitrary, albeit historically constituted practices of daily life are made to seem natural to insiders who take for granted the subtle cues that orient us to the world. Perhaps the most powerful illusion that contemporary Americans literally labor under is capitalism, an economic and social order geared for the creation of private profit that has been pervasive in structuring consumption patterns and landscapes since European encounters with indigenous peoples in the seventeenth century. Social scientists of various stripes would be remiss if they did not accord this phenomenon serious consideration in examining the constitution of society. Yet, just as capitalism erodes alternative forms of social interaction based in collective traditions of production and exchange, so too does it cover its tracks, making it notoriously difficult to monitor its pernicious social effects.

While untold gallons of ink have been spilled upon countless reams of paper under the capitalism regime, much of this writing serves to rationalize and reproduce the naturalization of the individual. In *The Archaeology of American Capitalism*, Christopher N. Matthews challenges archaeologists to use the tools at their disposal to move the discipline toward more ethical goals through a restoration of the justice that capitalism denies those working- and middle-class Americans who lack the resources to build alternatives to the systems of their oppression. Matthews begins with the bold and persuasive premise that capitalism is first and foremost a material process whereby people use the market to obtain the means to distinguish themselves from family and peers—that is, through the acquisition of commodities we can become who we believe we really are. Drawing on Marx, Weber, and other pertinent theorists, Matthews demonstrates the centrality of the promotion of the self in the creation of a new subjectivity under capitalism whereby everyone attains individuality by severing the "natural" bonds of the world into which they were born. Moreover, he argues, although the individual in capitalism is a powerful ideology, it is one that archaeology can be used to subvert.

The history of America is the history of engagement with material objects such as glass beads, ornate gardens, ceramic place settings, rubbish-filled back lots of tenements, alcohol bottles in old privies, and ruined knife blanks in waster heaps. The archaeological record of capitalism consists of the ways in which these and other materials were employed by people to construct themselves abstractly. They represent the means by which people became depersonalized commodities, and reveal how people used material culture to produce their individuality by forming relations with desirable objects. For historical archaeologists, this record documents the origins and developments of capitalism that are missing from or hidden by written accounts.

Employing case studies and plausible reanalyses from the seventeenth century to the present which examine various regions of the nation, Matthews demonstrates how individual distinction along class and racial lines was produced through material culture, examines signs of material resistance, and questions how archaeology reproduces capitalist relations. He posits that the fur trade, motivated by a desire for prestige, entangled Indians in the capitalist organization of Euro-American culture. As European activities made it increasingly difficult for Native Americans to sustain former ways of life, the evidence suggests that competition and notions of private property arose among them, and new forms of work positioned them in specialized roles in the capitalist division of labor. Ultimately, though not inevitably, social inequalities emerged that challenged communalism and relations of reciprocity—hallmarks of precapitalist modes of production.

Similarly, on the eve of the Revolution, colonial America underwent transformations that deepened the commitment to individual segregation at the expense of corporate models of behavior. For example, new labor relations led to the construction of more permanent buildings that no longer required the frequent maintenance that lent coherence to the community and underscored interdependency. Symbolically powerful didactic apparatuses such as place settings sent the message that diners were just interchangeable parts. The penetration of capitalist ideals was fully realized when these principles came to dominate everyday social life through the material construction of the domestic sphere and the spatial segregation of production, commerce, residence, and leisure, all of which can be read in changing landscape patterns, particularly in urban America.

The division between those who own the means of production and those who sell their labor lies at the root of capitalist culture. The abstraction of labor established that all were free to compete in the market in order to survive. In so doing, survival and reproduction were shifted from social to personal responsibilities. Capitalism also encouraged one to own the material requirements for respectability and to know how to use them, which led to the proliferation of etiquette books in the nineteenth century. Another result was the expansion of the market for products and services that would improve the quality of life, thereby naturalizing the capitalist foundations that led to increased consumption. Property-owning households embraced the rhetoric that tied well-being and virtue to cleanliness and sanitation, while unprecedented crowding and accordingly unsanitary conditions among the working class promoted the spread of disease and naturalized their condition.

Unsurprisingly, worker alienation was met with various responses that underscore efforts to assert agency in the face of exploitation. In the American West, miners and other disenfranchised workers like prostitutes turned to alcohol and other vices to ready their bodies and psyches for another day in the mines and brothels. The unskilled labor requirements of the frontier, coupled with limited investment in infrastructure and services, reveal that the West was an underdeveloped periphery characteristic of capitalist spatial organization globally. As is often the case in such marginal regions, what Westerners produced they did not consume, and what they consumed they did not produce, testifying to their role in broader economic markets.

The capitalist juggernaut has been continuously critiqued and rejected by segments of the populace. Archaeology is well poised to ascertain the efficacy of these resistance efforts. Laborers sought to regain some autonomy over their activities on the shop floor and often engaged in a dissident culture that harbored a hidden transcript which was used as a means of empowerment, albeit constrained by broader hegemonic power structures. Likewise, female reformers sought to create a community opposed to capitalism, and utopian experiments abound in nineteenth-century America. When women sought to establish the Ladies Library Association in Kalamazoo, Michigan, in the 1850s, they were encouraged by wealthy husbands to locate it not in the rural setting they proposed, but rather near the town square, so as to be under better surveillance should their readings become too subversive. The limits placed on alternative societal visions cannot be underestimated. Lest we miscalculate the power of capitalism when examining forms of resistance, we should be reminded that "capitalism was by no means a wimpy system," as a colleague once quipped.

Are we destined to labor under this system indefinitely? To what extent can a critical archaeology assist in piercing the ideology and transforming the practice into "right relations," to quote a ministerial friend of mine? Archaeology has long been a middle-class pursuit that simultaneously highlights human-driven progress and potential as well as the universal experience of humankind as it aspires to expose the roots of the capitalist bourgeoisie's ethos. Suffice it to say that the past should not be left to just anyone to recover and interpret. Increased community involvement in archaeological projects is having an impact on the sites that are examined, the questions that are being asked, the analyses that are being proposed, and the interpretations that are consistent with ways of thinking which lie outside of narrowly defined power structures mirroring capitalist concerns. As Matthews notes, in some cases burying or forgetting the past was an intentional act to dispose of evidence of wrongdoing. Perhaps so, but recovery is nonetheless necessary and often cathartic. Heritage sites need not be places to wallow in injustice, but rather can provide impetus to challenge inequities and create a new world in which community plays a central role and the isolated individual is recognized as an artificial construct of capitalism.

Michael S. Nassaney
Series Editor

Acknowledgments

This book grew out of my efforts in introductory and field archaeology courses at Hofstra University. My students' positive responses and comments on the material and how it describes the origins and materiality of so much of their experience in modern America deserve a great deal of credit, since they influenced how I structured and composed the text. I am also grateful to Michael Nassaney, Zoë Burkholder, Paul Mullins, Chuck Orser, Jenna Coplin, Mark Leone, Suzanne Spencer-Wood, Kurt Jordan, Nan Rothschild, Margaret Purser, and Patricia Rubertone for giving their time and attention to help make this a better book than I could have produced on my own. I also gleaned a great deal from my conversations on archaeology, capitalism, and modernity with Matthew Palus, Douglas Bolender, Sam Rebovich, Francois Richard, Sharryn Kasmir, Cheryl Mwaria, Maggie Abraham, Kirk Dombroski, Quetzil Castañeda, Lisa Breglia, Carol McDavid, Patti Jeppeson, Mark Warner, Rebecca Yamin, Anne Pyburn, Larry Zimmerman, Richard Handler, Kelly Britt, Shannon Lee Dawdy, Diana Loren, Bob Paynter, Warren Perry, Jim Moore, Warren DeBoer, Lindsey Weiss, Sarah Croucher, Dave Gadsby, Paul Shackel, Barbara Little, Jodi Barnes, Mark Hauser, Terry Weik, Randy McGuire, Rheinhard Bernbeck, Steve Mrozowski, Steve Silliman, and Chris DeCorse. Research and writing support was provided by the Hofstra College of Liberal Arts and Sciences as well as my colleagues in the Hofstra University Department of Anthropology.

I am grateful for assistance in acquiring the illustrations used in this book from Patricia Rubertone, Dean Snow, Melody Henkel, David Landon, Diana Wall, Rex Metcalf, Jenna Coplin, David Starbuck, Rebecca

Yamin, Leland Ferguson, Michael Nassaney, Margaret Purser, Thad Van Bueren, Suzanne Spencer-Wood, Ross Rava, Cornelius Holtorf, Beth Giard (Harriet Beecher Stowe Center), Jill Slaight (New York Historical Society), Stephan Saks (New York Public Library), and Rodney Leon. Thanks to Jamie Atkinson for her assistance in preparing the index.

Finally, I dedicate this book with love to Zoë, Dexter, and Hollis.

Introduction

> Man, in his *most intimate* reality in civic society, is a profane being. Here, where he appears both to himself and to others as a real individual, he is an *illusory* phenomenon.
>
> Karl Marx, *On the Jewish Question*

Over the last five hundred years, capitalism has become the most dominant social and economic force in the world, and the American historical experience best exemplifies the development of a nation-state based in a culture of capitalism. Capitalism's far reach is a result of its function as an economic order and social system explicitly geared for the creation of private profit, an emphasis that challenges and erodes alternative forms of production and social life based in collective and local traditions of production and exchange. Capitalism furthermore instituted a prevailing subjectivity based on possessive individualism, a rational objectification of social relations, and an embrace of fixed identities (MacPherson 1962, Althusser 1971, Wolf 1982, Leone 2005).

Historical archaeology provides a powerful method for tracing and critically understanding the development of American capitalism. Analyzing material culture such as architecture, settlements, landscapes, tools, machinery, burials, and artwork, as well as common household goods such as ceramics, glassware, and food remains, archaeology examines objects that, as commodities, implicated persons in meaningful capitalist systems of production, distribution, and consumption. Additionally, as archaeology penetrates the largely hidden everyday lives of past people through the recovery of the lost, buried, and forgotten traces of their social life, it exposes how capitalism emerged and replaced other forms of social organization and practice. Moreover, since it involves an intimate consideration of the human engagement with specific places and objects, archaeology allows for an understanding of the nuanced and mostly undocumented textures of social life, environmental relations, ideas, and ideals that can explain the specific events and processes that moved people to embrace their own commodification as individuals and, in some instances, how they resisted their capitalist transformation by developing alternative methods of sustaining a meaningful social life outside of the market. In fact, the tension between a community's control of its vital resources and the introduction of these resources into the market is the principal framework by which capitalism emerged and with which it should be studied.

This book considers the historical archaeology of capitalism in the making of modern America. I explain first how archaeologists may theoretically approach capitalism as a problem of subjectivity, specifically the making of individuals within yet against their own communities. I then present a sweeping and roughly chronological array of American material patterns from diverse settings to reveal the development of and resistance to capitalism in productive and social life. The theoretical basis of this book lies in an argument distilled from the work of Karl Marx and Max Weber presented in chapter 1. These foundational critics established that the study of capitalism requires its consideration as a revolutionary social phenomenon that transformed work from self-affirming and community-producing efforts to a devalued employment determined by an impersonal labor market. Marx and Weber describe the basic processes by which the ability of persons and communities to control the resources required for their reproduction was degraded, as well as the ideological mechanisms developed to rationalize and naturalize subsequent exploitative capitalist social relations.

I argue that the most potent ideological construction connected to capitalism is the naturalization of the individual as the starting point and purpose of production and social relations. As individuals, persons in capitalism imagine that they actively and freely construct themselves in order to exist in society (see Handsman 1981, Leone 2005). Any preexisting or what I call "natural" relations with kin and community are rebuffed, only to be deployed along with other appropriated markers of identity when they are advantageous attributes in the production of distinction within the market (Bourdieu 1984). In a society of individuals, the issue of authenticity therefore becomes paramount (Berman 1970, 1982). Severed from their "natural" conditions and communities, it is always a question of whether people actually are who they say they are or appear to be. As the focus of attention in socialization and meaning-making shifts from work, skill, knowledge, and material life to competency in discourse and interpretive symbolic expression, persons in capitalist societies are poised in a space between their material reality and the hoped-for ideas they construct of themselves despite that reality (Berman 1982, Leone 2005). This process has manifold material consequences since the encounter with and use of objects builds the world *as well as* the imagined roles people construct and adopt to identify themselves within it. As experts in the observation of modern material life and the interpretation of its meaning, historical archaeologists are extremely well-placed to recover and record the details and contours of the American capitalist experience. Guided by a theory of capitalist individual materiality, this book examines a broad range of examples that demonstrate this theory to be quite sound.

I coalesce my approach to an archaeology of capitalism around the idea that the material culture of capitalist American life has three simultaneous and competing levels of meaning that record the emergence of capitalism and its expansion to dominance. At the base of this tripartite meaning construct, all objects are what they are made of and what they were intended to be used for. Marx called this "use-value" and included especially the labor of human beings required for reproduction and happiness. A second level, seized on by capitalism but not exclusive to it, is the value of an object in relation to others in terms of its relative (usually monetary) worth. Marx called this "exchange-value" and included here the appropriated labor of individuals that came to be exchanged in the market for a wage that afforded them the objects required for life and happiness. In Marx's classic formulation, the primacy of exchange value in capitalism was based in the transformation of objects into commodities—that is, objects whose value was determined more by their place in the market than by their usefulness in work and other productions. Building on commoditization, a third level, perhaps unique to capitalism, comprises the attributes of objects that allow things to stand in for people. Marx called this "commodity fetishism," or the sense that those attributes of social production that make it possible to value skill and knowledge and recognize distinction become endowed not in the makers of objects or even their users, but rather *in the objects themselves*. It is the elicited associations of things that people seek to be connected with to construct themselves, making objects into agents, if not de facto citizens, in capitalist culture.

An analysis of the use, exchange, and fetishization of objects long ago lost and buried in American soil is the focus of this book.

In chapter 2 I examine the beginning of American capitalism as it was crafted in the Indian trade in furs and other extracted natural products. I focus on the simultaneous inclusion and exclusion of Native American people perpetrated by European traders, merchants, and colonial political authorities. Settlers were as eager to trade with Indians as Indians were to trade with settlers. However, Indian efforts to control the trade were rejected until these efforts evidenced conformity to individual commodification as well. Drawing on archaeological studies of Narragansetts in seventeenth-century Rhode Island and Mohawks in eighteenth-century upstate New York, I illustrate a history of marginality that ultimately produced great wealth and new possessions for the settlers, yet little more than an outsider Indian identity, as a sign of an imposed nonconformity, even for those Native Americans who fervently joined in trade.

In chapter 3 I turn from the expropriation of Native Americans to that of the middling and poor within colonial American society. Examining the classic studies of Georgianization by archaeologists James Deetz and Mark Leone, this chapter explores the use of material objects to naturalize a social order of inequality and exploitative labor relations. Drawing from my own research in Annapolis, Maryland, I present a particular biography of a stone foundation at the Thomas Bordley house illustrating how capitalist class formation can be read from the material culture of distinction. I follow this with a discussion of Deetz and Leone's analysis of Georgian-era ceramics and gardens to illustrate the material segregation of the individual from the corporate structure of the family, as well as how the individual came to stand in as an empirical subject of nature and a citizen of the natural American capitalist republic.

Chapter 4 traces forward the processes of capitalist segregation outlined by Deetz and Leone with a close examination of the making of an American capitalist city in New York. New York City changed radically in the early nineteenth century, growing from an important trading port in 1790 to an incipient industrial metropolis by 1850. This transformation has been examined archaeologically by Diana diZerega Wall, who focused especially on the reconstruction of society through the segregation of the home and workplace. This now-ingrained middle-class settlement pattern was a radical change intimately related to the capitalist transformation of city life. Also endemic to the making of the metropolis was the emergence of working-class residential neighborhoods, colloquially known as slums. Rebecca Yamin's excavation of several tenement structures in Five Points, a notorious New York neighborhood mostly occupied by impoverished recent immigrants, reveals that the world of working people was very much geared toward the symbolization of respectability. Archaeologists unearthed a wide range of objects that show an embrace of emergent middle-class norms, items notably at odds with the working-class status of their owners. Also recovered were occasional signs of ethnic identity. I bring these strands together by arguing that ethnicity in Five Points was one of many ways for individuals to gain an affiliation that could lead to work. As such, expressions of Irish or German heritage were less about memory of the past than hoped-for associations that proved effective in negotiating the working-class labor market.

By the end of chapter 4, I have shifted my discussion from the processes involved in making a culture of capitalism to how those living in the United States negotiated the limits and opportunities presented by an established capitalist social landscape. In chapter 5, I examine archaeologies of everyday life in nineteenth- and early-twentieth-century Washington, D.C., Lowell, Massachusetts, and in mining camps, company towns, and small settlements in California, Nevada, and Arizona. The common theme holding these diverse case studies together is evidence of what Weber called "victorious capitalism," in which sanitation, housing, work opportunities and routines, consumption habits, and community formation were wholly tied up in the profit-making system that enriched the few owners of the means of production. A key theme in this chapter is the consistency of isolation, such that material culture reflects the efforts of individuals and individual households to maintain autonomy. By prizing self-sufficiency over the making of community, the cost of reproduction increased, engendering a system that favored the often distant capitalists who profited thereby.

Having thus far presented a story of capitalist triumph, I turn in chapter 6 to examine archaeologies of resistance, which have documented a range of efforts to construct American communities outside of and against capitalism. Among the most obvious forms of resistance are efforts to challenge the system originating from those most directly exploited by it: deskilled laborers. Michael Nassaney and Marjorie Abel's archaeological examination of the Russell Cutlery factory in Massachusetts shows that workers inscribed a hidden transcript of resistance by intentionally damaging products and creating mountains of waste metal. Another group overtly exploited in the structuring of the American capitalist market was women, who became isolated and ever more dependent on male relations for their well-being. In many urban centers, a reform movement to "make the world homelike" was initiated by middle- and upper-class women aiming to change how home production would function. The failure of these efforts to create change adds an important perspective on the difficulty of challenging the culture of capitalism from within.

Alternative forms of resistance that present greater evidence of success in fact come to light when communities further removed from the center of capitalist interests are examined. Also, these communities formed through an ideological, rather than material, form of resistance to capitalist expropriation. Intentionally isolated communal utopian settlements represent an overt attempt to break from the American capitalist mainstream. Archaeologists have examined many of these sites, which typically show a strict adherence in material culture to the home group's ideology and practice. However, in most cases utopian communities failed after a few years as individuals struggled to maintain their commitments. A much longer-lived community, the Canterbury Shakers in New Hampshire, extensively studied by David Starbuck, shows a patent adherence in many ways to Shaker ideology. Yet Starbuck also shows that the longevity of the community results from its connection to the American mainstream through its marketable products rather than its cultural distinctions. Such connections belie a self-interested, profit-making focus and establish the Shakers as, in actuality, a group only minimally resistant to capitalism.

A more successful and powerful form of resistance, one that in fact illustrates an important critique of the capitalist ideology, has been unearthed in the archaeology of African diaspora in the United States. Drawing from a wide set of sources, I synthesize in chapter 7 an approach to African cultural retentions and religious practices that considers the construction of African American culture as intimately bound to an anticapitalist stance. More than isolated and everyday acts of defiance, I suggest that archaeology shows an ontological alternative embodied in African American consciousness, which presents an astute and powerful critique of their exploitation by the capitalist system both during and after slavery. My study amplifies existing work by considering African American

Christianity as vital to the social networks and critical ontology embodied in African American material culture.

The final chapter considers the ethical concerns that emerge when the history of archaeology as a discipline is tied to the origins and emergence of capitalist domination in the United States. Relationships between capitalist middle-class values, social scientific abstraction, and archaeological cultural constructs reveal a series of parallels that make it hard to imagine an archaeology not in the service of mainstream capitalist interests. Working against this grain, I suggest undertaking an "archaeology of archaeology" by looking at the materiality of the middle-class American culture that largely gave rise to and continues to hold a vital stake in archaeological research and results. I present studies of archaeology's materiality based on archaeologically and historically informed "reconstructions" in modern Las Vegas and late-nineteenth-century Annapolis, Maryland. I conclude this discussion by looking at contradictions in the public meanings of the past, especially new trends in the public commemoration of death. I examine in particular some recent debates related to memorialization of the African Burial Ground National Monument in New York City, giving this as an example of how mainstream conceptions of life and death have been challenged and rethought. This concluding chapter critiques the ethics and practice of archaeology through a reflexive engagement with existing resistance efforts that take aim not only at the oppressive power of the capitalist ruling class, but also at its middle-class technicians, including archaeologists.

The purpose of this book overall is to provide a synthesis of a wide range of studies in historical archaeology that speak to the dynamic processes involved in the making of an American culture of capitalism. I have tried to provide archaeologists working in diverse settings with familiar examples that draw on a variety of topics and analytical techniques to show how the making of capitalism should be considered a vital context in virtually any historical archaeological study of the United States. I draw extensively from published studies, supplementing these with my own research and writing. In some cases I present work in the manner that I believe authors intended it to be taken, but mostly I develop new interpretations of excavated and analyzed data that owe a great debt to those who originally performed and published the work. I am sure not all authors will agree with how I have reinterpreted their original findings, but I have done my best both to work with the materials as they were presented and to produce clear and compelling arguments. Ultimately, this volume also attempts to lay some groundwork for a type of archaeology that does not reify capitalism. I urge that, we, as archaeologists, more seriously engage with our own material worlds to learn how our training, expertise, and privilege alone cannot break a cycle of capitalist reproduction. It will only be through critical self-reflection and the rediscovery of archaeology by archaeologists acting with regard for *persons*—past and present—that the discipline will proceed in this new direction.

1

Freedom, Culture, and the Authentic Self in Capitalism

> To be precise . . . we were now wondering about whether we order our beer, our clothes, our loves and our lives on the basis of just whatever we happen to be used to, or do we make our selections just because some crap designer has stuck his label on whatever it is? Do we, in short, really choose at all, and if so, on what basis? Is there any authenticity of feeling left in a world where bushmen goggle at Baywatch, and every man in the halfway developed world has been systematically bombarded with pictures of half a dozen more or less identical blondes wearing nothing but little pants and underwire bras? And if there is no such thing as real authentic feeling, how can there be anything worth calling Freedom?
>
> James Hawes, *Dead Long Enough*

The archaeology of capitalism in its entirety is an overwhelming topic. Capitalism is really too complex to be summarized in a single archaeology. It is an economic system (Smith 2003), a social system (McGuire 1992), a mode of life (Marx 1967), and an ideology (Marx 1967, Marx and Engels 1967b, Weber 2003, Althusser 1971, Eagleton 1991). It is also all of these things at once. Furthermore, over the last five hundred years capitalism has reached virtually every corner of the globe (Wolf 1982, Orser 1996, Falk 1991, Frank 1978, Wallerstein 1974). It has affected directly or, in the sense that it casts a "general light" over all modern life (Marx 1973: 43), indirectly the whole of humanity in the recent past. This book, therefore, is not an archaeological study of capitalism writ large, for no book could be. It is rather about a common unifying feature in global capitalism that allows its historically unprecedented reach to be manageably approached and at least in part explained. Capitalism involves the promotion of a very basic sort of subjectivity, or a theory and practice of the self. Summarized simply, the subject of capitalism is the individual: specifically, when persons begin to regard their self-interest as distinct from the interests of their family and community, they are behaving as individuals. When this occurs in a context where value is largely determined by the market for commodities, especially human labor, the self is a capitalist individual. When persons use the market to obtain the means by which they distinguish themselves from their family and peers, then the self is authenticated by capitalism. In this book, I argue that this is a material process, one that creates a distinct and recoverable record. Thus, the study of the making of individuals in capitalism requires the perspective of archaeologists to be fully brought into view.

This book illustrates how historical archaeology examines the capitalist self in the United States. Drawing on a wide range of examples from the colonial to the modern era, from cities to the frontier, from the powerful to the weak, I focus on the rise and development of capitalism in America as well as the construction of individuals within and against the interests of their communities. Evidence from the remains of houses, landscapes, bodies, tools, household artifacts, activities, and professions depicts the largely unrecorded locations where the capitalist negotiation between individual and community took place. I emphasize throughout that revealing this story requires archaeology, because the individual self in capitalism is a powerful foundational ideology, one that this field is well-placed to subvert and help us to move beyond. This ideology peddles the sense that the lone individual, constructed as unencumbered and "free" in the context of capitalism, actually exists and is thus the natural starting point for productive social life. Those who created and organized the documentary record subscribed to this ideology, for the individual's ownership of self, property, and belongings underwrites much of what is officially documented in wills, probates, land records, taxes, ledgers, censuses, membership rolls, subscriptions, even diaries and novels (see Johnson 1996, Handsman 1983, Bhaktin 1981). These documents establish that the individual (as opposed to the community) is a legitimate and rightful owner as much as they establish what any given individual owns or owes. In other words, most historic documents assume and thus follow after the making of the individuals whose lives and actions they record. We require other records to understand how such individuals are actually constructed. It is thus from the undocumented remains that are lost, buried, or otherwise forgotten that we can gather an understanding of the processes that manufactured such individuals from within and against their original communities (Deetz 1996, Leone and Potter 1988).

Notably, the very process of creating individuals establishes capitalism as a distinct social formation. This chapter considers the theoretical basis of this process found in classic works of Karl Marx and Max Weber. In describing their contributions I seek to provide archaeologists with a means for conceptualizing and recognizing the material processes involved in the making of individuals in capitalist societies. Moreover, in elucidating Marx and Weber's standpoint on individuation in capitalism, I hope to show how archaeology may help to develop a perspective which challenges the ideology of individualism and reconnects persons with the concrete material communities that they are in fact already involved with.

Authenticity and Commodification

I wish to begin with a discussion of the opening extract from the novel *Dead Long Enough*, by James Hawes (2000). The book considers feeling deadened by modern life, and, because one of the four main characters is an archaeologist, I think it is pertinent to this study. The extract is a commentary aside within the book; its language is not characteristic of the rest of the text, and the comment is dismissed as rubbish immediately after it is presented. This dismissal describes the main premise of the novel: namely, that looking at the social ills of society causes modern people to feel dead since they are largely powerless to do anything about them, resulting simply in impotent observation and/or creative deconstruction, which stand in for "experiencing" life. I want to consider the implications of this extract in some detail, because Hawes' commentary on the failure of authenticity and the impact of commodification yields some observations important for understanding the making of individuals in a capitalist system. The capitalist sense of reality he describes—as representation rather than concrete material substance—offers a systematic way to approach the self in capitalism through its archaeological remains.

Hawes associates authenticity with freedom. While freedom is often conceived of as a freedom of choice, Hawes leads us past this simplistic notion to the problem of *feeling* free, which he pairs quite nicely with feeling dead. In the extract Hawes describes the problematic posed by modern freedom. We may take freedom to mean having options—whether to do this or that—which are moments in everyday life that bring a social consciousness to light. Making choices, we become aware of ourselves as people who selected this rather than that. This may at first seem petty. Most would say that persons are much more substantial than the result of their superficial selection of Rice Krispies rather than Cocoa Puffs or transfer-printed rather than shell-edged table wares, and I agree. Yet the belief in a more substantial depth to the self is exactly where the issue of authenticity comes into play. The notion of authenticity suggests that individually we are actually something real (Berman 1970, 1982). Here I disagree. I argue that this reality is instead the primary ideology, or mystification, of capitalism, and it is the reality of individualism.

In the Hawes extract, the narrator discovers that his choices do not represent freedom, but are rather dictated by the marketing agendas, or the specific distinguishing mechanisms, of commodity producers. This discovery tells us something more: that the choice of one product over another is a meaningful enactment of the self in capitalist society. Purchasing and consuming commodities, individuals act out the roles modern society offers for our selection: for example, rugged or docile, strong or mild, natural or artificial. In capitalism, products must be more than just useful to succeed as a commodity. A profitable product must evoke an association with some valued aspect of the culture (perhaps the best example is Coca-Cola's recent claim to be "the real thing"). Moreover, this power of association must be available to the consumers, who may freely associate themselves with those values through the acquisition of commercial products. What ruins everything for the narrator is that coming to understand the arbitrary associations of commodities with cultural values is also a realization that the commodity serves as a vehicle for his self-discovery. Its practical use is secondary to how it is used to construct the self (Miller 1987, Mullins 1999, McCracken 1990). Most destructive for the narrator is the realization that it is not only simple consumer products that serve this function of self-discovery. This process of individuation is equally evident in his relationships with others and even himself—what he finds and wants in people are traits not simply represented by commodities, but revealed through them. Personal qualities are only made real by the associations made between commodities and the meanings derived from the market.

In capitalism, commodities create meaning such that the things we consume include our social relations. Just as varying products are specified as containing certain characteristics, friends are types of friends, lovers are types of lovers, colleagues are types of colleagues, and the subject is a type of self. Far from authentic, the self becomes a replica or simulacrum of an image created by marketing specialists (including archaeologists and other brokers of social differentiation in the academy) seeking to associate meanings with things. For the narrator in *Dead Long Enough*, he, his friends (including the novel's archaeologist), and everyone else are commodities available for consumption, products representing the given qualities they would like to be associated with. His feelings for women in lingerie, for example, are counterfeit emotions, as the value of these women is not their person, their bodies, their sexuality, or their beauty, but rather the way these characteristics reveal associations he desires to have with himself. His values and even his feelings are inauthentic, merely associations that represent an affiliation with supposedly common and therefore natural yet individualized desires.

Hawes' description of the alienation of persons from their concrete social relations outlines the symbolic removal of the self from its material conditions which is involved in the making of individuals in capitalist society. On the one hand, objects are produced in the market not to meet demand, but to create desire for the pleasing image persons have of themselves in association with that object. On the other hand, the produced desire does not reside, as is normally assumed, within consumers, but is external in that it defines their relationship with the market *as* consumers. Consumption does not satisfy a demand for a product, as such, but rather for the consumer's affiliation with what the product represents. Ultimately, market participation enables an association of the self with meaningful belief and action, which is a product, if not the focus, of the market (Wurst and McGuire 1999).

Notably, most cultural systems operate along similar lines of meaning production (see Geertz 1973, Holland et al. 1998). Persons in virtually every cultural context are constructed through particular intersubjective relationships with peers, elders, enemies, spirits, and so forth. What is unique to capitalism is that these "intersubjective" relations are with things that stand in for people, specifically the commodities that help us to become the persons we believe we really are. In this way the self constructed in capitalism is twice removed from its material conditions: once by the market, which presents a limited range of possibilities in the form of competitive products, and again by persons themselves, who use their choice of products to "represent" who they really are to themselves and others. Furthermore, as this double removal of the self is bound to the common interest in the generation of profit, alienation of this sort is essential to creating wealth and the successful reproduction of capitalism.

In *Dead Long Enough*, this realization is a disaster for the characters, who face it with a mocking ambivalence by forcing meaningful engagements through reunions held in tourist destinations chosen solely to contextualize or give a storied backdrop to their relationships. Hawes is making the point that for the majority living in capitalism, this realization is uncommon, since as a system of production and a "culture," capitalism seems to make sense. It offers ample rewards for participation, including the potential for material wealth and comfort, and, more powerfully, it supports a very accessible sense of freedom in the form of self-reliance. Seemingly a system with few restrictions, capitalism appears to be undirected and thus the result of individuals freely associating with each other and guided by their self-interests (Smith 2003). Here again we confront the problem of authenticity. Seeing the self as an individual means that all social relations are "artificial," in the sense that *any* relationship is between self-directed, independent persons. Relations in this context are constructed by distinct individuals who, each believes, have entered into them freely. Elided here is that it is only through such artificial relations that individuals may actually exist. Beyond this contradiction, embedded in the modern relations of individuals is their non-modern antithesis: the unselected, social ties that encumber individual freedom typified by kin and community. However, family, community, and culture, if taken seriously, are not just an individual's background or heritage, but the real social conditions that frame their interests, opportunities, and responsibilities. They are the basis, that is, of that person's actual subjectivity. Yet these potentially "natural" relations have no place in a rational capitalist society, especially not in its productive realms. However, it is difficult to imagine what components of society are not related to production when we consider production in more than rational, economic terms—that is, as social reproduction through which persons are born, raised, labor, and ideally thrive within a system that is dialectically constructed by these very activities. This approach to society, which draws on Marxist anthropological theory (see, for example, Wolf 1982, Roseberry 1989, Sider 1994), regards the whole of social life as production and thus as relevant to the construction of culture and meaning.

Individualism rejects understanding the self as a social and cultural product in favor of a novel sense of self defined through personal freedom. Again, we often think here of freedom of choice, and this has relevance in that modern individuals appear to choose whether and how they engage and break off relations with others, including kin and community. However, underlying these relations is a much more profound sense of freedom that lies at the heart of capitalism. To explain this conceptualization I turn to a discussion of the way Karl Marx and Max Weber describe the making of individuals and freedom in capitalist society. I follow this with a sketch of a theory of the archaeology of capitalism that informs the case studies in the chapters that follow.

Marx: Abstraction, Labor, and Property

Individual freedom in capitalism is founded on the distinction Karl Marx makes between the use-value of objects and the exchange-value of commodities. Every object has some use: an automobile transports, the gasoline it burns creates energy, the pumping pistons power the wheels, the steering mechanism allows the vehicle to turn. These characteristics are specific qualities that reveal these objects' use-value. Gasoline cannot turn the car any more than the steering mechanism can power the wheels. These qualities are the "natural" aspects of these things, and, as they have unique natures, they cannot be made equivalent except abstractly, as in, "the steering mechanism is as good at turning the car as the gasoline is at producing energy." Capitalism reforms this understanding by making these qualitative aspects, the parts' use-value, less significant than the equivalence of their abstract aspects, known as their exchange-value. Exchange-value imposes a *quantitative* sense on things that allows them to become equivalent in reference to a common value—usually currency. Money establishes, for example, that a wonderfully effective steering mechanism is worth the same amount as are fifty gallons of gasoline. This assignment of value makes otherwise naturally distinct items theoretically equivalent as commodities.

Marx argues, however, that money by itself does not make things equivalent. Rather, it is that money stands in for a more foundational common factor that underlies all value: human labor. Marx posits that money is human labor in the abstract: "considered solely as the mere expenditure of human labor power, measured in its duration, irrespective of the concrete character of the work done" (Sayer 1991: 26). He also establishes that this abstract conception of human labor is the basic premise of capitalism. First, abstract human labor translated as money allows for naturally incommensurate things to be qualitatively equivalent as commodities, including labor itself. Second, the abstraction of human labor provides a basis for transforming laboring persons encumbered by natural social relations into individuals, or persons exchangeable for one another in the sense that they are socially free to be treated as commodities.

There is a great deal involved in this capitalist transformation of the self and the abstraction of labor that is detailed in the works of Marx and others (see Marx 1967, 1973, Marx and Engels 1967a, Simmel 1969, Thompson 1993, Williams 1973, 1976, Berman 1982, Sayer 1987, 1991). My focus here is on what freedom means within capitalism, and how this relates to the making of individuals and authentication of individual experience.

In *Capital*, Marx writes: "For the conversion of his money into capital . . . the owner of money must meet in the market with the free laborer, free in the double sense, that as a free man he can dispose of his labor-power as his own commodity, and that on the other hand he has no other commodity for sale, is short of everything necessary for the realization of his labor-power" (Marx 1967: 169). Having the capacity "to dispose of his labor-power as his own commodity" means that a worker may freely sell his or her labor on the market to a labor-purchaser, or capitalist. Capitalists require labor to operate the means of production they own—that is, the tools, machines, and other facilities that produce new commodities. From the perspective of the capitalist, these objects, along with the labor costs required to operate them, make up the investment he or she has made in commodity production. Thus, the labor a capitalist purchases is considered relatively equivalent to the machines and tools his or her laborers use, and all of these transactions, as costs of production, are similarly commodified. Significantly, the purpose of this system is not the production of new commodities for their use-value, but the production of money in the form of profit resulting from the sale of the commodities for more than they cost to produce. The basis of commodity production in capitalism as such is defined entirely by exchange-value, or the relative equivalence of all things to each other, including human labor.

From the capitalist's perspective, this is a straightforward, rational process. However, considering that the root basis of value is human labor, Marx reflects on the revolutionary character of capitalism. His focus is on how a laborer becomes free, which draws on the second half of the extract from *Capital* above. To have "no other commodity for sale" and be "short of everything necessary for the realization of his labor-power" describes a condition of poverty (Katz 1990, Goode and Maskovsky 2001, Grusky and Kanbur 2006). Marx explains that noncapitalist systems fail to produce poverty in this sense. While famine, violence, and what has been portrayed as a short, brutish existence may have been common in such systems (Hobbes 1996), poverty as it is now known was not, because such a state requires the particular characteristics that define the relationship between capital and labor. Laborers in capitalism are defined not by the work they perform, but by the necessity that they enter into a market-based relationship with a capitalist who will purchase their labor to be able to work at all. A laborer in this sense is free because he or she has nothing else which they may sell in the market, a position that Marx argues follows the "Decomposition of the Original Union between the Laboring Man and His Instruments of Labor" (Marx 1865, cited in Sayer 1991: 34). In other words, because workers are severed from the means of their own reproduction, be it the tools or skills of a trade, and, additionally, lack the substantial social relationships of family and/or community that might otherwise sustain them, they become "free" to affiliate with capital. This situation reverses the primacy of concrete labor over abstract labor in human life. In noncapitalist systems, concrete human labor directly produces the materials and conditions required for social life and reproduction. In capitalism, conversely, abstract labor generates the conditions of reproduction, because all production is conceived of as commodity production, wherein objects are produced not for direct use, but for sale, including human labor. Therefore, to produce the self and build social relations with others, laboring subjects must be conceived of abstractly in terms of capital.

The point to focus on here is the doubleness of existence which capitalism demands of its human subjects. Within capitalism persons simultaneously act out *and* construct their lives; while they inhabit the world concretely in the sense that they act in certain material conditions and social relations, they are also aware of themselves and the world abstractly in the sense that among their material conditions are vital representations that they use to organize and give meaning to reality. The antithesis here is that prior to capitalism, the productive system (monastic, guild, monarchy, feudal, and so on) prescribed action. Personal identities were based on the discrete qualities (noble, serf, priest, pauper, cooper, smith, merchant) that established subject positions within the system. "There [was] no gap between who the individual [was] and how his or her subjectivity [was] publicly represented" (Sayer 1991: 18).

Capitalism caused a revolutionary break from this structured order, such that individuals within capitalism now see the self existing prior to its social construction through status, gender, race, class, occupation, or belief, and they demand that all persons accept and operate from this preconstructed level. Only persons unencumbered by traditions and collective relations of class, race, gender, guild, union, or, more broadly, "culture" may live freely, for only these individuals may act in society from the position of their relative equivalence with other persons. As such they are not beholden to any particular agenda other than their own self-interest, which is posited as their common subjective position as well as the basis for creating a just society. So, as all free persons engage with each other in this manner, they actualize their common interests, which, as apologists for capitalism argue (Smith 2003, Rawls 1971), produces a free society.

Critics of this theory argue that the antisocial, noncultural, or pre-discursive location for individual subjectivity is the major component of the mystifying ideology supporting capitalism (see, for example, Marx 1967, Foucault 1977, Bakhtin 1981, MacPherson 1962, Eagleton 1991, Holland et al. 1998, LeFebvre 1991). Fundamental to this criticism is that subject positions only form within the dialogic spaces of intimate everyday social life, and therefore individualism is a result, rather than the cause, of the particular social relationship between capitalist and laborer. While this is key, there is another factor underlying the construction of individualism that needs to be further explored: private property, the main factor that explains why the conception of labor as something free to be sold was and is not contested more effectively.

Private Property and Competition

Private property is related to the first sense of freedom in the extract from *Capital* above: "as a free man [a laborer] can dispose of his labor-power as his own commodity." Labor-power here is regarded as the private personal property of the laborer. This construction is effected through both the abstraction of labor from its concrete manifestations and the realization of value for abstract labor in the market. The freedom to sell their labor on the market gives laborers within capitalism the impression of standing alongside, rather than in opposition to, capitalists. While they may have been deskilled and uprooted, the ideology professes, workers were also given possession of a valuable commodity. The ownership of their labor supposedly places them in a comparable position to the capitalists who purchase labor. Being free to sell their labor, there is nothing preventing them from envisioning it as an investment. In fact, being paid in money for labor-time reinforces this process by mimicking the money reward gained by the capitalist's investment. The point here is that abstracting labor as private property, as something not only for sale but also owned, establishes a common subjectivity between capitalist and laborer regarding the basis of social value, despite the oppositional relationship that defines them.

The private ownership of labor in capitalism leads to competition, which is the most profound effect of individualism. Accepting that labor and other commodities are privately owned and that owners have exclusive and free access to sell them marks individuals as living in distinct and private material conditions. The concrete, collective labor of the guild is replaced by the abstract labor of private individuals, a revolution that turns each laborer, and each capitalist, into a competitor. Most significantly, natural communalistic ties of kin and community are immediately severed when there are only enough jobs for some, leaving the others not only unemployed, but also dispossessed, impoverished, or dead. Thus, in some contexts siblings will be as much in competition with each other as they are with neighbors, strangers, or foreigners. This is not to say that by rule everyone chooses to compete with their kin and neighbors, but in capitalism those that do so gain an advantage. Furthermore, since many are already struggling with limited resources, the principled decision not to turn against one's community may be practically impossible.

Weber: The Ethic and Spirit of Capitalism

With this core understanding of Marx's conception of individual freedom within capitalism, I want to explore how the construction of the "authentic individual" reveals the powerful ideological force behind capitalism. As individuals are constructed through the aforementioned processes of social division, abstraction, commodification of labor, and the creation of competitive labor-owners, there arise barriers to experiencing what I have been calling the "natural" social life of kin and community. Yet for almost everyone relations with kin and community are obvious and typically paramount. So, given that one result of market competition is a loser—a laborer without a job, for example—we need to ask: How is the capitalist system maintained? Would not this laborer and others like him or her come to hate the system? Would they not, for their very survival, call on their kin and community, thereby privileging the very social relations that stand as the antithesis of the capitalist system? Max Weber's analysis of the basis of individual subjectivity within capitalism offers insight into why such occurrences fail to challenge the efficacy of the capitalist system (1981, 2003).

Weber emphasizes the high value placed in capitalist societies upon rational, predictable action, especially what he calls "calculated behavior." Rationally assessing the means, the ends, and the secondary results of action creates a space wherein persons may experience abstractions *as* reality. In capitalism, proposed actions or events, especially potential investments such as a new product design or a new factory plan, take on a sense of being real in a way that even hypothetical or what Weber considers "magical" conceptions in noncapitalist societies do not. A potential reality in capitalism contributes to the actual reality in a profound way. An investment involves the application of real value, as money and/or labor, which is brought to fruition even before the market for a product that results from the investment can be engaged and a profit realized. Rational calculation of all that is involved with a *potential* investment, as such, is obviously highly valued behavior. Weber's point is that this rationality is not just a feature of economic practice, but of the general subjectivity inherent to capitalism, what he identifies as its ethic.

Weber's famous analysis of the "spirit of capitalism" ties this behavior explicitly to the ascetic tenets of Calvinist Protestantism (2003). Principal to Protestantism is the rejection of a limited priesthood who may reveal God to others in favor of a more dispersed and individualized religious experience. Specifically, Protestants have equal access to God through the Prophesies, which may be analyzed personally and rationally rather than accepted dogmatically. This universal, individualistic approach to religion mirrors the Marxian notion of the abstraction of labor as something that applies to all persons and things despite their particular concrete conditions. This mirroring is amplified in Weber's discussion of Calvinist asceticism as being at the root of the modern capitalist subject. Based on the rational behavior of the monk—"only for him did the clock strike, only for him were the hours of the day divided—for prayer" (Sayer 1991: 119)—Calvinist asceticism emphasized individual conduct within the world rather than a rejection of corporeal existence. Worldly conduct was believed to reveal one's inner essence, and good conduct, including success in business and the accumulation of wealth, established one's worthiness of divine grace. This sense of an inner goodness revealed externally, Weber argued, internalized a responsibility for the individual self. In exchange for equal access to God, Protestants cannot be absolved of sin by a priest. Their relative goodness is determined by their ability to produce "a life of good works combined into a *unified system*" (2003: 115). This unity of experience, imagined as reaching across the whole of a life, reveals to each person their essential character. More powerfully, it establishes that "morality is thereby abstracted from all particular contexts, becoming an ontological attribute of the *subject* rather than of his or her discrete *actions*" (Sayer 1991: 121).

The self-interested, profit-focused aspects of capitalism were seized by Calvinism as a way to practice the discipline required to reveal one's inner goodness. Moral and ethical consistency in the market demanded self-reliance, for the self was not based on a person's relations with others, but resided solely within. Thus, increasing personal wealth was a moral imperative, and further, the means by which this was best accomplished was through "the conception of labor as an end in itself, as a calling" (Weber 2003: 51, 63). This "calling" was interpreted as the enactment by individuals of God's will.

The Protestant background for Weber is a corollary to the Marxian conception of capitalism as based in the abstraction of labor. It offers an understanding not only of how the capitalist system legitimates individuals, but also why persons were not only subjugated, but seemingly engaged with capitalism willingly. Laborers, according to this ideology, who lose their job and turn to their family to survive have not been failed by the system, but rather by their own flawed, if not sinful, character. As bearers of the system, an effect simultaneously of the ownership of their abstract labor and their internalized morality and self, individuals in capitalism are deemed responsible for their own successes and failures, just (and equally) as all other persons are for theirs.

Bureaucracy and the Public Culture

Weber extends this premise of the self as an abstracted individual to assess how modern rationality sustains inequalities inherent in both common social relations and, especially, the operations of the modern state. The function of modern state bureaucracies epitomizes the impersonal subjectivity of capitalism because they establish as mandatory the separation of official and personal interests. Bureaucrats must work objectively—they may not be influenced in their official work by private relations. Bureaucracies create a distinct public culture of capitalism, for they establish meaningful frames of social organization based on the assumption that capital is private property, so its unequal distribution does not hamper the operation of a just society. The very social substance by which human life is produced (that is, the control of concrete labor), when constructed as private property, is not a concern of public society. Weber's pessimism is worth considering here as well. He describes the subjectivity exemplified by rational bureaucracy as an "iron cage" (Weber 2003). As modern bureaucracies insist that persons operate in society objectively and rationally as individuals, collective action is severely limited, for cooperatives are irrational, if not illegal. Given the construction of modern social equality, if bureaucrats and other capitalist subjects allowed personal interest to play a role in their work, it would mean that they also would have to accept their own inherent inequality with others, realize that their "natural" relations should have authority in public life, and simultaneously demand this understanding from others. This process constructs, from the perspective of capitalism, the subject as a potential tyrant who must be controlled. The system therefore frames itself as indispensable: a way not only of situating the self within society as free and equal, but also of curtailing the presumed desire of some subjects to dominate others. This is only possible when the factors used to define equivalence are disconnected from productive social life.

Without Regard for Persons: The Archaeology of Capitalism

This exploration of subjectivity within capitalism has thus far outlined several key issues that archaeologies of capitalism should consider. The root of this discussion has been an examination of the authenticity of experience within capitalism. The abstraction of labor, which sustains the double removal of the self from its material conditions, is established here as the main focus. Experience in capitalism is seen as largely inauthentic insofar as the self is not realized through concrete labor and production. Rather, the self is a commodity seeking affiliation with capital interests that can sustain it, placing its locus in the market. Therefore, as Robert Paynter has noted (1988), the recovery and analysis of material culture from American historical archaeological sites needs to contextualize artifacts not solely as commodities, but as the material components of individual commodification, or the processes by which rational individual selves were constructed in the market. It is useful for archaeologists to see capitalism as a state of permanent revolution or crisis (Marx and Engels 1967a, Leone 1988). The idea of a permanent revolution underlies the meaning of modernity, in that everything is new all the time. The capitalist revolution, however, is not involved with the constant production of something new, but more the revolutionary destruction of the actual or "natural" social relations that define persons: kin, community, and culture. So, since all persons are born into concrete social worlds, it is mandatory for capitalism to constantly produce its detached, individual subjectivity anew. Importantly, everyone must *become* an individual by severing their irrational, unequal, and natural bonds with other persons, and they must repeat this process consistently throughout their life. This is the revolution and it is extremely personal, for the abstract individual is constructed by each person as they dissolve the significance of their personal life in their productive relations. This achievement is presented as realizing personal freedom and equality, but, as explained above, these come only with the subjugation of labor to capital.

Archaeologists are primed to recover the material histories of this individual-making with an analysis of the way persons were segregated and individually represented through their affiliation with the symbolic meanings of material things. Objects recovered from archaeological deposits related to capitalism cannot be treated as direct representations of those who made, acquired, used, and discarded them. The direct sense of self implied by this approach does not fit since the material remains of capitalism cannot in fact be equated with real persons. Rather, the archaeological record of capitalism consists of the objects that people employed to construct themselves abstractly in and for the market. Historic artifacts, architecture, landscapes, and the activities that produced these do not represent persons per se, but rather the way in which people became commodities and how, with material culture, persons produced their individuality in society by forming relations with desirable objects in the market.

Historical archaeologists can approach this problem in three ways. A widely applied effort is to examine the construction of the way that individual difference was produced through material culture (see, for example, Deetz 1996, Handsman 1981, 1983, Leone 1988, 2005). I show in the following chapters that this differentiation worked in two crosscutting social fields simultaneously. One field is interpersonal relations, where individualizing artifacts were used specifically to segregate persons from one another in activity and space. The other field is intergroup relations, where the capitalist core segregated as other those from whom they appropriated raw materials and labor but did not allow direct entry into the system. These others were the communities of Native Americans, African Americans, and immigrant ethnic groups who occupied spaces at the margins of capitalism (even if they were in the heart of modern cities). The margins became sites of ethnogenesis where these communities formed diverse, innovative relations with the capitalist core. Examining evidence of intergroup negotiations embeds archaeology in a study of domination, acquiescence, and resistance inherent to the dynamic ascendancy of capitalism in the United States. Studies illustrating this process comprise the material in chapters 2–5.

A second effort in historical archaeology has been to explore material signs of resistance by marginalized and impoverished peoples to the ill effects of individual difference. Examining an array of movements including utopian communalism, feminism, industrial sabotage, and alternative religious experience, I describe in chapters 6 and 7 examples where material culture was appropriated and re-signified by anticapitalist communities. These studies also allow for an assessment of the degree to which the replacement of "natural" relations with artificial ones was completed and the relative effectiveness of resistance to the penetration of capitalism into the recesses of community life. Notably, resistance to capitalism is not an individual event, for it is only those who organize and sustain themselves collectively that may stand outside of capitalism. The archaeology of successful forms of resistance to capitalism thus requires the recovery of materials that illustrate social relations of production in a realm exterior to the market, one where labor is self-directed, self-fulfilling, and is aimed at community versus individual reproduction. Moreover, such archaeology should also seek to identify and assess to what extent the structuring principles of potentially anticapitalist communities challenged the underlying principles of capitalism, like the commodification of labor and the individuation of experience.

A third form of the historical archaeology of American capitalism questions whether archaeology is even capable of operating free of the influence of capitalist structures. Typically identified as Marxist critical archaeology, research in this vein has shed light on the intersection between archaeological research and the production of aspects of capitalist culture in the present (see, for example, Leone 2005, Leone et al. 1987, Pinsky and Wylie 1989). Scholarship along these lines has supported the emergence of a vibrant effort to understand and improve the relevance of archaeology in contemporary society (McDavid 1997, Little and Shackel 2007, Castañeda and Matthews 2008). Included in this body of work has been research on the entanglement of archaeology with tourism, development, and the heritage industry, some examples of which I present in chapter 8. This research has in large part produced the assessment that archaeology remains complicit with key foundations of capitalism, especially the idea of private property and the authentication of abstraction through themes of cultural heritage and the abstraction of the archaeological record.

Yet, this work has begun to define spaces for archaeologists to develop a new, productive, and ethical form of practice. It is historical archaeology's job to record the origins and developments of capitalism missing from and hidden by the official documentary record. Only archaeology can look at the unrecorded, everyday effects of capitalism on a site-by-site basis as well as relate capitalism to long-term material and social change. But archaeology alone cannot offer a way out. All archaeology is guided by theory, or at least a certain commitment to purpose. A new ethics calls for us to embody this purpose in a more transparent way that will allow our own personhood and our own "natural" social relations to be increasingly a part of our work and public life. It is thus in the realm of praxis that an anticapitalist, critical archaeology will find the most success.

I opened this chapter with an extract from James Hawes' *Dead Long Enough* because I think that the novel captures a way to think differently about archaeology given its relationship with capitalism. Most poignantly, just before the end, the archaeologist in the novel is killed. Why kill this particular character? Perhaps there is something in this that nonfictional archaeologists might consider. As archaeologists, we are purveyors of the past and the dead in the modern age, yet despite our work, the past has no place in capitalism's endless revolution. Weber states plainly, "for civilized man death has no meaning" (Sayer 1991: 153). However, death does have a place in capitalism. As Marx said, the capitalist revolution comes into the world "dripping from head to toe, from every pore, with blood and dirt" (Marx 1967: 760). The point of critical archaeology is thus to break with capitalism's commitment to constant revolution. As Hawes suggests, life, including its archaeological representations, is not about having a choice. Rather, "balancing from stone to stone is all we have; that, and the people whose hands we are holding [along the way]." The point is for archaeologists to remember themselves and to know that the stones do not lead to the past, but forward, in a very simple, everyday sense. And the people who are supporting us are not our archaeological subjects, but our living colleagues, collaborators, kin, and community, who are too often entirely missing from our conceptions of our work as described in reports, books, and articles. Simply put, our focus on the dead obscures and hides our lives in the present. This is a choice we make. By rethinking this position, something I hope is aided by this book, archaeology can break away from simply interpreting fragments of the world and begin to find new ways to actively participate in it.

2

The Expansion of Capitalism and the Inventions of America

> In a majority of cases the [cultures] studied by anthropologists owe their development to processes that originate outside them and reach well beyond them, that they owe their crystallization to these processes, take part in them, and affect them in turn.
>
> Eric Wolf, "Culture: Panacea or Problem?"

This book reviews and organizes archaeological evidence of the social transformations caused by the introduction of capitalism into everyday American life. These transformations were outlined theoretically in chapter 1. They may be summarized broadly as the replacement of primary productive relations based on the "natural" affiliations of kinship and traditional communities with relations between abstract individuals formed and symbolized through market and commodity exchange. The result is the creation and reproduction of individualized social relationships within capitalism. This process is not just a social issue, but equally a cultural problem. The success of capitalism is realized in its effect not only on the social life of persons, but also that of groups as wholes, cultures in the anthropological sense as distinct and integrated formations productive of life, meaning, and identity. Within capitalism cultures often correlate with the division of labor, so persons become identified with members of their group as well as certain forms of work within the larger mode of production. Persons must therefore negotiate both the productive system and the order that places them in certain positions within it.

To explore this process, and to start the temporal sequence that structures this book, I examine in this chapter the normalization of capitalist social relations in the context of the fur trade in early colonial America. While capitalism was foundational to the colonial expansion of Europe, its particular effects in the American setting followed a developmental process distinct from that which took place in Europe (see, for example, Braudel 1979, Johnson 1996). An important part of this different growth pattern was the role of Native Americans. Largely excluded from direct participation in American colonial society, Indian peoples and groups were nonetheless integral to the colonies' success and thus were actively involved in the capitalist organization of American culture. The historical archaeology of Native America in fact situates Indian people precisely in the position where organizational networks based on kin and community confronted and awkwardly merged with networks based on individualized market exchange. As indigenous and settler systems contradicted one another, archaeology illustrates not just a blending of old- and new-world cultures, but the creation of entirely new Native American cultures that only incompletely healed the ruptures in Native life caused by their entanglement with capitalism.

The Social Organization of Colonial American Merchant Capitalism

The European market for extractable products such as fish, furs, minerals, and spices; agricultural goods like sugar, tobacco, rice, and cotton; and the (often enslaved) labor to produce these goods drove the expansion of merchant capitalist interests to new regions across the globe where these commodities were available. The "discovery" of America amplified this desire by presenting what seemed like a land of endless opportunity for accumulation, especially in contrast to the limitations posed by established old-world feudal manors. Furthermore, the politically small-scale American indigenous populations did not present a substantial impediment to acquiring these goods (Bodley 2008). This lack of leverage resulted from Native Americans' relatively small and dispersed populations, their non-state political organization, and further, their willingness to trade for readily available manufactured goods such as glass beads, woolen cloth, and iron and brass tools. In this chapter I archaeologically analyze the colonial American fur trade in New England and New York in order to examine European-American contact through the lens of merchant capitalism. I follow Eric Wolf in arguing that what the documentary record defines as Native American tribal groups or nations were in large part a product of the social organization of production resulting from the introduction of the fur trade (1982, 1984). Wolf, drawing on Fried (1975), argues that prior to European colonization, northeastern North American indigenous sociopolitical organization was more often village- than tribal-based. Villages were essentially extended kin-groups organized around the needs for subsistence, settlement, and social exchange (for example, alliance and marriage). By contrast, tribes are larger formations of multiple villages under the banner of a presumed identity such as language, systems of intercultural exchange, and at times, supra-village forms of leadership. Wolf does not reject the existence of American tribal groups prior to European contact. Rather, he suggests that such inter-village affiliations were more loosely organized than they became during the fur-trade era, and were organized more by a system of endogamous, totemic clans than through the expectations of tribal loyalty, tribute, and abstract identity.

This perspective does not reject Native American cultural continuities across the supposed prehistoric-historic divide. Clearly languages, forms of sociopolitical organization, religious expressions, and material culture and technologies "survived" contact (Nassaney 2000, Pauketat 2001). To think that the capitalist system simply replaced the indigenous one is ahistorical and deterministic. Rather, the increasing organization of social formations on the order of Native American tribal groups signifies adaptations made by indigenous persons and groups to the changes brought about by involvement with European merchant capitalism. Tribal affiliation, in other words, was expected by Europeans and in fact came to make sense to Native Americans given the evolution of the division of labor within the fur trade.

Inclusion and Exclusion in the Colonial Fur Trade

In 1737, representatives of the Iroquois Six Nations appealed to the British authority at Albany, New York, saying that, "wherever the Christians settled... hunting was destroyed for the Bever [sic] & Deer &c. Fled from the places they disturbed" (quoted in Parmenter 1999: 710–72). This statement describes early colonial relations and the concerns they produced as Native Americans and Europeans were brought into close contact in the northeast during the seventeenth and early eighteenth centuries by the fur trade. Driven especially by a burgeoning European market for beaver hats, the northeastern fur trade between Native Americans and Dutch, English, and French traders organized a great deal of productive and social life in colonial America. The focus of my discussion is on the cultural duality that the fur trade established within Native populations. The exchange of furs for "trade goods" was not just conducted between individual European traders and Indian hunters, but equally between the groups these individuals stood for. Despite the common interpersonal experiences and interests involved in the exchange, a defining feature of the fur trade was its insistence on the cultural difference between trading partners. While it is conceivable that trading partners may have developed a common bond that could have surpassed cultural difference and created a unified American culture, this bond did not emerge (not excepting here the "white Indians" and *"courier de bois"* who as much enforced as challenged the cultural divide between Native Americans and Europeans [Axtell 1975, Loren 2001]). The important result of this difference is that it was in part through their role in developing the fur trade that Indians became *Native* Americans, a novel cultural marker that has lingered in their identity definition since the seventeenth century (Sider 1987, Dombrowski 2001).

Approaching the fur trade through this lens of ethnogenesis (Sider 1994, Voss 2008)—or the creation of new cultural groups and identities specifically associated with being Native—allows early American intercultural relations to be placed in the active historical setting required to understand the underlying capitalist expectations of the trade. Not just an exchange between people of different backgrounds, languages, customs, beliefs, and resource access, the intercultural fur trade also produced a substantial qualitative difference between partners: one *kind* procured furs and similar American products, while another *kind* purchased them. Each side of the exchange was defined by both the person of the trading partner and their entire culture, a generalization from person to group that allowed the trading system as a whole to function, at least on one level, without regard for specific persons. On the one hand, assigning trading partners to different cultures turned everyday commodity exchange into rituals on the order of state relations. In this way, the power of the colonial relationship in its entirety was made evident in every trading act (Bourdieu 1977, Corrigan and Sayer 1991). More important, if each side of the exchange was its own cultural "universe," then the exchange did not carry with it the mutual responsibility for the well-being of the other group (compare Mauss 2002, Hyde 1983). While it may be thought that a culture can and even should care for its own, in this system a group was expected to do so necessarily, whether it wanted to or not. In other words, expectations of cultural difference dominated productive life, even if productive life could not meet the demands for reproducing the culture. The fur trade was thus structured to turn Indian culture upon itself.

Anthropologists see this as a common problem in modern colonialism. They often describe it as a process of simultaneous inclusion and exclusion (Sider 1987, Cooper and Stoler 1997). Natives were certainly included in the fur trade as its primary producers. This role in part organized their production as they devoted time and effort to procuring and trading furs. In fact, the colonial fur trade was at first a form of surplus production in that communities captured furs only after their basic needs were met. However, as the trade expanded and became increasingly competitive on both sides of the exchange, it grew to dominate many Native lives at the expense of subsistence labor (Cronon 1983, Jordan 2009). At this point the fur trade shifted from a peripheral to a central component of Native American life. In this way, inclusion in the system was evident at the level of production both for the trade and through the challenges the trade imposed on Indians' productive autonomy. However, the colonial organization of the fur economy did not allow for the inclusion of Indian people and cultures, which likely promoted a critical consciousness of the system's impact on the rest of Indian life. While Native hunters produced furs, Native persons and groups were structurally conceived of as outside and thus excluded from the system that purchased them. Because of differences in language, religion, social life, technology, and so forth, Native autonomy was emphasized by all parties even after Indian production itself became dominated by the trade.

Anthropologist Gerald Sider suggests we consider this as a form of mutual self-deception (1987), arguing that although the common interest and even codependence of Indians and Europeans were evident in every moment of exchange, both sides seemed empowered by their opposition across a supposedly vast cultural divide. As much as each was invested in the other in terms of production, they did not see it this way in the cultural realm. On the one hand, Native autonomy allowed Europeans to ethnocentrically assert their cultural superiority (Berkhofer 1979, Drinnon 1980). Europeans also remained free from the responsibility of mutual welfare and the moral obligations that a shared cultural standing demands. It is less obvious why Native people chose to stand apart. For most, it was less than one or two generations before their autonomy was undermined and replaced by varied forms and levels of dependence on the European commodity market (White 1983). These effects were not hard to see, and the aforementioned complaint of the Six Nations representatives shows that they were aware of the drastic social and ecological changes that had emerged. Nevertheless, even in complaint, these Indians played out a key aspect of the trade's emphasis on cultural difference by identifying Europeans as "Christians." While it is certainly difficult to imagine that Indian people would abandon their religious beliefs, the use of this framework for identifying difference is self-deceiving. It emphasizes that because of religion, Indians and colonists were different. While different religions do produce different perspectives, in this case the problems these Indians were citing were the result of their unequal position in the colonial fur trade's division of labor, the basis of their *common* cultural standing.

Next I will examine Indian constructions of cultural difference as I reconsider the identification of Native American cultural persistence in the archaeological record as resistance to colonization. Simply put, in the context of the fur trade distinct Indian cultures were as much a means for distinguishing groups *within* the system as they were a way to situate persons outside of, and perhaps, against the system. Furthermore, as the fur trade developed, it destroyed the ability for many Native groups to stand apart from the system as separate cultures. Many northeastern "cultures" were eliminated altogether, and their surviving members merged with other Indian and non-Indian communities (for example, the Pequot, Montaukett, Mashpee, Huron, Neutral, Erie). Some turned to armed resistance, such as those who fought with King Philip in 1675 (Drake 1999), some moved away to the Great Lakes or southern Canada, some intermarried with local African American populations, and some accommodated and to a degree accepted their subordination. None, importantly, became a part of the white European mainstream. I will proceed to explore the problems of resistance and self-deception with a look at both the archaeology of a seventeenth-century Narragansett cemetery in Rhode Island and the eighteenth-century Mohawks in upstate New York.

Narragansetts at RI-1000

Among the most important and informative single archaeological discoveries related to the Native American role in the fur trade is a late-seventeenth-century cemetery associated with the Narragansett tribe of

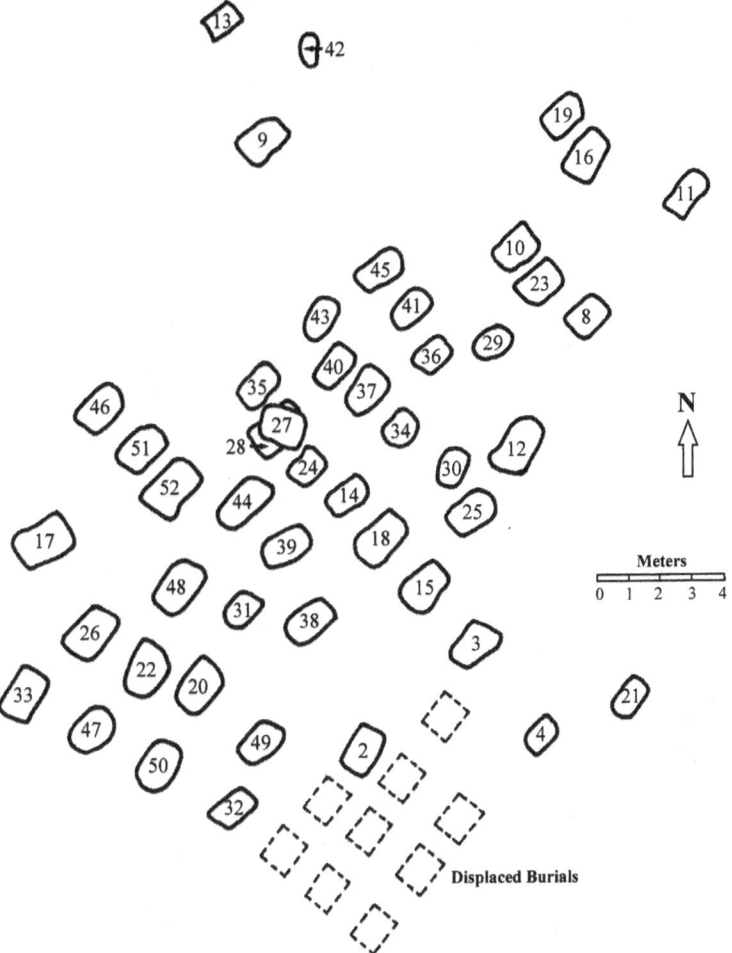

Figure 2.1. Plan of burials at Narragansett Cemetery known archaeologically as RI-1000 (drawing by Ross Rava after Rubertone 2001: 198).

western Rhode Island. Known as RI-1000, the cemetery was located on the western shore of Narragansett Bay in North Kingstown, Rhode Island. It was discovered in 1982 after a bulldozer digging in preparation for a new housing development uncovered several graves. Negotiations among the landowner, the state historical society, and the representatives of the descendant Narragansett community ultimately led to the excavation of the entire cemetery, which, including those disturbed by the bulldozer, consisted of fifty-six burials (Rubertone 2001: 133, Brown and Robinson 2006) (see Figure 2.1). The information obtained from these burials as well as research on related Narragansett sites offers insight into the strategic accommodations Narragansetts made to take advantage of the opportunities created by the fur trade. I draw in this discussion on the work of the many scholars whose research allows us to understand this data, especially Patricia Rubertone (1989, 1994, 2001, also Robinson et al. 1985, Robinson 1990, Turnbaugh 1993, Nassaney 1989, Brenner 1988). My discussion critically expands on interpretations presented by these authors, specifically in the manner that the materials from the cemetery illustrate Indian complicity in emergent American capitalist relations.

To begin it is important to situate the Narragansetts buried at the site in their historical context. European interaction with Native people in Narragansett Bay began in the 1520s when Giovanni da Verrazano anchored for two weeks near present-day Newport to explore the interior, trade with the Indians, and acquire provisions. While contact between Europeans and Americans over the rest of the century was irregular, it was not infrequent, and after 1600 Dutch traders made the Narragansett Bay a regular stop. The English competed poorly with the Dutch in this trade until English Pilgrims occupied the lands at Plymouth, Massachusetts, in 1620. While far from a booming colony at the outset, the group at Plymouth managed to survive and stay, becoming a colonial permanence that affected the Narragansett and their neighbors in profound ways. English survival at Plymouth was based on an economic well-being fueled by the colonial fur trade, a fact that spurred several additional English settlements which competed with one another as well as Native groups to survive and prosper in the region.

The two most profound effects of colonialism on Native Americans were the introduction of epidemic diseases and the expansion of the fur trade. Smallpox and other epidemics initially devastated Native populations, but widespread disease is reported to have waned by the 1630s. The pressures of the fur trade, however, did not similarly subside. As the trade developed in the late sixteenth and early seventeenth centuries, focusing on beaver fur in particular, new forms of productive life and political relations among Indian people emerged. Beavers are largely northern animals, thus coastal peoples like the Narragansett in southern New England did not have direct access to the most desirable furs. In order to acquire beaver pelts, they traded with neighbors, a process that constructed lines of exchange relations between coastal and interior groups. Wolf highlights this exchange network to describe the process of Indian tribal formation (1982). As each occupied a distinct link along the chain of exchange, groups became associated with their position in the trade. This was not simply a matter of identity through association, because the resources each group controlled required not only procurement but defense in order for the group to maintain its position. The fur trade thus established an active rationale for tribal affiliation. Given these relatively rapid and significant changes to their way of life, why did Indians so eagerly enter the trade?

It appears that the fur trade exploited a desire for prestige. Traditional intergroup exchange among Indians was largely defined by the exchange of gifts and persons through marriage, acts which cemented alliances between regional villages. Outside of these exchanges, other trade relations were driven by the desire for prestige within such alliance groups. Prestige was earned through success in battle or through effective leadership. It was also gained through the control and exchange of limited resources. For the most part, Native societies suppressed the private accumulation of key resources such as arable land or hunting territory, but the access to desirable and prestigious resources such as marine shells or crystals, which had potential spiritual associations (Miller and Hamell 1986), was not as tightly controlled. While Native societies typically reserved control of these resources for spiritual specialists who had demonstrated the ability to serve the community, access to imported goods nevertheless drove the fur trade.

Coastal groups with access to European trade goods such as glass beads, glazed pottery, mirrors, marine shells, and smooth metallic objects like spoons, all of which functioned like crystals in that they reflected the soul, or groups who controlled and/or produced shell-bead wampum (which was used by inland groups to cement new sorts of political relations) traded these goods inland for furs. The quality and quantity of European trade goods, however, quickly unbalanced economic relations. As coastal groups controlled access to valuable European goods, they demanded from their trading partners great numbers of furs. In fact, disputes between Indian groups were not infrequent. Archaeologist Peter Thomas illustrates that fluctuations in annual quantities of furs captured in the Connecticut River Valley were the result of inter-Indian conflict more than variations in natural supply (1981, 1985). Furthermore, the effects of this competition on peaceful trade were not restricted to Native Americans. To ensure the production of furs in a changing and competitive system, English, Dutch, and French colonial authorities regularly inserted themselves to resolve Indian-European as well as intertribal disputes through negotiation and, as often, violence. Among the most dramatic intercessions was the Pequot War of 1638, a violent assault that directly involved the Narragansetts.

By the late 1630s, the Narragansetts and the Pequots, their western neighbors, were intense competitors. Each sought special arrangements with English traders and more control over wampum produced by Native Americans on Long Island. In the midst of this tension a Pequot sachem and two English traders were killed between 1634 and 1636. These killings prompted an English incursion. As the Narragansett lived between the Pequot and the Massachusetts English, both groups sought their alliance. The Narragansett sided with the English and joined them in a predawn raid on the Pequot fort near Mystic that ended with the massacre of nearly seven hundred Pequot men, women, and children (Rubertone 2001: 76, Strong 2001: 11). This destruction of the Pequot as a viable polity resulted in a regional power vacuum as various groups including the English, Dutch, Niantic, Mohegan, Montaukett, and Narragansett sought to gain control of Pequot territory, alliances, and the surviving Pequot refugees. To resolve the conflict, the English called a meeting of Indian sachems at Hartford, Connecticut, in 1638. Building on their violent reputation, earned after the Pequot massacre, the English pushed through a treaty that forced the Narragansett to make annual wampum tribute payments to the English and more fully accept the authority of English law in cases of intertribal and Indian-English dispute. As a result of the treaty, all Indians in the region (allies of the English or not) became subject to English authority without becoming English subjects themselves.

Rather than accepting this as the start of a slow decline of the Narragansett, it should also be noted how their subjugation involved the less spectacular, yet no less violent, process of English land appropriation and use. Described by the Narragansett sachem Miantonomi below, English farming techniques destroyed the ecological conditions that sustained the Narragansett way of life (Cronon 1983: 82–156). In order to survive this ecological attack, Indians across New England were forced to shift virtually all of their productive energies to the fur trade. The Narragansett sachem Miantonomi spoke of the problem in 1642 to the Mountaukett of Long Island, who he hoped to enlist in a revolt:

> For so are we all Indeans as ye English are, and Say broth^r to one anothe^r; So must we be one as they are, othe^{r}wise we shall all be gone shortly, for you know our fathers had plenty of deare & Skins, our plains were full of dear, as also our woods, and of Turkie, and our Coves full of fish and foule. But thes English have gotten our land, they with Sithes cut downe ye grass, and with axes fell the trees; their Cowes and horses eat ye grass, and th^r hogs spoyl our Clambanks, and we shall all be starved: therefore it is best for you to doe as wee, for wee are all the Sachems from East to West, both Mouquakes and Mowhauks Joyning with us, and we are all resolved to fall upon them all at one apoynted day. (Cited in Rubertone 2001: 79)

Similar to the 1737 complaints of the Six Nations noted earlier, Miantonomi records how the Narragansetts' way of life could not withstand English expansion. Rubertone urges us to recognize that this complaint and the suggested violent response are not just objective assessments, but pointed political *and* moral arguments. In the fur trade, which after the Hartford Treaty was firmly under English control, Native partners were still expected to stand on their own, an expectation which implied they could actually do so. The call to join a revolt comes only after Miantonomi "speaks of insults and cries for dignity" (Rubertone 2001: 79). The moral outrage evident in the extract results from the inability of Natives to stand on their own and the fact that the English had no interest in doing anything about it. Despite this claim to a common moral ground, Miantonomi describes the English as an other in the opening phrase, just as the Six Nations Iroquois did by referring to colonists as Christians. It is my point here that othering the colonizers enacted the self-deceiving premise of the colonial merchant capitalist system. The fact that the sachem Miantonomi (a rank that was in large part created and sustained by the fur trade [see White 1991: 142–85]) stated that it was *not* his system but someone else's shows that he placed the integrity of Native culture as defined outside of its involvement in the fur trade. His assassination after delivering this speech by Uncas, sachem of the competitive and English-loyal Mohegan people, is evidence that he may have fared better by seeing the role of the fur trade (and his people's productive life in general) differently. Looking at the archaeological remains of some of his Narragansett descendents at RI-1000 amply illustrates this.

The RI-1000 Cemetery

Following Rubertone (2001: 132–64), the burials at RI-1000 may be divided into three age groups: children (3–9 years), adolescent male/female (11–28 years), and adult male/female (29–58 years) (see Table 1). I will consider the patterns Rubertone identifies as associated with these groups, though I will develop my own interpretations as I relate the evidence to the Narragansett people's struggles for inclusion (or, in some cases, the opposite) in colonial English society.

Table 1. RI-1000 burial data

Burial Number	Age	Sex	Adornments	Other Artifacts
2	33	M	Buckle, brass, double; Headband, brass; Ring, brass, signet; Ring, brass, "set"	Nail, iron, rosehead; Nails, iron (5); Pipe, English; Spoon, latten, seal top
3	16	M	Comb fragments, carved bone; Headband, shell	Axe, iron; Button mold, stone; Knives, iron blade, wooden handle (3); Spoon fragments, brass; Spoon, brass
8	43	M	None	Fragments, brass; Fragments/strips, iron; Pipes, English (2); Scissors, iron
9	43	F	None	Awl or mux, iron; Spoon, brass
10	3	?	Bracelet, glass; Bracelet, shell; Headband, shell with glass closure	Apothecary jar, tin glazed; Bell fragments, brass; Hoe, iron; Spoon, latten, slipped stem; Swivel (?), iron
11	3	?	Bracelet, glass and brass	Bottle, glass, medicine; Hoe, iron; Spoon, latten

Burial Number	Age	Sex	Adornments	Other Artifacts
12	43	F	None	Disk, glass with metal
13	4	?	None	None
14	11	F?	Fragment, shell	None
15	28	M	Rings, brass, Jesuit "HIS I" (3); Rings, brass, Jesuit "L-heart" (2); Ring, brass, Jesuit "L-heart-IV"	Abrader, grooved; Abrader/whetstone; Adze, iron; Ceramic, Native; Cylinders, lead (4); Fragments, brass; Hoe, iron; Musket ball, lead; Nodule, graphite (3); Pipe, European; Rod, iron; Spoon, brass
16	22	M	None	Container, iron
17	16	F	Hoops, brass (2); Ring, brass, signet; Ring fragments, brass	Bottles, glass (3); Clips, brass (2); Hooks, iron (5); Kettle, iron lug with legs; Mirror box, wooden; Spoon, brass with animal effigy
18	20	F	Necklace, brass and glass; Rings, brass Jesuit "IHS I" (4); Ring, brass, Jesuit "double heart"; Ring, brass, Jesuit "L-heart"; Ring, brass, signet; Ring, brass, signet, "asterisk"	Apothecary jar, tin glazed; Box fragments, brass
19	14	F?	Glass; Rings, brass, Jesuit "IHS I" (3); Ring, brass, Jesuit "L-heart IV"	Nodule, graphite; Spoons, latten, short seal (2)
20	48	M	None	None
21	4	?	Headband, brass; Hoops, brass with shell (10)	None

continued

Table 1—*Continued*

Burial Number	Age	Sex	Adornments	Other Artifacts
22	15	F?	Comb, brass; Headband, brass and shell; Necklace, glass, shell, and brass; Ring, brass wire	Bottle, glass; Nodule, graphite with animal effigy; Object, brass with cordage; Scissors, iron; Spoon, latten; Spoon, Native/English
23	53	F	None	None
24	7	?	Bracelet, glass and shell; Misc., glass	Bells, brass (hawk's bells) (2)
25	28	M	None	Knife, wooden handle; Muxes, iron (approx. 10); Pipe, English
26	17	F	None	None
28	29	F	None	Ceramic, Native; Nodules, graphite; Kettle, brass
29	24	F	Necklace, glass and shell	Bottle, glass; Spoon, latten, seal top
30	13	F?	None	None
31	57	F	None	Hoe, iron
32	58	F	None	Awl tip, iron; Hoe, iron; Pestle, stone
33	3	?	None	Spoon, latten, seal top
35	33	F	None	Hooks, iron (5)
36	4	?	Bracelet, shell; Buttons, cast metal (5); Buttons, glass (5); Headband, shell	Ceramic, Native; Scissors, iron; Spoon, latten, seal top
37	3	?	Earring (?), shell	None

Burial Number	Age	Sex	Adornments	Other Artifacts
37	3	?	Belt or girdle, glass; Bracelet, brass; Bracelet, brass, incised; Bracelet, glass and shell; Earring, shell; Earring, glass; Necklaces, glass and shell (3); Pouch, glass	Bells, brass (hawk's bells) (11); Container fragments, brass; Container fragments, iron; Misc. fragments, mica and brass; Spoon, brass; Spoon, latten, seal top; Spoons, latten, slipped stem (2)
38	28	M	Headband, shell	Abrader, groundstone; Adze/chisel, iron, reworked; Claw hammer, iron; Flint/gunflint; Fragments, brass (cache?); Horseshoe fragment, iron; Knife, iron blade, wooden handle; Knife, iron blade and tang; Nails, iron, rosehead (2); Pintle, iron; Pipes, English (3); Rod fragments, iron, reworked; Spike, iron; Spoon, brass; Swivel, iron; Wedges, iron, reworked
39	13	F?	None	Cup or box fragments, brass; Knife handle, antler, bone; Spoon, latten, seal top
40	15	F?	Bracelet, glass; Bracelet, shell; Necklace, glass and shell	Bottle, glass, medicine; Cup, tin glazed
41	7	?	Buttons, lead, Native (13)	Clip, brass

continued

Table 1—*Continued*

Burial Number	Age	Sex	Adornments	Other Artifacts
42	4	?	None	Nails, wrought iron, rosehead (2); Saw blade, iron
43	38	F	None	None
44	39	M	None	Kettle, brass; Knife, wooden handle; Wedge, iron
45	43	F	None	None
46	43	F	None	None
47	15	F?	Bracelet, glass	Bottles, glass (2)
48	26	F	Necklace, brass	Clip, brass; Disk(?), glass; Nail fragments, iron; Spoon, latten, slipped stem
49	15	F?	Shell	None
50	43	M	None	Pipe, clay, Native; Pipe, English
51	42	F	None	Bails, iron; Hoe, iron; Kettles, brass (2); Knife, iron, antler/bone handle; Pan, brass; Pestle, stone; Rods, iron, reworked (2); Spoon, latten, slipped stem
52	48	M	None	Container, iron

Source: Table follows Rubertone 2001: 191–94.

Because of their age, the youngest group of nine individuals cannot be sexed, thus they are seen generally as representative of Narragansett childhood and child-rearing practices. The most noticeable feature of these graves is the large number of items included with burials as either bodily ornaments or grave goods (objects buried with, but not on, the body). Children had by far the most objects per person of any group, suggesting that material culture was an important medium for childhood to be expressed and defined. Although young children (3–4 years) as a group had a high number of burial objects, some burials contained more than others. Accounting for two low-count burials by their association with evidence of disease and their burial away from the main group (Rubertone 2001: 145–47), the remaining seven still show a discrepancy. Rubertone accounts for this variation as an effect of differing maternal expectations for survival in an attempt to discount the possibility of inherited ranking. I suggest an alternative. Rather than inherited rank, these distinctions may be the sign of the achieved rank of a child's family or clan. Within competitive systems, as exemplified by the fur trade, children often display their family's status (Baxter 2005). Variation in the quantity and quality of grave goods and body ornamentation associated with children reflects internal competition within the community. The use of wampum in virtually every "wealthy" child burial suggests that involvement and relative success in the colonial fur trade may have been the root of this competition.

Six of the buried children had adorned bodies. Their ornaments consisted mostly of bracelets, necklaces, headbands, and ear embellishments made of shell, glass, and metal beads. Rubertone shows that encircling ornaments (2001: 143), especially bracelets, represent the binding of children to the earth, their parents, and the larger social group. Bracelets especially may have been mnemonic devices reminding young people of their place and the people they belong to. It is notable that this sort of ornamentation is not as common among adolescents and not found at all among adults. The association of children with bracelets thus suggests a reaction to the threats to group and family integrity caused by the fur trade, which will be discussed in more detail below. The challenges to culture arising from the internal competition of the fur trade may have demanded a way for children to be tied explicitly to their group. It is important to remember that this is not just a benevolent interest in reproducing the culture, but a way to control the significant material resource that children represent to any group as its future leaders and laborers, citizens who will act in the interest of the group to which they belong. Consideration of the burial patterns of older males and females shows the cultural challenges surviving Narragansett children faced.

Identifiable females in the cemetery may be grouped as either adolescents or adults. Adolescence typically marks a transitional phase from childhood to adulthood, and the RI-1000 burials reflect this pattern. As with children, many adolescent female bodies were adorned with necklaces and bracelets of wampum, glass, and brass beads. Among females and almost unique to adolescents were rings, perhaps a sign of their young adulthood. Rubertone suggests rings may have been associated with dexterity (2001: 149), a developmental and social skill perhaps related to beadwork and likely also to the manufacture of shell-bead wampum. Two adolescent burials were also associated with clan emblems (bear and turtle), which may indicate clan initiation and thus adulthood.

Older women show a very different material pattern. None of the older women were buried with bodily ornaments, and their relatively few grave goods consisted mostly of the tools associated with horticulture, cooking, and crafts such as beadwork or basketry. This sharp age-based distinction separating older females may indicate their married or, more likely, their maternal status. Far from being children who could bear the possessive signs of their parents or clan, these older women were among those most responsible for the material foundations of their family's and their community's survival and social standing. Rubertone argues that this standing was pronounced through the symbolization of women's work, as the majority of tools buried with older women were "heavily used and highly curated" (2001: 156). This symbolic marking of everyday labor through the preservation and public burial of tools may illustrate one way that the Narragansett mitigated the corrosive effects of the fur trade on their traditional subsistence patterns. As Indian lands diminished and hunting declined, to be replaced by trapping and trading for furs, the basic activities that signified being Indian—to Indians and non-Indians alike—withered. Yet Indian people were expected—again by both parties—to make do with what they had. Symbolizing traditional women's labor associated with farming and craftwork focused the group on the aspects of their communal life that were obviously "Indian." This process made women more than ever into bearers of Indian culture, allowing men to operate in other realms largely defined by the colonial market for furs, labor, and similar products and services. Male burials provide evidence to support this interpretation.

Burials of men at RI-1000 indicate that male "life passages were not as clearly marked, which seems to imply that transitions in life cycle were not as meaningful for [men] as they were for women" (Rubertone 2001: 159). Instead of representing life's stages, male burials illustrate "complicated individual histories." These conclusions are based on the presence of material ornaments and grave goods that make each male quite distinct from the others. Burial 25 was found with ten graduated iron awls in two kits that were likely used for making wampum. Burial 15 was found with cast-lead cylinders and a lead musket ball, perhaps indicating a practice in leadwork. Burial 38 was found with a claw hammer, horseshoe, nails, reworked iron artifacts, scrap iron and brass, and a whetstone, items commonly used in metalworking and blacksmithing. These three graves display different specialized strategies which these men may have employed to situate themselves in the colonial market for labor and goods. Especially in the case of Burial 38, these remains show a competence that follows traditional forms of Indian craftwork. As such, I agree with Rubertone that this is not simply blind acculturation or even evidence of Indian apprenticeship (2001: 162–63), but rather "a compelling story of Narragansett resourcefulness." However, I do not agree that this is, therefore, resistance to colonialism.

Rather, the evidence of the founding of the cemetery by this Narragansett community suggests a great deal more cultural accommodation, though the persistence of Narragansett communities to the present marks this as an excellent example of resistant accommodation. It is hardly surprising, given the expectation that despite the loss of resources the Indians would still care for themselves, that some Indian men would take up marketable work even if this work was contradictory to a culturally distinct existence. Burial 2 at the cemetery shows how this complicated picture perhaps made sense. This thirty-three-year-old man was buried with a set of brass ornaments, including a buckle that may have held up a sword belt, a double headband, and two rings. One of the rings was a signet ring with a heart-and-anchor motif. Signet rings were used by Europeans to make an official mark on documents and commodities in order to verify their proper owners. The signet ring found in Burial 2 may have served a similar purpose. Perhaps offered as a gift to this individual, it would have established an official relationship between a Rhode Island trader or government official (the anchor was the emblem for Rhode Island and the heart was a sign common among Rhode Island family seals, including merchant families) and this person, who perhaps acted as a representative of his community. The ring likely marked this man as the community's leader, its spokesperson, a position he apparently gained only by submitting himself as the symbolic property of the Rhode Island family who laid claim to him. As Rubertone writes (2001: 160), "it was an expression of personal and tribal history, of autonomy and submission, and of appropriation and rejection." It was a sign of the simultaneous inclusion and exclusion of the Narragansett within colonial Rhode Island society, a plural status that allowed them to be Indians for better or, as is likely, for worse. Inasmuch as this understanding holds true, the signet ring may be considered further. Along with the symbolization of women's work discussed above, the ring produced, on the level of cultural discourse, a sign of Indian otherness that made Indian productivity *within* colonial society possible. Only by accepting their otherness—that is, all that being Indian entailed in terms of living with the potential for markets to be closed as well as the looming imposition of other unfair trade practices such as treaties, tribute payments, or war—would competitive Indians be able to sell their craftwork to colonists. Wearing this ring made this man a leader, but only of an Indian community which was otherwise already dominated by the English colonial system. For the remainder of the community, this submission allowed their way of life and the few advantages they had by virtue of being Indian to be maintained on their ancestral lands.

This precarious situation may help explain one other distinguishing aspect of the RI-1000 cemetery, a pattern commonly found in Indian burial practices after colonization. In the generations before the fur trade, Indian people in southern New England located cemeteries on marginal, rather than arable, lands. Arable lands were instead the location where men cleared fields and women planted, tended, and harvested the corn and beans that made up the core of the Native American diet. In contrast, RI-1000 and other formal bounded cemeteries of its era were located in pockets of arable soil. This shift in practice is no small event. Giving fertile ground to the ancestors may be seen as turning over one of the basic characteristics that define any human relationship with the natural world: specifically, the way in which groups define and signify their culturally determined productive activities. This move, however, also has a political aspect. As Rubertone states:

> The appearance of this communal burial ground in the archaeological record of this ancestral homeland at this time tends to support the interpretation that this sacred place may have been used primarily by a localized segment of a particular descent group or

clan claiming exclusive access to land, corn, and other resources of increasing social and cultural significance in the seventeenth century. (2001: 131)

The Narragansett dead were no longer just ancestors, they also signified exclusive, though communally held, Indian lands. They served to mark a community's claim on the resources (that is, the land and its products) that alone could sustain them against the otherwise entirely destructive effects of English colonialism. The RI-1000 cemetery was a mark of history, the history of kinship *and* the history of being Indian, that made Narragansett survival in the Rhode Island colony possible.

The Mohawks at Fort Hunter and Indian Castle

After over a century of armed resistance, highly successful trading, and skilled political maneuvering, the Mohawk people west of Albany, New York, agreed to allow the British to construct Fort Hunter at the eastern edge of their traditional homeland along the Mohawk River in 1712. The construction of this fort marked a moment of great transition, for the Mohawks were among the most powerful Indian fur traders. The Mohawks sat at a strategic interstice of European colonial control. Their homeland, known as Kanienke, was in the space between the territory controlled by the English in New England, the Dutch in the lower Hudson Valley (who were replaced by the New York English after 1664), and the French in Canada. The value of this location was enhanced by the Dutch settlement at Fort Orange, which was built in 1624 at the mouth of the Mohawk River on the Hudson. Because it was an isolated Dutch settlement, the settlers were authorized to trade with the Mohawks not only ornaments, but also munitions (Grumet 1995: 180). This rare practice certainly emboldened the Mohawks toward their Indian allies and adversaries, since they not only had superior weapons, but also held a virtual monopoly over the trade with Fort Orange after they had defeated the Mahicans in 1628. This trade control and resulting wealth elevated the Mohawks to a supreme position within Indian America. As such, it is not surprising that a Mohawk raiding party was reported in 1661 along the Maine coast, that Mohawks collected tribute from Connecticut River Valley Indian communities, or that they were identified as the formidable ally of the Narragansetts by Miantonomi (P. Thomas 1981: 363, 367, Rubertone 2001: 79).

Mohawk power was so pronounced in the middle and late seventeenth century that they, along with their Iroquois neighbors, conquered competitors to the west like the Neutral, Petun, and Erie nations, ensuring Iroquois mastery over a vast area of fur production reaching from eastern New York to the eastern Great Lakes. Protecting their main source of power, the Mohawks alone then made an alliance with the English, who took over Fort Orange in 1664. This alliance marked the beginning of a several-decades-long struggle among the Mohawks as they became a significant party in a series of conflicts between the French and English colonial interests between 1667 and 1710.

Problems began when a French raid in Mohawk territory in 1667 was not avenged by their English allies. The English ambivalence toward the Mohawks was alarming, for it was made clear that their relationship was based not on an alliance, but the fur trade alone. In fact, if not for the continued English interest in that trade, the Mohawks would likely have sided with the French and attempted to expel the English from the region. Instead, they were put into an untenable position, which led eventually to the collapse of the Mohawks' regional supremacy. Over the rest of the seventeenth century, the pull of the French and the English literally tore the Mohawk nation apart. Several Mohawks converted to Catholicism under the guidance of French Jesuit missionaries, leaving Kanienke to resettle in Canada where there were fewer Europeans. Others stayed behind, and at sites dating from 1680 the absence of Jesuit artifacts is a conspicuous sign of their preservation of traditional religious beliefs as well as their loyalty to the English.

When colonial wars between the French and the English ensued in 1689 and again in 1702, the remaining Mohawks in Kanienke found their duties as English allies increasingly hard to avoid. Any potential for neutrality had withered with their regional authority. Worrying that their participation in a British war party would spark French retaliation, they invited the British to build Fort Hunter. The fort became the center of an eighteenth-century Mohawk community known as Tiononderoge. The remainder of the Mohawk Valley Indians settled in the western edge of Kanienke at Upper Castle. The archaeological remains of these settlements illustrate the extreme effects of colonialism, as the Mohawk community not only accommodated the capitalist expectations of English colonial culture, but some actually sought out advantages within it to the detriment of the larger community. While a few Mohawks found prosperity because of their alliance with the British, this accommodation became a liability after the American Revolution, when American soldiers first plundered and burned their homes, then expelled them from Kanienke altogether.

Archaeologist Kurt Jordan inventoried the accommodations to colonialism made by the Mohawks during the eighteenth century in several aspects of their productive life and material culture (2009). While European trade goods such as glass beads, white clay tobacco pipes, and iron, brass, and lead tools are common from Mohawk sites dating as early as the 1620s, the eighteenth-century European presence in Mohawk life is evident in much more than just artifacts. Mohawk housing in the eighteenth century was constructed almost entirely via European techniques and materials. Stone foundations, frame and log structures, and even two-story houses made up the stock of small, Mohawk family homes, even as their Iroquois neighbors still lived in communal (though often creolized) longhouses. The majority of animal remains consisted of European domesticated animals. Fifty-three percent of the deposits from Fort Hunter and Indian Castle were European species. A 1777 war claim shows that most Mohawk households owned a small number of pigs, cattle, horses, sheep, and oxen. This document also records that barns were common, indicating that domestic animals were tied to specific Mohawk properties (Guldenzopf 1986).

The use of domesticated animals may be paired with evidence of intensive agriculture. Rather than the extensive slash-and-burn techniques used for generations, eighteenth-century Mohawk farmers intensively plowed fenced-in fields. While these techniques were not used at all by most Indian peoples, they had become normal to the Mohawks. The key, as Jordan emphasizes, is not simply the presence of new tools and techniques, but the additional labor involved in their use. Plowing and fertilizing fields and building and maintaining fences involve a great deal of extra work that radically transformed both the Mohawk way of life and the material environment, which this work only prepares for use. We see here, in other words, labor undertaken not directly for reproduction, but simply to make it possible to perform the labor that will eventually meet these needs. This abstraction from primary production is a hallmark of capitalism.

These problems were further complicated by the tendency for eighteenth-century Mohawks to own property privately. In one example of this, individual Mohawk household settlements were dispersed along the riverfront rather than grouped together as a village. The 1777 war claims document shows as well that these lands were privately owned, and, in contrast to the communal ownership of the land by matriarchal clans, the property owners were almost always individual men. This detail, as much, if not more, than the others, reveals the very powerful transformations of Mohawk life that resulted from their colonial subjugation. However, this was not solely the result of an active acculturation process by which the Mohawks were shown the light of modern life and thereafter leaped at the chance to join in. Rather, illustrating the capitalist premise of these structural changes to production, Jordan shows that Mohawk accommodation is best explained by the relatively intense competition between Indians and colonists for basic resources in their locality.

The construction of Fort Hunter was taken as a sign of Mohawk submission, as the British settled five hundred Palatine German refugees on "vacant" land near the fort in 1713. By 1720 there were more Germans than Mohawks in the area, and by 1723 Germans had expanded to new settlements at German Flats and Stone Arabia. With these new settlements, just ten years after Fort Hunter was built, the Mohawks were hemmed in both up- and downriver by new settlers. This situation worsened for these Mohawks over the next decade, as colonial speculators adopted various means to defraud Mohawk families of their lands. By midcentury Guldenzopf estimates that six hundred and fifty European houses were built in the Mohawk region (1986:55). Still, these newcomers alone were not the whole of the threat. Their introduction of European agricultural practices, including forest clearance, field drainage, fence building, road building, and the elimination of predators, was also damaging to Mohawk communities. These "rational" actions produced safe pasturage for cows and other domesticates and protected fields for cultivation. They also destroyed the Indians' traditional habitats by disordering the food chain, encouraging erosion, and making hunting, extensive agriculture, and even trapping impossible.

It was thus for their own protection that Mohawks built fences to guard their fields from deer, feral pigs, and other animals whose forest habitat was fast disappearing. The threat of fraudulent land dealings that in part challenged communal land ownership also forced men to stay close to home, instead of going hunting or trapping, so as to demonstrate their claim on the highly desirable floodplain lands. Land grabbing also likely led Mohawks to acquire legal title to their lands, making the widespread ownership of private property at least in part a result of local political relations. This may also explain the common male ownership. As the European legal system expected male ownership, it may be that Mohawks assigned male names in print to avoid further complications. Yet even though these accommodations may be explained as a response to "European encroachment and directed-culture incentives" (Jordan 2009: 17), it is not enough to let the discussion end here.

Evident in this process is the intensity of competition for the control of resources, most specifically land, and the effects of this competition on the Mohawks as well as everyone else living in their former homeland. Unlike the Narragansett buried at RI-1000, there is no sign among the eighteenth-century Mohawks that anyone was even "playing" at being Indian. There was nothing the Mohawks could do within Kanienke to preserve the material basis for being Indian; their was no incentive or space where their Indianness served a purpose in colonial life. This may indeed be why so many Mohawks left for Canada. For those that remained, however, there was still no shaking the stigma of their Indian heritage, as the widespread destruction of their homes by American soldiers during the Revolutionary War demonstrates. In the era between the initial period of direct colonialism beginning with the construction of Fort Hunter and ending with the community's destruction, we can see how the contradictions of accommodation were handled.

The eighteenth century, for most Mohawks in Kanienke, was a time of great struggle. I have shown how their traditional ways of life became virtually impracticable as they were forced to spend more of their time protecting the few resources they could still claim. I also described how this protection involved the investment of significant labor into intensification of agriculture, an activity which involved their segregation from other community members, who were each facing the same troubles. If all such families were struggling to survive and had to demonstrate their control of the land by working it in some productive way, there was little incentive or even opportunity to work together. In other words, the Mohawks did not walk away from their formerly communal productive life, it was taken from them. Given these circumstances it is expected that Robert Grumet would conclude that "Indians living in Kanienke owned little more than the land beneath their towns" (1995: 374). Excavated ceramics associated with these households confirmed this relative impoverishment, as they consisted mostly of common "redwares and other less-refined earthenwares." Unexpected is that among these sites are a few that demonstrate that some Mohawks "had a higher standard of living than most of their non-Indian neighbors" after 1763 (1995: 375). How did these few prosper while the majority of Mohawks struggled? How did Mohawk communalism not only break down, but so disintegrate that some were wealthy alongside, and in spite of, a majority who were impoverished? Examining this process shows how inter-household competition became legitimate within the Mohawk community, providing a specific example of the capitalist transformation and virtual destruction of this Indian culture.

The Brants are the most well-known eighteenth-century Mohawk family. The remains of their homestead are now preserved as part of the Mohawk Upper Castle Historic District. Excavations by Dean Snow and David Guldenzopf defined two stone foundations (20' x 40' and 10' x 15') and an associated stratified midden deposit (Guldenzopf 1986). The two structures were built in the third quarter of the eighteenth century and are associated with Molly and Joseph Brant. Molly was known for her intimate relations with English colonist Sir William Johnson, a powerful local merchant and New York's superintendent of Iroquois affairs after 1755. Joseph Brant was the last Mohawk chief in Kanienke before they were removed after the Revolutionary War.

The remains recovered from within the cellar holes and surrounding midden illustrate that the Brants were not only well-known, but also relatively well-off (Grumet 1995: 373–75). Peter Schulyer, who occupied the Mary Brandt house after American troops ransacked loyalist Mohawks, recorded the house to have "yielded gold, silver, and silk clothing" (in Snow 2006). The excavated cellar hole also showed that the house had wooden floorboards with rose-head iron nails and plaster walls. The associated midden deposit contained the following (see Figures 2.2a and b): "catlinite and slate beads, a harness bell, a frizzen, white-clay tobacco pipe bowls, bone-handled [utensils], iron kettle fragments and a variety of European ceramics [including] Jackfield type teaware, white salt-glazed stoneware plates, clouded wares, tin-enameled earthenwares, creamwares, [and] underglazed blue and overglazed enameled Chinese porcelain" (Grumet 1995: 373–74). In contrast to the simple assemblages of the commoner Mohawk sites, the wealth of this one truly stands out.

One likely explanation for the Brants' wealth was their association with Sir William Johnson, who as a merchant and an Indian agent was

Figure 2.2. Prestige artifacts from the Mohawk Indian Castle site (photographs by Dean Snow).

motivated to maintain good trading and political relations with Mohawk leadership. While this explanation is likely, I want to contrast the Brant assemblage with the remains associated with RI-1000 Burial 2, the likely Narragansett leader, to elaborate on the meaning of colonial Indian wealth. The remains associated with Narragansett Burial 2 suggest that he may have been a spokesperson for his community within colonial Rhode Island society. This was also the role that Joseph Brant played for the Mohawks in New York. However, the remains associated with Burial 2 illustrate a man laid to rest with objects highly charged with a distinctively Indian symbolism. His brass ring, headband, and buckle, while of European manufacture, made sense to Indian eyes. I am not suggesting that their meaning was only legible to Indians—in fact, his dress was likely necessarily obvious as "Indian" to Indians, Europeans, and others in the community. Rather, I am citing how the assemblage from RI-1000 Burial 2 contrasts markedly with the midden assemblage of Joseph Brant. While expensive "stemmed glassware, fine porcelain, [and] leaded glass" may have once had charged symbolic and spiritual meanings (Grumet 1995: 374, Miller and Hamell 1986), their association with weapons (the flintlock frizzen, for instance), plaster walls, and tea sets suggests Brant's "Indian" associations were downplayed, if not altogether replaced.

In what way was Brant an Indian? I suggest that he was an Indian only inasmuch as Johnson required Indians to trade with and represent. So, if the Narragansett women and the leader buried at RI-1000 were in part being Indian to secure their claim to a fragment of their ancestral territory, it appears that Brant was at best an Indian farce constructed with Johnson in order to acquire "a higher standard of living" for each other. If, in fact, Miantonomi failed to grasp the situation of the Narragansett in 1642, which led to his untimely death, then it seems Brant similarly did not understand the situation of the Mohawks when he brought his people into an alliance with the British after 1775, also leading many to their untimely deaths or, at best, lives in Canada as propertyless refugees.

Conclusion

The similarities between these examples of the seventeenth-century Narragansett and the eighteenth-century Mohawks are based in the themes of inclusion and exclusion from colonial society and a related pattern of self-deception. For Miantonomi, Joseph Brant, the Narragansett man known as Burial 2, and the impoverished Mohawk "property owners," the colonial fur trade, as an extension of European capitalism, produced entirely new worlds to understand and negotiate just to survive. My argument has been that these worlds were imagined as much as they were real, and that this duality was necessary to their practice.

The fur trade established real economic relations between European traders and Indian persons, but these relations were imbued with a sense that a substantial cultural divide existed between the people involved. I have tried to show that these "cultures," though seemingly substantial and imagined as preexisting the actual encounter, were, instead, among the trade's principal products. The fur trade was based on the association of Indian people with Native American products like fur, skins, fish, foods, and crafts. But the fur trade was equally based on positioning Indian people in specialized roles within the capitalist division of labor. As "natives," Indians knew the land and had the necessary technology for extracting its products. In this way, they were part of the larger system at work. As persons, Indians were considered irrational, savage, weak (both from the effects of disease and their susceptibility to it), childish, and easily manipulated. In this way too they were part of the capitalist system. As "Indians," however, Indian people were different and incomprehensible. In this way they were legitimately excluded from the system, and thus any concern for their personhood or humanity was regarded by the majority within the system as inappropriate.

Although some (like the Brants) gained in material ways and as such seemed to be finding a way into the system, in the end they were never seen as anything but Indians, a point no doubt driven home to the Brants by the American soldiers who burned down their fellow Indians' homes and then occupied theirs. Only those within the system are able to truly prosper free from the possibility of exclusion, and this is the real threat of capitalism. By imagining that the most basic foundations for life, things like land, its products, and especially the labor to produce these and other necessary goods, are alienable, all persons in capitalism live in a system wherein their life is conceived and defined as a commodity within the market at least in some way, though for most in very powerful and obvious ways. The means by which people deny their implication in a system that does not regard their personhood are often considered an ideology, in the sense that they mask reality and justify inequalities. The example in this exploration of Native America is that the idea of "the Indian" is one such ideology within capitalism.

In the next chapter, I shift my focus to explore the archaeology of American capitalism from inside its home base, looking at the rise of individualism as the dominant operating ideology within colonial society. Inasmuch as I have explored here how archaeology shows the way Indians, through forms of deception, were excluded from colonial society, I show next how those positioned inside the colonies found ways to demonstrate their inclusion as appropriate, despite the costs that they had to bear to gain this standing.

3

Georgian Practice

Defining Nature in Colonial America

> The Georgian era was one which took cultural conventions into nature and placed them where no one could see their origin and use in society.
>
> Mark Leone and Paul Shackel, "Forks, Clocks, and Power"

Alongside Native Americans, European settlers constructed a different kind of colonial culture. While the productive process within Native America was only partially (yet powerfully) determined by capitalist practice, colonial societies were more completely subsumed. A parallel to the persistent Native kin and community networks was not tolerated within colonial society. Specifically, after an initial phase of settlement, a critical threshold was reached when market exchange within colonial communities reached beyond a focus on the extraction of American commodities through relations with Indians. In varied moments across the colonial landscape, yet through common processes, colonial societies became productive on their own and established a series of new nodes in the Atlantic commodity-exchange network. Relatively less structured by the material legacies of European feudalism, persons in these new American societies were highly driven by a competitive desire to accumulate wealth and market recognition. In the cultural sphere—where the novel practices of the colonial system were normalized—archaeology shows effects of this change, during which early colonial corporate models evident in houses and domestic routines were replaced by practices highlighting individual segregation and competition. Ultimately, the individual became the basis for a new ideology of the natural human experience.

Archaeologists James Deetz and Mark Leone have examined colonial individualism by recording changes in material culture and social practice during the eighteenth century (Deetz 1977, 1996, Leone 1984, 1988, 1995, 2005, Leone and Shackel 1987, 1990, also see Handsman 1981, 1983, Paynter 1982, 1988). Both identify these changes as part of the Georgian order, a movement associated with England's Georgian monarchy (Kings George I-IV ruled from 1714 to 1830) as well as important aspects of Enlightenment philosophy (Glassie 1975). Deetz and Leone highlight that individualism involved a new theory of nature. Rather than a spiritual, supernatural, or irrational force, nature was seen as knowable because it followed calculable, coherent, and observable laws relevant to both the physical world and social life. In fact, the distinction between the human and natural worlds was one effect of this new theory of nature. Positioning human beings where they could objectively observe nature, as if they were outside of it, proposed a discursive shift directly attributable to the revolution associated with Enlightenment philosophy and science (Newton 1999, Horkheimer and Adorno 2002, Trouillot 1995).

American historical archaeology has made a major contribution to understanding the meanings of this profound philosophical and practical shift. Tracking changes in domestic material culture, archaeology shows that the application of natural law to social life is visible in the remains of houses, gardens, and the artifacts associated with the relations formed around the family dining table. While these spaces and objects are typically seen as reflecting Enlightenment ideas, they were more important for their recursivity (Leone and Potter 1988), or the didactic manner in which they acted back upon their users. Their use, in part, produced the modern individual, for it established spaces and implements through which persons could observe differences between themselves and others in their family and community. Additionally, self-assessment could be accomplished by evaluating one's relative competence. Only those who knew where to sit at a table, how to use a fork and napkin, when to show up to work, or that they should retreat to a private room for sleeping were behaving appropriately. Only these persons had standing within society and enjoyed the entitlements of citizenship. Failing to know these rules was cause for embarrassment, but more important, poor manners also impeded one's ability to find the way into proper social standing (Shackel 1993). The main factor underlying this argument is that the mechanisms used to organize social practice, while clearly arbitrary and placed into nature, were instead described as being discovered in nature. They were proposed not as constructions, but formal realities that established the premises of a natural human life. This chapter explores the materiality of this ideology.

New and Different: The Georgian Order and Modernity

Following Deetz and Leone, we may approach the Georgian cognitive order as a revolution. It epitomized a radical and specifically modern transformation of everyday cultural life that broke with long-held traditions associated with Europe's medieval feudal system. Deetz explains (1996: 63), quoting art historian Alan Gowans: "more than a change of style or detail is involved here: it is a change in basic tradition . . . a new and different concept of the relationship between man and nature" (1964: 116–17). This conception was pronounced in material forms, activities, and ideas that emphasized "order and control." The Georgian order was "mechanical where the older was organic, balanced where the older had been asymmetrical, individualized where the older had been corporate" (Deetz 1996: 63) (see Figure 3.1). Deetz considers the Georgian era as an archaeological horizon, or a pattern in material culture that evidences widespread use of culturally distinctive materials resulting typically from "rapid military conquest or effective religious mission" (1996: 64). The Georgian order, however, was the result of neither. Deetz explains that horizons are usually short-lived, yet he considers that the Georgian order "lasts to the present and accounts for much of the way in which we ourselves look upon reality" (1996: 63–4). This contradiction between the sense of the Georgian era as both short-lived and lasting is a sign of its association with modernity as an age that defies history.

The Georgian order makes the arbitrary natural by also making the temporary permanent. It prescribes a way of living based on the state of always becoming, or striving to be, something else. The Georgian order proposes that perfect lives can be led despite and essentially alongside the struggles and limitations people face every day. Leone concludes that the Georgian order is a rationalization of the contradictions between theoretically possible utopian societies and natures described by Enlightenment philosophy and those that people actually experienced as dim and brutal realities (Leone 2005, MacPherson 1962). The Georgian order as such reveals another premise of modernity in the way it poses itself as natural. It claims that what it replaces is not only unnatural, but exactly that which

Figure 3.1. Westover, a Georgian manor house illustrating the style's emphasis on symmetry, balance, and harmonic proportion, as seen in the façade (Virginia Department of Historic Resources, http://www.dhr.virginia.gov/registers/Counties/CharlesCity/Westover_photo.htm).

must be surpassed in order to achieve humanity's ultimate potential. The Georgian model, therefore, carries along its opposites—the traditions of the medieval, primitive, and dogmatic—to show modern people how they can know their failings. Knowledge and experience of the Georgian, or more generally the modern, therefore, is only through a constant failure by most to ever be modern (Latour 1993). In considering the Georgian era a horizon, therefore, Deetz was both right and wrong. Georgian material culture did emerge and spread rapidly, but the fact that its worldview is largely still in place suggests it has become more of an "archaeological tradition," or a discrete set of persistent cultural practices (Deetz 1996: 64). It is the basic character of modernity, however, that recognizing the modern as a tradition is heretical, since the modern is defined by the ceaseless reinvention of itself in opposition to the past (Berman 1982, Matthews 2002). Archaeological studies of the Georgian era help to identify the origins of this contradiction.

The archaeological evidence of Georgianization that Deetz and Leone interpret are materials used to demonstrate that perfection can be achieved. Georgian houses, landscapes, furnishings, utensils, and their associated behaviors allowed persons to practice being modern individuals. Georgian material culture, therefore, does not reflect an inner sense of order, but rather an order based on a hoped-for state of being (Leone 2005: 81, 94). The Georgian materials that emerge in the archaeology of later colonial America are mechanisms by which persons confront the expectations of their own modernity. In no small part through their successful ownership and use, Georgian materials underwrite the dominant senses of belonging and entitlement in modern society. This review of the archaeology of the Georgian era in colonial America shows that such a stance is arbitrary by exhibiting the Georgian model as a naturalizing ideology. Quite contrary to what the Georgian system claims, archaeology shows that more "natural" kin- and community-based social relations and engagements with the material world make up the precursors of the Georgian era. Archaeology also explains how the natural basis of postmedieval culture was overturned and replaced by what amounts to an unnatural, arbitrary, supposedly "natural" arrangement in the explicit service of capitalism.

Organic in the Extreme: Social Relations and Early American Material Culture

Prior to the cultural revolution of the Georgian order, early American colonial societies illustrate what may be considered "natural" forms of social organization and material production based on traditions tied to kinship and the social production of value. Most households, especially in rural settings, were independent in the sense that they controlled production themselves, owned their own capital and tools, and provided for their own subsistence directly or through limited market and barter exchange. Deetz generalizes early colonial communities as "peasant societies" (1996: 61), highlighting their rural, insular, and conventional character. We should take this assessment with a grain of salt, as many Europeans in colonial America, even those who did not participate in the Indian fur trade, came with an eye for engaging in international mercantile trade (Kulikoff 1989, Bushman 1998). Still, we can work with Deetz's archaeological observations to record how, despite the specific character of their economic motivations, early settlers essentially reproduced traditional "medieval" culture.

Deetz's study of the material culture of early America positions early colonial communities as relatively closer to nature than their followers in several respects. Nature here is a crude gloss for environmental, social, and cultural forces that limited human choice such that access to raw materials, community size and integration, as well as conventions of social life and belief were considered more directly relevant to life than these factors are for most Americans living after the emergence of the Georgian era. Again, this may be overstated, but the patterns that Deetz defines show that certain practices in early colonial communities followed routines that have limited parallels in modern capitalist societies. I illustrate this closeness to nature in the architectural evidence Deetz presents.

Early colonial houses were vernacular constructions. They were not planned by architects, but followed building traditions that colonial settlers imported from England and elsewhere. Deetz illustrates this process in two ways. Architecture in early colonial Massachusetts, for example, shows a variety of forms and styles, including post-in-ground structures, longhouses, and hall-and-parlor, central-chimney structures which may in turn be related to distinct regions in England such as the English uplands or East Anglia (Deetz 1996: 133–38). This persistence of architectural designs is hardly surprising, but for Deetz it shows an attachment to both materials and forms as well as a worldview that made the adjustment to colonial life in America less culturally daunting. He emphasizes that these building styles were traditions, meaning that their reproduction through time likely happened without any thought. Such thoughtless action is one important aspect of the "natural" character of these houses. Incorporating research by folklorist Henry Glassie (1975), Deetz further describes how early colonial houses were not simply stylistic and technological survivals of English regional traditions, but also were signs of deep structural or grammatical norms associated with rural English culture generally. Glassie's analysis of folk housing in rural Virginia shows that a spatial norm, defined as a sixteen-foot square, underlies the multitude of floor plan variations found throughout the region. Without architectural plans, it is clear that this unit and the spatial sense and order it produced resided solely in the minds of the region's builders. In this space, Deetz summarizes, "an Anglo-American feels most comfortable" (1996: 155). Glassie further shows that this natural unit was a generative force in that other

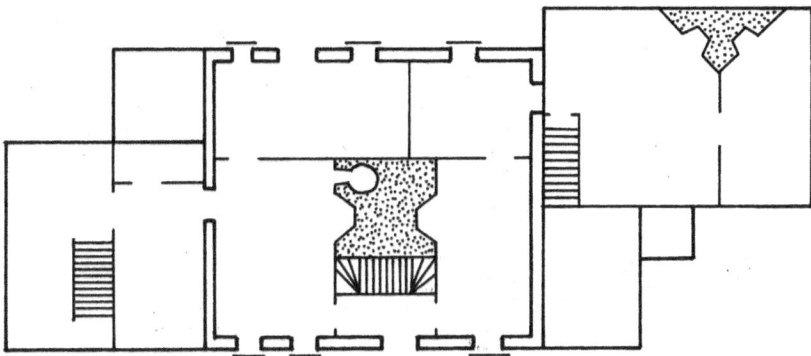

Figure 3.2. Floor plan of the Fairbanks House in Dedham, Massachusetts, showing accretionary "organic" growth in the structure to accommodate changes in household composition (drawing by Ross Rava after Deetz 1977: 110).

dimensions were defined by common variations such as half (eight-foot) or quarter (four-foot) sections or additions. Thus, the houses themselves conformed to dimensions that enacted long-held values about the organization of space. In this way, again, the relatively natural basis of early colonial culture is revealed.

Significantly, houses are not just materials and constructions—they also embody human beings in important ways. First, houses provide humans shelter. In rural New England, houses were typically family dwellings, and they contained in their growth family histories which are important records of the colonial story. One example is the Jonathan Fairbanks house in Dedham, Massachusetts, built in 1637 (see Figure 3.2). The original part of the house followed the common central-chimney, two-room, hall-and-parlor form. Over time several new rooms were added on and enlarged to accommodate new household members and productive activities. By the early nineteenth century, the two-room house had become a ten-room arrangement around the original core, with lean-tos and other additions and alterations. This growth by accretion followed no organized plan, but is rather described by Deetz as "organic in the extreme [because] the houses of this early time grew according to need" (1996: 138). At the Fairbanks house, change was prompted by family growth and developments in productive life. Vernacular houses like these are not a style, because they do not reveal a preexisting plan or claim to reveal principles of order and beauty that lie behind nature. They are material forms determined by everyday confrontations with the limitations and opportunities imposed and created by nature.

Besides those they shelter, buildings also embody humanity in the labor required for their construction. For the present discussion, in fact, the work of building is the most important architectural aspect to consider. The renaturalization of labor (whether for building or other productive work) associated with the Georgian order illustrates the practical actions that made the radical capitalist transformation of modernity seem rather ordinary. Among the displacements of social life associated with capitalist production in the colonies was the redesignation of the relations between builders and owners. Prior to the Georgian era, buildings show two aspects of the noncapitalist corporate foundations of early colonial communities. First, building on Glassie's idea of an architectural grammar, Deetz states, "most important, these concepts were those of the builder, who was intimately a part of the society for which the house was produced, and as such closely reflect that society's values" (1996: 156). In their works, builders revealed aspects of the shared corporate culture that tied together those living in early colonial communities. However, this intimacy describes another aspect of these early societies that ties them more closely to the natural roots of a social life based on kin and community.

Referencing a study by Robert Blair St. George (1983), Deetz notes that seventeenth-century craftsmen such as carpenters, masons, and thatchers "spent a disproportionate amount of time in maintaining their work after it was completed, more than income from such repairs would suggest" (1996: 147). The conclusion to be drawn from this is that maintenance was part of a builder's work. This was not a formal arrangement; rather, this work was part of the larger circulation of value within a community. As builders maintained houses, those who lived in them would in turn provide services, as a matter of custom, to builders. In this way the whole of the community was housed as part of the standard norms of obligation. The point is that this exchange was not a barter of services between builders and homeowners, but rather part of a wider "set of reciprocal relationships that lent coherence to the community" (Deetz 1996: 147). Even more so than building in the grammatical traditions of rural England, I think this tradition nicely illustrates how builders were an intimate part of their communities. Through such "maintenance relations," builders remained a part of their work, and their continued presence at homesites helped bind communities through the ongoing nature of such relations

(St. George 1983). As much as aging, bearing and raising children, and death and decay, maintenance is a natural part of human community life. Notably, Georgian architecture, defined not by traditions of maintenance but by the idea of houses as completed works, brought about new building practices that distanced builders and other laborers from their work. Even though this part of Georgianization has explicit archaeological correlates in that it is tied to new forms of building in and on the ground, it remains underreported in historical archaeology. I will consider next an archaeological study of historic architecture that speaks to this issue directly.

Stone Foundations: Breaking the Community

Thomas Bordley is calculated to have been among the five wealthiest men in Annapolis, Maryland, in 1720 (Baker 1986). Bordley was a prominent politician and a successful lawyer. He was appointed by the proprietary governor—Maryland was a privately operated colony under the rule of the Calvert family—as attorney general, and he held a seat in the upper house of the colonial assembly. These positions were the most prominent in Maryland that could be held by nonproprietary family members. Bordley's standing, however, was relatively short-lived, as the proprietor accused him of giving "councel of pernicious Consequence" (cited in Morton 1964: 14), leading to his removal from all appointed posts. In response, Bordley shifted his loyalty to Maryland's emergent "Country Party," an oppositional faction demanding self-determination for Maryland's colonists. During this time, he built an impressive house in Annapolis. The story of its construction relates the movement away from traditional community relations to important aspects of colonial politics in the early eighteenth century.

The Bordley-Randall house is located on the interior of a five-sided city block off of State Circle in Annapolis (see Figure 3.3a). The main section of the original house is a two-story central element that exhibits obvious symmetry. Archaeological and historical examination of the landscape immediately surrounding the house suggests that the two wings, a kitchen and an office, were built concurrently with the central block before 1726 (Matthews 1998). Several architectural characteristics of the Bordley house stand out. First, it was made entirely of brick. Even as late as 1715, most houses in Annapolis were frame (Yentsch 1994: 18, 240). Large brick manor houses were associated only with the wealthiest plantation owners

Figure 3.3. The Bordley-Randall House in Annapolis, Maryland. *Top:* Front view in the 1890s, though the house was first built in the 1710s (courtesy of the Historic Annapolis Foundation, Inc.). *Bottom:* The east wing foundation, showing the massive stonework that was originally exposed when the house was constructed (photograph by Christopher Matthews).

in the surrounding Chesapeake countryside. Furthermore, the brick pattern of the façade was all headers, a style that required twice the number of bricks as did the more popular running, Flemish, or common bonds that employ a majority of stretchers. The expense of brick construction was, therefore, doubled in this instance. Second, the house design follows the principles of the Georgian order in its symmetry, which includes a central doorway and an interior passage, two window bays on each side of the door, and the opposing placement of the wing structures in relation to the central block. In this manner the plan is very formal. Related to building this formality is a telling indicator of the construction technique that was discovered archaeologically: its stone foundation.

Excavations adjacent to the structure in areas that were undisturbed by nineteenth-century renovations and additions indicate that the east wing was built on top of and along the edge of a slope that dropped off to the southeast. To accommodate the slope, the depth of the stone foundation under the wing varies quite a bit, being only two feet deep under the north or back wall of the wing, but over five feet deep under the south or front wall (see Figure 3.3b). This variation allowed the wing to stand level with the rest of the house and be situated in the visual center of the five-sided lot. In other words, the natural topography of the site was altered as a result of being subjected to a gaze that saw the house as a visual element of a larger formal space. According to this gaze, the site was then transformed to fit the house, even though at the time the house was only in the builder's (and in this case likely the owner's) imagination. This construction can be contrasted with the Mott farmhouse in Portsmouth, Rhode Island, discussed by Deetz (1996: 159–60) (see Figure 3.4). The Mott house was remodeled in the mid-eighteenth century, incorporating several elements of Georgian symmetrical design. However, an obvious violation of symmetry is evident in the façade, and the roofline reflects the accommodation of the house to the existing sloping landscape, a feature that was not or could not be altered during the renovation.

The Bordley house design and construction were not just stylistic, they also illustrated the shifting social discourse associated with the Georgian order. Like brick walls, stone foundations were a relatively uncommon and expensive building component in early-eighteenth-century Annapolis. Stone, however, was a solution to a problem that men like Thomas Bordley faced. Before the use of stone foundations, most Annapolis houses were post-in-ground structures. Using inground wooden support

Figure 3.4. Front view of the Mott farmhouse in Portsmouth, Rhode Island, showing an effort to construct a symmetrical house mitigated by a forced adjustment to the preexisting landscape (drawing by Ross Rava after Deetz 1977: cover).

columns, then a norm across the Chesapeake region, early colonial houses were often considered impermanent architectural forms (see Carson et al. 1981, Deetz 1996: 20–22, Shackel 1998). These structures illustrated for some the hard work and short-sighted, profit-focused goals of colonization that left little time or interest for investment in more permanent architecture. Still, post-in-ground foundations required a great deal of maintenance over the years, and this maintenance would have materialized the relations that bound homeowners with laborers in communities like Annapolis. The shift to stone, therefore, was a sign of wealth and permanence, but also a statement on the nature of community relations. Paul Shackel recorded one instance in Annapolis, the Sands house, where a post-in-ground foundation was replaced with stone under the existing house in the early eighteenth century (1998). The visible foundation at the Thomas Bordley house is even more clearly pronounced.

Rather than being hidden under the house or placed entirely underground, the upper courses of stone on the front-facing foundation under the east wing of the Bordley house were originally set above grade. This is evident in two ways. First, unlike the roughly laid east and north walls, stones used for the south wall were smoothly faced. This suggests that the wall was intended to be visible. Second, within an early-eighteenth-century stratum adjacent to the foundation, a concentration of brick, shell, plaster, and artifact debris was located exactly where a stairway would have allowed entry into the east wing through a doorway. It was in the three feet of space between the ground surface and the interior floor level that the foundation was visible. A visible foundation matters because it embodied and publicly expressed the new relationship between laborers and owners. Stone foundations were permanent constructions that eliminated the need for maintenance relations. When builders completed the work, their relationship with homeowners was complete. Where buildings had been previously a source of community intimacy, Georgian houses, especially those with stone foundations, now created social distance. That Bordley built a foundation that was both permanent and highly visible suggests that he was aware of this fact.

This story takes on additional meaning when it is related to local politics. Bordley built this house around the time he switched his allegiance from the colonial proprietor to the opposition. Bordley's construction of a stone foundation and brick house may have symbolized independence. Breaking from traditions such as maintenance relations provided a way to establish his capacity to stand on his own within the community. Thus, even though he was putting himself effectively at odds with those who labored to build his house, he was doing so in the spirit of breaking free from the bonds of service and obligation that defined the arbitrary rule of the colonial proprietor. Considering other aspects of Bordley's life and livelihood that may have supported these politics helps to further explain his motives.

As with many of his class, Bordley was simultaneously a lawyer, planter, landlord, and merchant. These varied interests went hand in hand, because the Chesapeake was a tobacco plantation region and most people there were involved directly or indirectly in that dominant trade. For example, towns were rare, so centralized settlements that supported full-time merchants were few. Instead, leading rural planters functioned as part-time local merchants for smaller planters, providing consumer goods in exchange for tobacco futures. It appears that Thomas Bordley served in this role for his Annapolis neighbors. A listing of items included in his 1726 probate inventory is stated to be from his store, which was presumably located within his house. Further probate account details show that he was also involved in other forms of productive labor and debt relations common at the time. He owned plantations in three Maryland counties and owned and rented extensive property in Annapolis itself. These ventures were extremely profitable, and they were generative in that those who could invest in them claimed more and more of the profits created by local communities. Notably, in Maryland, proprietary control placed restrictions on the accumulation of such profits by private individuals, and this was in part the basis for forming the oppositional Country Party.

For an oppositional movement in the name of unfettered private accumulation to succeed against the colonial authority, it had to gain support from those outside the uppermost ranks of society. The use of new construction methods was one way to do this. Even though stone foundations undermined the security of skilled working people who relied on long-term maintenance relationships for their livelihood, they instituted a new way of thinking about social relations within the community. Rather than obligation, new communities were based on economic freedom defined by contractual relations between individuals. The subordination of builders to owners (and similarly of renters to landlords and debtors to creditors) could be seen as lasting only for the time of the contract. This market-based sense of freedom was the basis of the opposition to proprietary control, and members of the Country Party in turn applied it to the way they practiced social life in their own communities. Highlighting the free individual, contract-based relations separated persons from their productive lives and productive work from community organization. As work was defined by agreement, it was not a traditional pursuit, but one invented and reinvented with every contract.

Contract relations embodied a "new and different" order in which individuals engaged in social life of their own volition through agreements defined by their legitimated self-interest. This modern order replaced one wherein social life preexisted and determined the individual because people's work and self-interest were bound up with their community's needs. Contracts created a new community that enabled the expansion of capitalism, one where the perspective of the individual was given standing in nature though it had previously been subordinate to the community at large. Placing the individual in nature, as the perspective we use as a starting point for social interaction, also forced the normalization of labor abstraction essential to capitalism. Despite the material presence of other persons and relationships, workers were expected to imagine themselves as discrete entities who engaged in social relations independently and in the specific settings and times defined by contracts (also see Handsman 1983). Beyond social and productive life, that is, there was proposed another reality, which, because of the artificiality of the contract, was seen as the natural basis of an individual's existence. The function of the Georgian order was to enable the experience of this reality beyond social life and work and, by opposing community life to individual experience, to illustrate the possibility of constructing a society of individuals.

Therefore, the archaeology of the Georgian order examines how Georgian forms segregate experience into what is real and what, because of contractual relationships, is both temporary and artificial. Mark Leone argues that this division is a naturalizing ideology in which the natural and artificial aspects of social life are reversed (2005: 24–26). Within the Georgian order, productive labor and the social relations that organize it are not seen as a basis for meaning, but instead are taken to be simply work undertaken to support the fulfillment of the self through more consequential "off-duty" activities. Included among these activities, as Leone shows (1988, 1995, 2005), are didactic apparatuses such as place settings and formal gardens that teach persons how to be individuals. It is particularly the way material forms enable individuals to construct themselves and their realities that allowed the Georgian order to succeed since, as it was based on abstract principles, it relied on individual experience and perspective to be fully understood. That is, the principles of the Georgian order cannot be told to someone as truth, but must rather be presented so that an individual can come to know the truth as a result of their own actions.

Setting the Table: Breaking the Family

Considering the materials within the houses of early America, Deetz uses both probate inventories and archaeological remains to construct a sequence of change for domestic activities that describes the emergence of the Georgian order in the everyday lives of common people. The development of modern dining practices, evident in ceramics and other material culture, is one of the most telling examples. Ceramics are an important data source because they were a component of the basic activities associated with cooking and eating. Changes in ceramic use and meaning therefore illustrate the very deep influence of capitalism, since ceramic analysis shows how even the most common activities became charged with new significance as people sought ways to distinguish themselves from others. The most notable result of these changes was how the family was redesigned, transforming from a cooperative, productive unit into an assembly of persons learning how to be individuals. Due to the Georgian order, moreover, the family became a symbol of the intimacies and irrational responsibilities that had to be overcome for individuals to succeed in the market.

Following Deetz (1996: 75), ceramic use patterns may be arranged as a three-stage sequence among domestic sites in colonial America. In the first stage, which runs from initial colonial settlement until about 1660, sites produce relatively few ceramics, and most are utilitarian earthenwares. The second stage, which lasts until the mid-eighteenth century, includes more ceramic variety, including greater numbers of fancy types like delftware plates and Rhenish stoneware mugs. The third phase, which lasts until the early nineteenth century, is dominated by mass-produced earthenwares known to historical archaeologists as Creamware and Pearlware. In third-stage sites, ceramics are found in much greater numbers than in earlier phases and show signs of being replaced more often. Deetz associates third-stage ceramics with the Georgian order partly because, like Georgian architecture, they were popular styles, used by homeowners to set a table in the current fashion.

To explain these patterns, Deetz tracks the relationship between domestic ceramic use and eating. In the first stage, ceramics play only a small role in eating. The utilitarian vessels recovered were used instead for dairy work, especially cheese making, which called for glazed vessels and varied and specific forms like pans, colanders, and crocks that local potters could produce. Comparing contemporary probate inventories, Deetz concludes that food was eaten either directly from the pots it was cooked in or from wooden trenchers that were shared by multiple persons. Drinks were also taken from shared vessels, typically made of leather, pewter, or sometimes clay. This finding shows that in the early colonial period eating was a corporate activity. In fact, eating may have been an activity used to reinforce family ties and obligations. With shared vessels the norm, even in times of scarcity, what was had was presented to all.

In the second stage, the ceramic pattern is defined by the addition of more expensive wares such as large delftware plates and stoneware mugs. Deetz records that the delftware plates most often recovered are unique in several ways. They are the only plates found, they are larger than expected, and they show little use wear. These observations suggest that they functioned more as display items than tools for daily food service. In fact, citing room-by-room probate inventories, it was more common for these plates to have been located in the formal parlor than the hall where cooking, cleaning, eating, and similar everyday labors were performed. The implication is that these vessels were used to display household status, conveyed by their fashion and the fact that they were *not* used for mundane purposes. This pattern suggests a spatial and likely intellectual separation of domestic activities by their relative social value. This may also mean that, at this time, activities associated with household production came to stand below those related to presenting social standing. We might take this as a sign that even in a two-room house, people sought to segregate what they had to do from their efforts to illustrate who they were or, perhaps, hoped to be. This distinction in value is mirrored by the increase in stoneware mugs. The finding in probate records that stoneware mugs were kept with trenchers suggests that the greater number of mug fragments relates to their increasing presence on the dining table. Deetz concludes that while eaters continued to share common vessels for food, they were now more likely to drink from individual mugs. Stoneware mugs are thus seen to have been material signs of individuality within the household. This demand for material forms of individual distinction became even more clearly asserted in the third-stage ceramics.

The popular ceramics now known as Creamware and Pearlware were among the first mass-produced products associated with the English Industrial Revolution (Miller 1991). These types were available as matched sets, a quality related to their mass production as well as to the demand for individual place settings, each consisting of multiple vessels. Deetz explains that matched sets of plates demonstrate the Georgian symmetry of one person per dish that individualism demands (1996: 86). Arriving at a dining table, diners found that there was a place for each person defined by a plate, cup, set of eating utensils, and more (see Figure 3.5). These artifacts contrasted with trenchers and shared mugs, as they declared the separation of each diner from the others. However, because not only did each person have the same set of objects, but the sets themselves matched

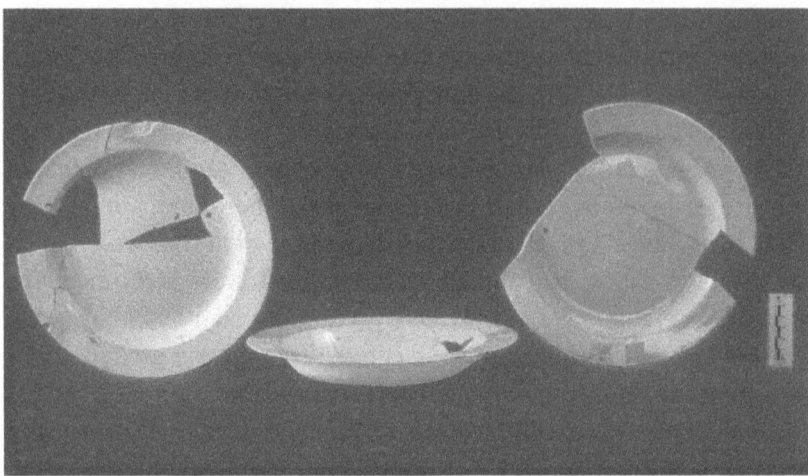

Figure 3.5. Matched set of Creamware plates, first manufactured by Josiah Wedgewood in Staffordshire, England, in 1763. These examples were recovered from the Hoffman household, that of a late-eighteenth-century German baker, in the Five Points section of New York City (photograph courtesy of Rebecca Yamin, John Milner Associates).

as a whole, the message was sent that all diners were at once individuals with their own place and interchangeably equivalent in that each place was essentially the same as the others.

These attributes of matched sets project the principal social messages of capitalism, excluding one key element: competition. Additional analyses define the meaning of other elements of Georgian ceramics, showing that competition was evident, on the one hand, in market variation, and, on the other, in the performance of dining etiquette. The roots of interhousehold market competition were first revealed in the delftware plates displayed in parlors. These plates spoke of their owners' relative success in the market, since they were both expensive and unused. The sharp increase in ceramics during the third phase may be related both to increased supply due to mass production and a competitive demand driving stylistic variety (Leone 1999). Compared to earlier types, Creamware and Pearlware ceramics show simultaneous uniformity and variety in terms of decorative attributes, such as molded shell-edge or transfer-printed forms and decorations (see Figures 3.6). These variations in part ensured sets could be matched, because these techniques were easily replicable and thus suitable for mass production, but the decorative variety was also pronounced enough so that consumers could select from different styles

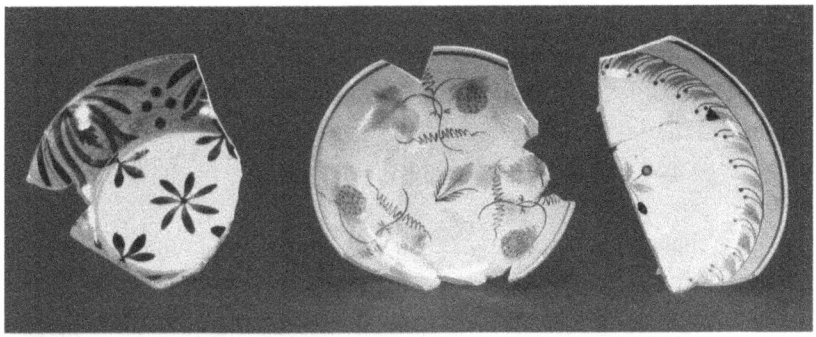

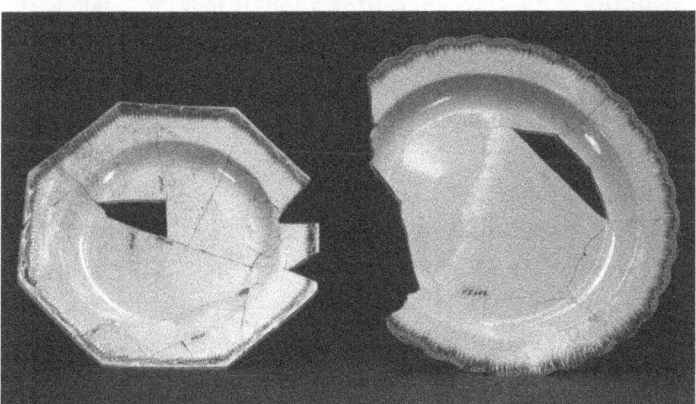

Figure 3.6. Common decorated ceramics from late-eighteenth and early-nineteenth-century archaeological contexts. *Top:* Hand-painted Pearlware saucers. *Middle:* Willow pattern transfer-printed whiteware platter. *Bottom:* Green and blue shell-edged Pearlware plates (photographs by Melody Henkel, courtesy of The Andrew Fiske Memorial Center for Archaeological Research, University of Massachusetts, Boston).

in order to choose the one that marked them as "different" from their neighbors. In fact, George Miller's widely used ceramic pricing indices are only available because of the exacting distinctions that ceramic mass producers made to allow matched sets to stand apart from one another in obvious and meaningful ways in the market and at the dinner table (1991).

The archaeological evidence of a sharp increase in ceramic use in the late eighteenth century indicates an important additional factor in the way ceramics enabled persons to become individuals within the market. The key is mass production and the collapse of the distinctions between the market and sites like the family dining table. With mass production eliminating the demand for skilled labor, a great deal about the market changed. Rather than an actual place where the work and products of skilled labor might be bought and sold, the market for mass-produced goods became increasingly abstract. It was still a market defined by buyers and sellers, but these were less persons someone knew in their community than abstract souls who may or may not actually exist, let alone be personally known (Agnew 1986). To compensate for the shift of the market from a concrete place to an abstract notion, competition became manifest at other social locations like the dining table. Importantly, the competition at the dining table was not symbolic of the market, but was rather the materialization of its abstraction.

Yet, unlike in the market, where getting a job or making a sale is the result of competition, competition at the dinner table was also didactic, and was never resolved. Furthermore, the dining table presented persons with those most likely to hamper their individual standing in the market: their family. Even within capitalism, it is normal for working people to share a home with their family and be primarily responsible for the care of their family members from birth to death. Such kin relations and responsibilities, however, stand opposed to the contractual relations that define work in capitalism, where one may break off business relations without unforeseen consequences. The dining table and the paraphernalia it included thus served two simultaneous purposes. It was a site where the rational (market relations) and the irrational (kin relations) could be distinguished and opposed; and, through the consumption and appropriate use of the paraphernalia, it was a location where persons could realize the substance of their individuality in the presence of their most intimate community.

In order to prepare children for market relations, families were expected to teach them about competition and expectations of individuality. The dining table was the ideal site for this training. It put persons in a situation where, as a family, they were focused on a common activity, and thus created a moment in which they might feel most obliged to share. Individual place settings, however, restrained this impulse by segregating portions and family members from one another, essentially positioning diners as competitors for food. Eating off of matched sets taught that, in other situations, members of the family sitting at the table were interchangeable, and might very well find themselves in competition for jobs, clients, and wealth.

Competition at the dining table was also pronounced in the appropriate use of the varied objects included in a place setting. Rather than simply containing and conveying food, the matched plates, bowls, cups, and utensils each required a set of learned techniques for their correct and mannerly use. The fork, which became common only in association with matched sets in the eighteenth century, offers a good example (Deetz 1996: 168–70; Leone and Shackel 1987, Shackel 1993: 146–50). Prior to the common use of forks, eaters either used their hands or the pointed tip of a knife to convey food into their mouths. With the emergence of the fork, knife tips began being rounded. This change in knife form indicates that eaters were expected to cut their food into small bites with the knife blade, then transfer proper bites to their mouths with the fork. This extra, technical step ensured that grease or gravy would not be smeared on the diner's face or drip off of their chin onto their shirt. This new etiquette made the signs of eating that might have been evident on a person's body or clothing after a meal disappear. With the aid of forks and napkins, proper diners were to leave the table bearing no visible signs that they had eaten at all. This compulsion for cleanliness may be paired with the separation of production and status symbolism associated with the large delftware plates noted above, except here the person is equivalent to the plate in that their social status is revealed by their ability to show no use-wear from engaging in work.

This construction of the individual as distinct from their productive labor (including eating food) is a principal component of capitalism. All persons must work, but who gets hired or promoted is a result of the evaluation of the relative qualities that are thought to be inherent to each individual. Irrational social ties like family connections and traditional community relations have no role in the capitalist labor market. Only the qualities of an individual matter, and with the growing use of unskilled labor associated with mass production, these qualities became increasingly represented by the way persons presented themselves for inspection, measured in terms of how they dressed, took care of their bodies, ate, danced, worshipped, showed up for work, and so forth (Leone 2005: 55, Upton 1997). The presentation of the self in capitalism is framed in the same way as the presentation of mass-produced plates: persons become individuals only when they see themselves as comparable commodities, and, as with varied decorative styles, this vision focuses attention on how they manage to stand apart from others who are increasingly just like them. Therefore, the archaeological recovery of matched sets of ceramics indicates that families adopted dining activities that were primarily about teaching and practicing the techniques of mutual individual inspection.

Leone identifies this as the masking ideology of possessive individualism (2005: 35, 155). Following MacPherson (1962), this theory suggests that individuals in capitalism must own themselves, such that personhood is regarded through the lens of property relations. In practice, this meant that personal talents or skills were alienable. They may reside within people—in fact, they may define them as, for example, a carpenters, doctors, or mothers—but they may also be separated out as solely what the people do, rather than wholly who they are. To know one's self required that one find different sources than work for one's identity. The demand for knowing the self outside of productive work thus cycled back on the other activities that sustained life like eating, sleeping, shelter, and elimination. Matched sets of dishes at the dining table therefore not only enabled persons to practice manners and discipline, but also allowed them to discover—in their relative ability to properly manipulate the paraphernalia—more about who they really were as a mannerly and disciplined person. This search for the self outside of work also allowed persons to survive if the market for their talents or skills disappeared. Thus it was not the individual who failed, only the individual's skill set, and with new training that person could find another source of work. This extension of the theory is especially important, for with industrialization, less and less skill was demanded of laborers, placing more and more emphasis on the other parts of their life that would allow them to distinguish themselves from the growing mass of interchangeable laboring individuals.

The Georgian House and Garden: Breaking Nature

This approach of using matched sets as evidence of an ideological masking of reality has not gone without criticism (for example, see Hodder 1986: 63–65, Beaudry et al. 1991, McGuire 1992: 140–42, Wilkie and Bartoy 2000). Some question whether working people would adopt new practices that alienated them from the means of production. Why would they accept that the self was to be found in the performance and evaluation of actions associated with personal discipline rather than productive labor? Did they not resist this exploitation? These important questions demand solid responses. I think that the evidence for the validity of the Georgian order as an important component of the ideology of possessive individualism comes from a serious consideration of Gowans's conclusion that the Georgian order promoted a "new and different concept of the relationship between man and nature." We can see this in the most expressive forms of the Georgian cognitive order—houses and formal gardens.

Georgian architecture was part of a radically new way of thinking. Enlightenment philosophy redrafted the cosmic order from one based on the supremacy of God to one based on the supremacy of man as a knowing, reasoned, and self-determined creature. In other words, the order of the universe, once envisioned as the work of God, came to be seen instead as the result of natural laws that could be observed, calculated, and applied in the betterment of human life. Sustained with the Enlightenment is the sense that behind what we observe is a functional apparatus or plan, but this shifted from a divine to a natural origin, one which by experimentation could be appropriated and put to use by human beings who understood its rules. The idea that there is a plan that follows formal rules and which can be copied is what stands out in this "new and different" sense of nature. No longer was nature a force that persons confronted as they grew, built with, navigated, and mined its resources to meet their needs. Nature could be understood, tamed, and in turn put to use by educated, modern persons. In fact, people who knew how to put nature to work no longer needed affiliations with those in their community or family to survive, but could instead willingly engage fellow persons on a new plane of positive, individual relations apart from productive work.

The formal designs of Georgian buildings captured the essence of this proposal. Deetz contrasts Georgian architecture with its vernacular predecessors in part by way of the architectural plans used in its construction (Deetz 1996: 126). These plans were not just drawings, but manifestations of orderly and natural designs captured by classical Greek and Roman architects, whose genius was rediscovered in the Renaissance (Wittkower 1971). The epitome of this sense of order was formally expressed in the Georgian commitment to producing the harmonic proportions illustrated in dozens of architectural plan books published in English beginning in the 1720s (Matthews 1998). Rather than utilizing spatial dimensions, Georgian house plans often simply include single numbers that define the size and arrangement of rooms and elevations. These numbers are scaled proportional ratios that allowed builders to create perfect forms in actual buildings of any dimensions. In fact, some such books included charts that translated these ratios into actual measures. While this is a simple functional application, it represents how the new natural order was seen, produced, and, importantly, published. The rules of nature could be boiled down to sets of interrelated numbers, or abstractions, that could theoretically be produced by anyone.

Examples of Georgian architecture that illustrate this way of thinking are evident in Annapolis, Maryland, and other prominent towns and cities that date from the late colonial period. The Chase-Lloyd house (see Figure 3.7) was built in Annapolis between 1769 and 1774 by two wealthy Maryland planters under the architectural direction of William Buckland (Matthews 2002: 56–58). The housefront exemplifies the symmetry characteristic of the Georgian style, and it demonstrates the use of harmonic ratios to enhance the stylistic effect. Each story, as the building climbs upward, is proportionally shorter than the one below it. The ratio of the stories employs the Pythagorean standard of 3–4–5, in which the first floor translates as 5, the second floor as 4, and the top floor as 3. While there is no surviving architectural plan of the house, these ratios indicate that one was followed. The purpose of the plan in this case, however, was not simply to show a hidden though underlying order, but to produce an illusion. The proportionally related stories work together to make the house appear taller than it really is. It is this use of natural rules, here the laws of optics, that makes the Georgian order function as an ideology. It is not simply that behind the material world lie abstract principles and laws, but that those who know these most thoroughly may use them to produce material forms that can expand on, or in a sense reconstruct, reality for human use.

Figure 3.7. The Chase-Lloyd House in Annapolis, Maryland. Constructed in 1772, the design illustrates the detailed attention paid to the reproduction of a neoclassical emphasis on symmetry, balance, and harmonic proportion (photograph by Christopher Matthews).

Leone's analysis of elite, formal gardens built in Annapolis during the 1760s and 1770s makes the same case by using landscape data. After studying the reconstructed William Paca Garden (Leone 1984, 2005: 63–83; Leone and Shackel 1990), Leone devised that similar illusions were explicitly crafted in both published and built forms. Authors like Batty Langley commented extensively on the use of harmonically proportional ratios in the construction of garden terraces, such that spaces could be made to appear larger or houses further away than they really were (Langley 1726, Leone 2005: 69). At the Paca Garden, a structure known as the Summer House—which was defined archaeologically in a 1960s reconstruction effort and thus was part of the original plan—indeed appears father away than it really is because of the garden's nonuniform, sloping terraces. Langley describes another technique: "All walks whose lengths are short, and lead away from any point of view, [should] be made narrower at their further ends than at the hither part; for by inclination of their sides, they appear to be of a much greater length than they really are" (1726: 196).

Leone shows how gardens could be made to make lines of sight converge through the use of nonparallel hedgerows or varying shades of color. These findings were confirmed when surviving gardens built in the 1770s by John Ridout and Charles Carroll in Annapolis were mapped, showing that the construction of garden ramps and garden beds followed suit (Leone 2005: 73–77).

Georgian houses and gardens in Annapolis thus present a diverse set of data that may be tied together. They each employ illusions that reconstruct reality. They were all built at the same time, in the decade before the American Revolution, a fact that stands out because many of the published sources on Georgian architecture and gardens were available thirty or more years earlier. They were each built by the leading wealthy men of the Maryland colony, who, like Thomas Bordley, were stuck in a colonial system that imposed limitations on their ability to accumulate wealth. Each also owned a large number of slaves, operated plantations, and was involved in the colony's politics. Like Bordley, these men built in the context of a struggle for power. The difference is in how they related to the audiences of their visual works.

While the point of Bordley's construction was to distance himself from his builders by establishing a contractual basis for community relations, Paca's garden and Chase's house were about reincorporation. Over the course of the eighteenth century, the proposals made by Bordley became essentially accepted, and most free, laboring people became engaged in work that was contractual and based on the ownership of their labor. Yet, as Leone shows (2005: 16), during this period there was also a significant realignment of wealth, such that by the 1770s the top twenty percent of the population owned eighty-seven percent of assets recorded at death. Notably, this pattern was first pronounced in the era of Bordley's death in 1726, thus the intervening half-century only saw an intensification of this process. Still, for those free persons in the middle and lower classes, this was not a time of simple acquiescence. Rather, their participation in the antielite religious movement known as the Great Awakening, affiliations with independently backed merchants, and a slow but steady growth of rural towns all challenged the political and economic hegemony that Bordley and his peers instituted (Isaac 1982, Kulikoff 1986, Matthews 2002: 50–54). There is no evidence of a desire by the leading gentry to expand on their power during this period. Given their rather extreme local authority despite these social challenges, why would they? However, at end of the Seven Years' War in 1763, a substantial threat to their position emerged in the form of British parliamentary taxes like the Stamp Act and navigation taxes aimed at making colonists pay for their protection and related imperial services. This threat was not as easy to mitigate as was the Great Awakening, since it was directly aimed at the profit-making system of the colonial elite.

Given this particular challenge, one response was to seek American independence, a proposal that required the support of those who would be soldiers and later workers for the new republic. This is how Georgian architecture and the theory of nature it embodies fits in. Following authors like Langley, Leone writes:

> While walking through the garden, the owner was to be like Isaac Newton, observing and recording the laws of nature and explaining them. But because the owners had actually created the environment using these laws, there was an element of reproducing nature that used Newton as a model. All these actions were to impress a visitor, but never exempted the builder from being the most impressed of all. (2005: 79)

The illusions produced by Georgian gardens and houses were not meant to deceive the viewer and thereby place the owner above his visitors. They were conceived of instead as placing all viewers, owners and visitors alike, on a common plane where they could experience the illusions and the theory of nature they revealed. This plane is where the abstractions that theory posited as underlying reality could be known and owned as knowledge.

The aspect of Georgian design that makes this ideological technique work is its basis in an individual's experience of nature. Nature, revealed in these examples through the laws of optics, was not a blunt or brute force against which humanity as a whole struggles. Rather, nature became a set of laws that operate on persons individually through the intersection of their senses and the knowledge they have about how nature is organized. Georgian gardens and houses put the individual in nature by making nature knowable only through an individual's experience of it (Leone 2005: 83). This is an ideology because the knowledge that people have about nature is not natural at all, but is rather cultural knowledge that describes natural processes, taken to be lessons on how persons fit into nature as individuals.

Conclusion

Did the Georgian ideology work? Likely not all on its own. But the theory of the natural individual was integral to the eventual war for American independence. During and after the Revolution, America was envisioned as a natural republic by more than one founding patriot (Morgan 1975, Dain 2002). This state of nature has many roots, but among them was the idea that citizens were natural persons that a subservient government merely enabled by clarifying and guaranteeing the meanings of contracts made between individuals. It is important to also consider that proclamations of a natural republic of free citizens were made despite the several hundred thousand enslaved laborers whose role in the Georgianization of America was essential. Men like Thomas Bordley, Samuel Chase, and William Paca each owned a substantial number of captive Africans, whose laborer and outsider/noncitizen status helped guide the reorganization of relations among free persons as individuals.

American historical archaeology has made substantial and important strides in recovering details about enslaved persons and their status as Africans, African Americans, or other racialized outsiders in American society (Orser 2007), and I consider examples of this research in detail in chapter 7, where I explore African American alternatives to capitalism that those situated outside of its mainstream developed. Before turning to this study, however, it is important to consider how capitalism itself was elaborated and incorporated into American national practice. I consider this in chapters 4 and 5, which explore the archaeology of New York City as a capitalist metropolis and the archaeology of places and lives conceived from the ground up as components of the American industrial-capitalist complex.

4

The Capitalist Metropolis

> Thus the metropolitan type of man—which, of course, exists in a thousand individual variants—develops an organ protecting him against the threatening currents and discrepancies of his external environment which would uproot him. He reacts with his head instead of his heart.
>
> Georg Simmel, "The Metropolis and Mental Life"

The segregation of persons evident in the individualizing artifacts of the Georgian order was elaborated in the years after the Revolutionary War as the early American republic faced the political and economic realities of independence. Struggles and opportunities on various fronts supported local innovations in production and social organization that advanced merchant capitalism toward an urban-based industrial capitalism. I consider the archaeology of nineteenth-century industrial capitalism in detail in chapter 5, but to lay the groundwork for understanding later forms of capitalism, I consider in this chapter the archaeological record of the urban capitalist revolution. Simply put, it was in the city that Americans first learned how to live and relate to one another as a society of modern individuals (see Simmel 1969, Weber 1969, Bender 2002). This urban capitalist subjectivity then extended out from the cities as it rationally organized virtually all of America in an urban capitalist mode.

Focusing on nineteenth-century New York City, I highlight two interrelated processes of modern urban society in order to illustrate how capitalism came to dominate everyday social life. The first was the material construction of the domestic sphere and the re-symbolization of the private family. An extension of the private individual, the private, nuclear family became the ideal American social unit. The family was envisioned as the principal site for producing well-formed individuals, and with its assumption of control over establishing moral behavior, the family also publicly symbolized a successful head of household, who was predominantly male and worked outside of the home. Archaeologist Diana diZerega Wall has explored various dimensions of this process, especially the development of distinct gender roles that rationalized the segregation of work from home and men from women in capitalism. I consider her research in detail in this chapter.

A second development in urban America was a rational spatial segregation of production, commerce, residence, and, somewhat later, leisure. Embodied within this organization was not only the separation of the workplace from the home, but an association of social status with the relative ability of households to distance themselves from the workplace. While homes distant from productive zones of the city were attributed higher status, those close to docks, warehouses, factories, and workshops were by contrast considered impoverished. This segregation of the home from work epitomized the underlying rationality of capitalism in that private domestic life rather than public productive life became the primary basis for defining social and public action. However, the segregation of residential areas by wealth produced distinct forms of experience and opportunities that fostered class consciousness as different groups unequally confronted the common expectations for appropriate public and private behavior. One district in New York City where working-class class consciousness is archaeologically visible was known as Five Points. Archaeological research at the Five Points neighborhood directed by Rebecca Yamin illustrates the struggles of urban poverty and the class strategies, most notably ethnicity, that some residents adopted to establish a relatively secure footing in the capitalist economy.

The Urban Revolution

The idea of an urban revolution comes originally from archaeologist V. Gordon Childe, who posed that urban growth led to primary state formation in the ancient Near East (Childe 2003). Childe's subject matter as such has little direct bearing on the archaeology of American capitalism, but nevertheless, his discussion presents issues worth considering in the examination of the modern city. Childe argues that urban growth resulted from two factors: surplus production and specialization. Utter reliance on the domestication of plants and animals was possible only when early farmers discovered that they could produce a surplus which would sustain them through periods when no other food was available. During these off-seasons, craft workers perfected various skills. Demand for their products led them to shift from part-time to full-time specialization based on the exchange of their products for surplus food produced by farmers (Brumfiel and Earle 1987). Childe proposes that these craft specialists, cognizant of their value to society, organized into cooperative guilds to control their quality of production and manage exchange with farmers. Craft guilds were located in central areas to take advantage of trading opportunities with more dispersed farmers. These centers became early cities when, alongside craft workers and farmers, juridical priest-administrators emerged to resolve disputes and normalize social relations among the various interest groups. At this point, cities became the centers of larger, more complex societies. Managing complexity gave administrators additional control over not only social relations, but also economic redistribution. This division led to class formation, and, Childe argues, civilization as we know it.

Many have highlighted flaws in Childe's reasoning, especially the lack of empirical support for his sequence of events in the archaeological record. Some have in fact argued that he improperly imposed a rational capitalist model on ancient cities (Clark and Blake 1994). However, because of this error, Childe presents a highly simplified representation of the modern city. His emphasis on surplus production—or profit—and specialization—or the social division of labor—is key to understanding the capitalist metropolis. Adding to this the dimension of the individualistic basis of modern subjectivity and cultural authority, we may appropriately conceive of the urban dimensions of the American experience of capitalism as a similar yet constant revolution (Marx and Engels 1967b).

Making the Home: The Archaeology of the Urban Middle Class

To explore the modern urban revolution I consider research presented by Diana diZerega Wall (1991, 1994, 1999, 2001). Wall focuses on patterns in ceramic assemblages associated with middle-class homes in early to mid-nineteenth-century New York City. She conceives of this process in various ways, considering the intersecting effects of changing household organization, the segregation of work and home, class formation, and shifting gender roles. She especially highlights the new expectations and achievements of women in constructing the urban domestic sphere, and their use of material culture to negotiate, practice, and reinforce their social position. I consider the principal processes she highlights below as illustrative of the several important material aspects of urban capitalism that archaeologists might consider.

Specialization and Class Formation

Following the American Revolution, colonial-era restrictions on trade, production, and American wealth accumulation were removed. With wars in Europe and demand for local production, the era between 1790 and 1840 was a relative boom time for American capitalism, which, despite intermittent declines, fostered the radical transformation of New York into a modern metropolis. Among the most powerful changes was the specialization of productive labor, as opportunity and competition supported the separation of once-unified, general businesses into specialized and interrelated commercial pursuits. With this process a generalized merchant elite class who claimed patriarchal authority in all areas of life (men like William Paca in Maryland and DeWitt Clinton in New York) was replaced. These elite merchants, along with many others who found space to compete, specialized and focused their efforts into certain goods, such as textiles or hardware, or certain pursuits, such as banking, insurance, wholesale, or retail trade. Specialization also occurred within businesses, which were broken down into increasingly various interrelated occupations such as managers, accountants, brokers, jobbers, factors, and auctioneers. Diversification depersonalized business practices, as individual merchants—who had relied in large part on reputation and personal relations—gave way to corporations whose standing was increasingly determined solely by their market value.

While this pattern was first pronounced among elite urban merchants, artisans followed soon after. Artisanal work in colonial New York was largely under the control of master craftsmen who directly organized production and training. Various trades were in fact organized as informal guilds, assuring the quality of work produced (Wilentz 1984: 23–103). With the expanding markets and reorganized commercial structures that emerged after the Revolution, many artisans broke standing relations with elite merchants and sold their products themselves. Competition with elite merchants and other newcomers in the market also led artisans to explore cost reduction in order to sustain profits. It was the laboring class that felt the effects of this effort the most. Simplifying, routinizing, and mechanizing production, master artisans became early industrialists, overseeing larger, more specialized works that were centralized under their authority. This shift inculcated a novel class distinction. Whereas artisanal production in the eighteenth century was organized by trade—so, for example, cobblers of any rank had more in common with each other than they did with coopers—in 1833, the General Trades Union established that wage-earning journeymen of any industry shared more with each other than they did with their masters (Wilentz 1984: 219–96). Capitalist specialization in New York thus included not only the diversification of pursuits and occupations within elite sectors of the market economy, but it also specialized those who lost control of the means of production as wage-earning laborers. From the perspective of capital, that is, class division was secondary to the specialized role that working people played as owners and sellers of the labor required for production to proceed. It is this conception in particular that is most pronounced in the archaeological record of modern urbanization.

The Spatial Reorganization of the City

Capitalist class formation rehearsed the same processes of segregation that individualizing artifacts did in separating persons: persons were segregated as they became specialists in different aspects of the productive process. The novelty of this construction is that it played out the emphasis placed by capitalism on the universal equivalence of abstract labor. As owners of the means of production, whether labor or other productive materials, all persons were theoretically in the same position. To enact this equivalence, many masters separated domestic life from production, in turn expecting their workforce to do the same. As each person arrived at the workplace, whether master/owner, semiskilled craftsperson, or unskilled laborer, and despite the conditions of their neighborhood or home, they materialized their *equivalency* to one another as persons in the eyes of the market.

Diana Wall examines the effects of this process in the archaeological record of New York City. Evidence from city directories, for example, shows that in 1790 only 2 percent of household heads maintained separate homes and workplaces, while by 1840 this figure had reached 70 percent (Wall 1994: 21). In this fifty-year span, in other words, the relationship between the workplace and the home radically changed. In the colonial period and immediately after, it was typical that the home and workplace were a combined entity. Merchants, for example, usually operated stores out of the front rooms of their homes. After the transition, most merchants reorganized so that the store and warehouse merged into a discrete unit known as a countinghouse. The merchant's home and family were thus separated from the workplace. The same sort of unified home and workplace was also common among artisans, who typically operated shops within the same building or lot as their homes. As artisans turned toward commerce, they followed suit and established separate manufacturing operations where they elaborated production into more diverse and simplified stages to reduce labor costs.

While still in their home workplaces, merchants and artisans oversaw a diverse household, as apprentices and journeymen, as well as their own families and servants, all lived together under their supreme authority. Separating families from the workplace reduced production costs because household heads, rather than being responsible for the reproduction of both their family and a dependent labor force, shifted this burden to the now-independent, wage-earning laborers themselves. The personal relationships embodied by home workplaces were thus replaced by impersonal relations of capitalist equivalency as both master and laborer were similarly responsible for reproducing themselves. Wall highlights that this shift brought about not only new financial arrangements, but also a new morality as well. As independent persons, masters and laborers were *individually* responsible for their behavior. Separate homes materialized this separate and equivalent social standing.

City directories show that urban capitalism promoted the separation of work and home in a very straightforward process related to the production of an individualized subjectivity. This separation is evident in the character of individual archaeological sites. Sites with combined domestic and commercial activities reflect the phase of merchant capitalism, while sites containing only domestic or productive remains indicate the shift to industrialization. This material transition is also evident in a new urban landscape created by functionally distinct districts devoted predominantly to productive or domestic life, which also invoked new distinctions between wealthy and poor residential sections in the city.

Wall tracks these changes by showing how the general social and spatial organization of the city changed as families were separated from the workplace. The colonial cityscape in New York was defined by a preindustrial spatial distribution of wealth. A core near the East River docks, which formed the center of commercial activity, was also where most elite merchants lived and worked. Middling and poorer areas surrounded this core to the west and north. Notably, no district was wholly made up of a single group, creating what Wall calls a "jumble of classes" throughout the city (1994: 45). By the mid-nineteenth century, the jumbled colonial city was built over by a radically different order. New York's 1790 population of thirty-three thousand exploded to more than three hundred and twelve thousand in 1840, making it the largest city in the United States and one of the largest in the world. An important part of this growth was the 1811 Commissioner's Plan, which created a uniform grid of numbered streets and avenues over the whole of undeveloped Manhattan (see Figure 4.1). This rational organization of space and property led urban development to proceed predictably, which facilitated the construction of new districts that came into demand as the independent workforce sought new places to live. While the uniformity of the grid epitomized the egalitarian spirit of American democracy, it also materialized the objective equivalency of humanity essential to the success of capitalism. As a single artifact, the American urban grid is one of the largest materializations of the capitalist ideology ever constructed.

The city built upon this grid reflected the segregation of home and work. For one, the commercial center expanded from the East River waterfront inland as management and finance came to stand alongside the commercial marketplace. This downtown was filled with structures used solely for work, and residents in the area were mostly poor. Those from the middle and upper ranks left this district behind at the end of the workday, riding commuter omnibuses to zones that had become almost entirely residential and segregated by wealth.

This social and spatial organization of production was also revealed in new architecture. In the commercial center, especially after an 1835 fire, new buildings were made to meet the specific demands of business. The particulars of given buildings notwithstanding, a unity among these structures was their distinctly commercial architecture. Granite columns, pediments, large windows, and other grand stylistic effects of the popular Greek revival separated the architecture of downtown from that of the rest of the city. Greek revival styles were also common in wealthy residential neighborhoods, though such expressions were more subdued. The most pronounced architectural characteristic in the residential zones was the

Figure 4.1. Map of New York City drawn by D. H. Burr expressly for "New York as it is in 1833"; engraved by S. Stiles & Co. Note that the grid plan includes both developed and undeveloped sections of the city (The Lionel Pincus and Princess Firyal Map Division, the New York Public Library, Astor, Lenox, and Tilden Foundations).

Figure 4.2. Midsummer in the Five Points, 1873 (Picture Collection, The New York Public Library, Astor, Lenox, and Tilden Foundations).

row house, a type of structure built by developers along the street fronts of the new grid. Long lines of townhouses with common walls and a uniform roofline extended the orderliness of the grid to architectural form. New construction also reflected the status differences of the different city districts. Older sections such as Five Points, which I explore below, retained the architectural variety of the preindustrial era (see Figure 4.2). Additionally, as many of the structures in poorer neighborhoods like Five Points were subdivided by landlords into multiple, smaller apartments, the district stood in contrast to the new, single-family row home districts, appearing crowded and noisy. These characteristics came to be associated not only with working-class neighborhoods, but their residents as well. The modern homes built in newly developed areas further from the city center thus represented both prosperity and, especially due to their uniformity and repetition, a commitment to a presumed common humanity that a family home was expected to produce.

The Domestic Sphere

The segregation of the workplace from the home also reorganized the way most people conceived of their daily routines—and, more powerfully, of themselves—within the capitalist city. The conception of the home as separate from work established a set of additional contrasts, most notably the opposition of private and public life, such that family and society, tradition and modernity, competition and morality, and women and men became culturally opposed in novel ways. The home, as the domestic sphere, balanced the effects of the workplace. Research on the home, therefore, must be conceived of as integral to the way the workplace functioned in productive life. As the separation of the workplace embodied the ideology of capitalism, so too did the new home that was simultaneously created. Most obviously, perhaps, since the male head of the household was typically away from home during the day, the home became a separate, female-dominated sphere, with the wife and mother assuming much of the cultural authority for raising children, managing the household (for example, provisioning, overseeing servants), and maintaining family status, which came to be tied to the display of proper morality. Just as with the specialization of the workplace, these tasks were part of the new division of labor which the capitalist urban revolution brought about.

Diana Wall's archaeological investigation of the new urban home focuses on ceramic use and the ritualization of family meals. Dinner, as Frederick Law Olmsted noted, became at this time a "constant and familiar reunion" where family members who spent the day doing separate activities in segregated sections of the city were once again together (Wall 1994: 113). Notably, gatherings under these conditions create the sort of setting that Marx and Engels highlight as having the potential for developing a critical consciousness, as the contradictions of the system were highly evident in the fact that the family had to be *brought* together, rather than simply *being* together (1967a). Quite the opposite, family meals became ritualized events wherein discipline of the individual by enforcement of their segregation from kin was played out. Wall cites Catherine Sedgewick's 1837 novel *Home*, which describes meals in modern New York as "'opportunities of improvement and social happiness' as they taught eight lessons three times a day with each enactment: 'punctuality, order, neatness, temperance, self-denial, kindness, generosity, and hospitality'" (Wall 1994: 112). These lessons were created by the invention of family meals as rituals that followed prescribed actions. During the early nineteenth century, Wall shows that family meals took on ritual aspects such as sequential order, repetition, and performance of activities in a collective setting involving others. Like all rituals, these acts were undertaken to reveal a community to itself, with membership defined by those who knew how to perform the ritual correctly. It is no small matter that those who were coming to know themselves as a community, as a family in this case, were already kin! What they were learning was how to be a modern family of individuals.

Ceramic vessels were integral to the dining ritual. Based on ceramic teawares and tablewares collected from eleven sites in Lower Manhattan, Wall recorded patterns of decoration, relative cost, and the use of matched sets for assemblages dating from the late eighteenth through the early nineteenth century (1994: 136–47, Appendix E). Considering teawares and tablewares together, she shows that ceramic vessels became more decorated with colors and printed designs between 1800 and 1840. Early in the period, the majority of dinner plates were minimally decorated, while early teawares were adorned with Chinese landscape and floral decorations. This distinction indicates the importance of having decorated wares for the more public social teas, in which neighborly competition was common. The simply decorated dinnerwares conversely emphasized the commonality of the family, since what was visible was the food they contained, which the family shared at the meal. While the distinction in decoration between teawares and tablewares was maintained, tablewares became increasingly decorated over time. Citing evidence from period descriptions and etiquette books, Wall suggests that the use of decorated plates was part of a growing middle-class acceptance of the ritualized aspects of the family meal (1994: 120–21). Thus was the stylization of the dining ritual elaborated, with greater emphasis placed on the ritual vessels than the food itself. In some instances, the food was removed to a sideboard, leaving the table set only with plates and utensils. Later, this separation was accentuated as decorated covered vessels were used to serve, in effect entirely removing the food from a direct role in the ritual.

This ceramic evidence has ramifications in understanding both the cost and cultural meaning of the ritual meals. Selecting increasingly decorated ceramic types, families in New York City spent more and more on tablewares up to 1840. Moreover, Wall found that the relative cost of tablewares was less than teawares only until about 1820, after which the value of each set was roughly equal. This suggests that the family meal became as important as the highly competitive social tea, and that the competitive, public aspects of the social tea were introduced into the arena of the family itself. Combined with the distancing or hiding of presented food, the ceramics enabled the commodification of the ritual meal as the public exchange-value of the vessels was highlighted in place of the private use-value of the food.

This interpretation follows from Wall's discovery that many families started having more than one matched set of dishes beginning around 1800. These sets typically varied such that one was more decorated and expensive than the other. The implication is that families were segregating their meals into more and less formal occasions, using different ceramic sets to distinguish formal family dinners from less formal breakfasts and lunches. While this would have established the family dinner as a special occasion, it also pushed family members to live up to the status of the meal itself, a status which was determined at least in part by the external, public, and competitive exchange-value of the ceramics. Moreover, as ceramics increasingly stood in for food in defining the ritual meaning of family meals, they mirrored the manner in which commodities came to stand for people in capitalist social relations. As middle-class families succeeded and advanced in the capitalist city, it makes sense that they would institute rituals where exchange-value was situated at the root of even kin relations. The moral lesson taught in this venue regards being a disciplined individual committed to understanding how value is produced through the social division of labor across all parts of the city.

Gothic Women and Wicked Men

This interpretation of the ritual family dinner expands on Wall's observations, which do not directly address the role of the exchange-value of the ceramics used in the ritual family meals. To support this new interpretation, I draw on Wall's research on the meaning of the Gothic revival style, positioning it in the culture of capitalism. Wall shows that in mid-nineteenth-century New York, domestic ceramic patterns changed in a counterintuitive way, given her findings from earlier periods (1991). While tablewares and teawares were increasingly decorated during the time period covered by her aforementioned study, after 1840 tablewares returned to being minimally decorated as a pattern known as "Gothic," a white-paneled ironstone, became popular (see Figure 4.3). During this era the

Figure 4.3. White granite tea and tableware forms in the popular Gothic pattern recovered from features associated with the sewage system at 472 Pearl Street in Five Points, New York (photograph courtesy of Rebecca Yamin, John Milner Associates).

Gothic revival was under way in architecture and, more broadly, social criticism. The premise of the Gothic revival was summarized by architect and reformer Andrew Jackson Downing in 1850 as being "of the quiet, domestic feeling of the library and the family circle" (Wall 1994: 160), material spaces and identities that for the most part did not exist a generation before. Because of its association with medieval European Gothic cathedrals and their heavenward-pointing spires and arches, the Gothic revival brought an explicit sacredness to the profane street in New York's modern church architecture (see Figure 4.4). In domestic architecture, adornment, and ceramics, the Gothic form simultaneously emphasized the sacredness of the American home.

Returning to an exaggerated religious symbolism at the height of a secular capitalist social transformation stands out. The Gothic style was a ripe symbol for institutions such as the Church and the home that stood in opposition to the impersonal, competitive marketplace. However, it is worth considering whether the promotion of the Gothic revival is itself not also marking the point at which the individualized capitalist subject became fully normalized. My point is that the Gothic, as a sign of an irrational, devotional community in submission to a dogmatic authority, presents the presumed opposite of capitalism. I suggest, therefore, that the meaning of the Gothic in nineteenth-century New York was not established in

Figure 4.4. Trinity Church at the west end of Wall Street in New York, 1847 (Picture Collection, The New York Public Library, Astor, Lenox, and Tilden Foundations).

a positive sense, but rather through the lens of a capitalism that sought simultaneously a superficial absolution from the sins of the market and an obvious oppositional symbol with which it could be contrasted, yet still related. Additionally, identifying the home as sacred through the use of Gothic architecture and dinner plates expands upon the idea that the home is the moral balance of an immoral marketplace. Thus, the Gothic revival, like the home itself, was a creation of capitalism. Just as it was wealthy New York capitalists who helped finance the rebuilding of the Trinity Church at the end of Wall Street in the Gothic style in 1846, so too did they create the Gothic home. The point of these efforts was simple: it extended the social division of labor and did so by couching it in sacred terms. The Gothic revival may be considered a capitalist farce by which those institutions believed to stand apart from the market—the Church and the family—were brought under its control without their obvious dissolution as independent entities (compare Marx 1964).

The simultaneous inclusion and exclusion of the home as a women's sphere explains the widespread adoption of Gothic-pattern ceramics among middling and wealthy New Yorkers after 1840. Wall specifically relates this shift in style to the establishment of women as the moral guardians of the home (1991, 1994, see also Fitts 1999). She highlights evidence showing that women were active in the production of the home as a separate sphere, including its construction as a moral space apart from the market. She cites documentary evidence that female household heads purchased household ceramics. Women's choice of Gothic ceramics illustrates an effort to materialize the sacred meanings of the family and the home, and by association their function as its guardians. While such activity, in terms of selecting what was brought into the home, clearly illustrates women's agency, the implication that they became moral guardians of family and home through their own volition is less convincing.

Alternatively, I suggest that women's domestic role was the result of the formal division of labor between husbands and wives (and by extension the definition of dominant roles for men and women), and that it was organized largely in response to the capitalist construction of a labor market. Just as laborers were freed to sell their labor and similarly freed from the support of their master's care except through formal, impersonal, contractual relations, so too women, as wives and mothers, were freed to take up the work associated with being the moral authority at home. Dispensing of these responsibilities to workers and wives in a similar fashion, middle-class men in turn were freed to pursue profit unfettered by irrational matters such as family, morality, and community relations. Rather, having de facto ownership of the principal sources of value—that is, the labor of workers *and* the family—middle-class men could afford their wives' independence. This severance was not the creation of a partnership, but one that forced women into positions of awkward subordination. They were simultaneously beholden to their husband's control of the means of production and responsible for their own well-being and success, which required the production of a respectable household. Perhaps as much as allowing persons to practice their individual discipline, ritualized family meals and Gothic dishes functioned to constantly reestablish the marriage that lay at the root of the family. Set at the table as equals, spouses played out partnership roles as husbands and wives, mothers and fathers, despite the fact that the inequality of their relationship challenged their capacity to stand together at all. Through the ritual, that is, the sacred farce of the separate spheres was reproduced.

Children of Capitalism: The Archaeology of the Immigrant Working Class in New York

The capitalist system clearly served the partisan interests of property-owning men who could stand apart from others on the secure footing of personal capital while also asserting their equivalence with others, including their wives, thanks to the ideology of the individual and the capitalist division of labor. The division of labor, however, created distinct perspectives within capitalism, and the division between capitalists and laborers lies at the root of the culture of capitalism. To consider capitalism, it is necessary to record how laboring people lived and constructed social positions, an effort for which historical archaeology is truly invaluable. The urban working class is poorly represented in the historical record because of several factors. They have left few personal historical documents, in part because many were illiterate, but more so because their everyday lives were defined by the contingencies of a labor market that left little leisure time for recollection. Equally problematic, the history of the immigrant working class is burdened by negative stereotypes produced by middle-class outsiders emphasizing the inherent moral failures of working immigrants, rather than admitting the limitations of their material and social conditions (see Yamin 2001, Fitts 2001, Reckner 2001). In New York City, the excavation and analysis of materials from a series of buildings located in the nineteenth-century immigrant, working-class neighborhood of Five Points shows that, despite the negative stereotypes, working people constructed vibrant communities and engaged in various forms of work and social life also prized by the middle class. I will now explore some of this archaeological evidence of working-class cultural life as expressed in Five Points.

I noted above that the population of New York exploded in the first half of the nineteenth century, the majority of which resulted from immigration from Europe, especially Germany and Ireland. Various push factors like the 1840s famine in Ireland and political and religious oppression in Germany may be cited. However, following Bodnar (1985), these factors should be related to the simultaneous development of capitalism in both Europe and the United States. Flares and lulls in the movement of populations to the United States relate to the European *and* American capitalist organization of production, including changes in transport, labor, and mechanization, as well as the reorientation of markets that changed everyday life in uneven ways. Simply put, immigrants "did not leave pre-industrial worlds but worlds which were already encountering capitalism and experimenting with ways to deal with its realities" (Bodnar 1985: 56). Immigrants were, as Bodnar argues, the children of capitalism.

The American immigrant working class, therefore, was aware of both positive and negative aspects of living within the system of capitalism. We may assume as well that they had at least a passing familiarity with the subjectivity that capitalism expected of individuals. With this sense we may apply a degree of capitalist agency, if not complicity, to immigrant persons and communities as we consider the archaeological record of their cultural life. I make this point because a great number of historians and archaeologists regard the working class as victims of capitalism and thus conceive of their successes, in terms of community formation and levels of material consumption, as unexpected. I, on the other hand, do not regard working-class community formation or relative prosperity as surprising. A laboring class is necessary for capitalism, and it is in the best interest of capitalists to have a large, competitive labor pool to draw from. Moreover, the capitalist system requires a consumer market for the commodities it produces, and the free laboring class was primed to fill this role. My discussion of the archaeology of Five Points thus highlights how competition and consumption defined the way working-class communities formed. First, though, I discuss the historical and material contexts of the Five Points neighborhood and the two-block project area that produced the archaeological remains that are the focus of this section.

Becoming Five Points

Originally confined behind a palisade wall to the southern tip of Manhattan, New York City expanded northward after the American Revolution (Yamin 2001). Among the first sections to be developed was the area surrounding the Collect Pond, which had been the location of a powder magazine, a poorhouse, African and Jewish cemeteries, and industrial operations such as slaughterhouses and tanneries, which are known for their unpleasant odors and noxious byproducts. After 1790, the burial grounds were covered over, and during the next decade the Collect Pond was filled in. New neighborhoods sprang up and were occupied by the emerging urban working class, who took their place in this outer ring of the city. The first new residents consisted of African American and white laboring families, who lived alongside the home businesses of clothiers and shoemakers.

Within the two-block archaeological project area, census records show the population rose from 227 people in 1800 to 948 by 1840. A noticeable trend in the population was a decline in African Americans from 19 percent to 4 percent of the total population, a trend matched by a commensurate increase in the white immigrant population, at least based on the presence of suggestively ethnic, mostly Irish, surnames and the growing number of households officially containing "aliens." By 1855, European immigrants made up the bulk of the area's population—for example, 71 percent of the 1,334 people were recent Irish immigrants. For the remainder of the nineteenth century, Five Points continued to be a destination for new immigrants, even as Irish residents were replaced as the dominant group in the project area by Italians and Eastern European Jews in the 1880s.

Large households were common in Five Points. Most immigrants were working-class, unskilled laborers, though some were employed in skilled trades or shopkeeping. Very few residents were property owners. To make rent, many households consisted of families spanning multiple generations as well as boarders. For example, in 1855, Margaret Barry's eleven-person household in the project area consisted of herself and two daughters, a young couple, and six unmarried boarders. Hers was one of eighteen total households consisting of ninety-nine persons living in a single tenement building. The development of the neighborhood reflects this crowding. Over time, most lots in Five Points were developed to the extreme, as smaller, street-facing houses were replaced with larger tenement structures and, on some lots, morphed into additional structures in the back. This architectural growth impacted the open space of the lots, with backyards becoming entirely filled with sewage systems, some of which were partially built over to provide yet more tenement space. Images of the excavations (see Figure 4.5) show the remains of this complex, urban working-class landscape in the common walls of the tenements and intersecting privies, cesspools, cisterns, and school sinks, which all together contained at least eighteen primary archaeological deposits reflecting the daily life of Five Pointers in the nineteenth century. It is from these deposits that Rebecca Yamin and her colleagues have amplified the story of New York's historic working-class community.

Competition, Ownership, and Ethnicity

I have described how the division of labor within capitalism encourages competition. The market, as a neutral space, was open to all those who

Figure 4.5. Features J, cesspool (left), and Z, cistern (right) visible during the excavation of Lot 6 in Five Points, New York (photograph by Dennis Seckler, courtesy of Rebecca Yamin, John Milner Associates).

owned a saleable commodity, and the abstraction of labor established that all persons, even those with nothing other than their unskilled labor, were free to enter into and compete in the market in order to survive. This democratization of the market sustains capitalism, as it makes everyone's self-interest primary, because survival and reproduction shift from a social to a personal responsibility. Competition has many attributes. As property owners compete, they seek advantages to distinguish themselves so as to gain better access to purchasers of their products. Commodity producers do this in various ways. They can lower the costs of production, allowing them to lower their prices, they can identify or create new consumers, or they may develop marketing strategies which distinguish their product through its affiliation with more desirable associations than their competitor's product achieves. Laborers can follow these strategies as well. Working to maximize their market value, laborers can distinguish themselves by working for lower wages, defining new skills or specializations, or finding desirable associations with which to affiliate. It is especially the latter that appears in the archaeological materials from Five Points.

Five Points was already a notorious neighborhood in 1842 when Charles Dickens described it as a place where "poverty, wretchedness, and vice are rife [and] debauchery has made the very houses prematurely old" (Cantwell and Wall 2001: 218). As the productive aspects of New York coalesced around capitalism, the workplace became established as an independent meeting point for masters and laborers, who were each expected to maintain a separate home. Those with greater means settled further from the new commercial and productive zones, while poorer people found housing closer to the city center. This trend changed the urban landscape by resituating what had been the working-class fringe into the central-city slum. Working-class neighborhoods stood out in part because their crowded, subdivided dwellings were commonly older, derelict buildings that did not meet the standards of new, middle-class housing found in other parts of the city (see Figure 4.2). In New York, Five Points was such a neighborhood, and by virtue of its proximity to the commercial and manufacturing districts as well as its visible representations of "poverty, wretchedness, and vice," it received a great deal of public attention. "Slumming," or taking police-escorted tours through impoverished neighborhoods, became a middle-class diversion in the nineteenth century. The characteristics of urban slums in fact led to their romanticization in the United States and elsewhere, and this aspect of working-class neighborhoods is significant to understanding their archaeology. Historian Alan Mayne argues as such that "slums are constructions of the imagination: a stereotype that was fashioned in the early nineteenth century by bourgeois entertainers and social reformers, and that obscured and distorted the varied spatial forms and social aspects to which it was applied" (Mayne and Murray 2001: 1). To counter these myths, Mayne and archaeologist Tim Murray promote the unique perspective of archaeology by way of entering working-class neighborhoods not through the eyes of outsiders, but through the remains of residents whose material lives were part and parcel of their reputation and aspirations:

> In light of archaeological and historical evidence . . . how should daily life in such neighbourhoods be described? Not as constituting an homogenous underclass. Nor as drip-down imitations of bourgeois prosperity and propriety. The material culture from such sites, researchers agree, is "mundane." By and large one finds cheap and mass-produced home-wares and domestic knick-knacks. . . . These objects—a decorated plate, for example, or a moulded clay pipe—are simultaneously functional and symbolic. They express personal and local identity. They exude a pride in self and place that is at variance with outside constructions by elite observers and later historians. (Mayne and Murray 2001: 3)

The archaeological view of the urban working class thus records material efforts to challenge social marginalization, which was compounded by both limited access to capital resources and a negative reputation concocted by the middle classes, who cited poverty and other failings as personal and cultural attributes. Archaeologists highlight that working-class strategies were driven by a quest for "respectability" (Mayne and Murray 2001: 3, Yamin 2001). I critically evaluate and extend this approach here by describing how the evidence that "exude[s] a pride in self and place" served also to establish markers of community and cultural affiliation that distinguished competitive individuals from one another in the labor market.

Being Irish in New York

The Irish were among the most stereotyped of immigrant groups in America. This was in part because they came in such large numbers in such a short period of time in the late 1840s. Following Ireland's Great Famine,

Irish immigrants to New York and other American cities shocked existing communities by rapidly introducing, along with their great numbers, a population of people differing from the American norm in origin, language, wealth, social life, and religion. The archaeological record reveals that the Irish in Five Points are recognizable through material culture in ways that emphasize a pattern of simultaneous accommodation and exclusion or insularity that supported their standing in American capitalism. This evidence integrates ethnicity with class standing, producing ultimately a sense of Irish ethnicity as an "owned" attribute with particular characteristics constructed to negotiate capitalism. Despite its common meaning outside of capitalism as descent or heritage, ethnic identity in nineteenth-century New York allowed immigrant laborers to situate themselves in particular ways that would provide distinct material advantages in the market. These are evident in various sources, including the archaeological remains from Five Points (also see Orser 2007).

Among the pronounced factors of immigration in Five Points was the association of certain groups with certain occupations. Though not a set rule, it was typical that "Irish men were laborers, bricklayers, and stonecutters, while German men worked as cabinetmakers, tailors, cigar-makers, bakers, and shoemakers" (Cantwell and Wall 2001: 217). Additionally, Irish women became the standard choice for middle-class household domestic servants. Irish women also did industrial out-work such as sewing garments in their homes (Griggs 2001). The association of immigrant groups with specific trades and occupations should be seen as part of the social division of labor in the city, a factor which I believe casts a new light on archaeologically defined patterns of ethnicity in Five Points. Most significant is how Irish ethnicity was constructed as part of the social discourse by which laboring people distinguished themselves in the market. We may think of it this way: successful affiliation would work for any person if they could enter the social and economic networks that ethnic groups established; that is, some immigrants may very well have sought to pass for Irish, much as some Irish persons may have sought to pass for white (Ginsberg 1996, Ignatiev 1995, Roediger 2005, also see Gaffney 2006). Thus, being Irish or German in New York may have been only partially tied to a person's point of origin. One's presumed background was equally relevant in distinguishing them in the city's capitalist market. It is thus important to examine both how ethnicity was symbolized and, equally, how it was *not* in the patterns found in material culture.

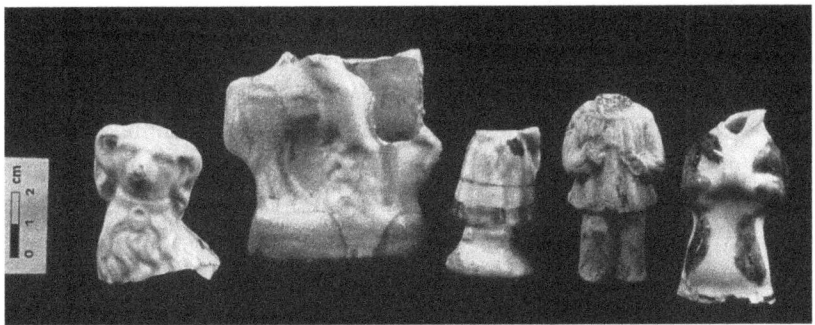

Figure 4.6. Personal artifacts from Five Points site, New York City. *Above:* 4.6. Staffordshire dog (far left) and other ceramic figurines. *Left:* 4.6. child's personalized drinking cup recovered from the sewage system at 472 Pearl Street, in Five Points, New York (photographs courtesy of Rebecca Yamin, John Milner Associates).

Notably, material markers suggestive of Irish or German heritage are conspicuously few at Five Points. For example, the remains from mid-nineteenth-century shaft deposits at 472 Pearl Street—a predominantly Irish-occupied tenement—in large part consist of artifacts that conform in important ways to middle-class norms of consumption and personal discipline, such as the following: matched sets of dinnerwares, including many examples of white granite Gothic wares, ceramic figurines, glass lighting vessels, flower pots which morally prescriptive literature and reformers highlighted as essential for home décor, didactic children's tablewares, including a personalized "John" cup, and temperance-related paraphernalia such as a Father Matthew temperance teacup (see Figures 4.6a and b) (see Yamin 2001, Brighton 2001, Griggs 1999). Patterns in the material remains of beverage consumption also suggest an adherence to the tenets of temperance. Figures from remains associated with three tenements excavated in Five Points have lower percentages of alcohol bottles as a total of all glass vessels than were found in assemblages associated with contemporary, native-born, middle-class households in the city.

Similarly, relatively high numbers of soda and mineral bottles, as well as a sieved pitcher for straining fruit juices, reflect the use of commonly suggested alternatives to alcohol found in middle-class temperance writings (Reckner and Brighton 1999: 79–81, Fitts 2001). At least among domestic material remains, it seems ethnic or other practices divergent from the American middle-class mainstream were not pronounced in Five Points.

One reason for this pattern may be that a pronounced ethnicity was not called for or desired inside the home. If ethnicity was tied to chances for employment within ethnically dominated occupations, it may be that its appearance was more evident in public spaces. In fact, the contradiction of the pattern of temperance found in the domestic archaeological remains at Five Points with the prevailing stereotypes of the "working-class immigrant drunkard" may be evidence of a distinction made between the private home and public spaces such as could be claimed by laborers, like the saloon and the street. As these spaces were also the focus of slum tours, it is not surprising that such public displays of ethnic, racial, and class difference were obvious to and seized on by outsiders.

The archaeology of working-class public spaces is not well developed, as their remains are much harder to come by than are those in sealed domestic deposits. Nevertheless, abstracting from some of the patterns defined in domestic remains, we can associate ethnicity with the imagined public lives of the working class. The most pronounced ethnic signs evident in the archaeological remains of 472 Pearl Street may be seen as an appliqué layered over what was otherwise a largely typical middle-class material assemblage. Along with a pattern showing the selective consumption of relatively expensive pork, especially pig's feet, which were commonly used in rural Ireland to prepare *crubeen* (Cantwell and Wall 2001: 223), items such as a diamond-cut cruet and a castor of Anglo-Irish origin, a Lea and Perrins Worcestershire sauce bottle, and a pepper sauce bottle lead archaeologist Heather Griggs to conclude that in some ways, Irish tenement dwellers "were consuming foods according to cultural tastes, even if this [was] more costly than other alternatives" (1999: 94). What stands out about these items of relative expense, however, is that many are related to or are condiments, substances that flavor or complement food. By extension, I suggest that the ethnically "Irish" aspects of the tenement's material culture are related to selective public and personal actions, such as adding flavor (that is, ethnicity) to an otherwise strategically prepared, undistinguished domestic life.

In this manner these artifacts reveal a two-part strategy that working-class New Yorkers enacted through ethnicity. On the one hand, working-class people seem to have aspired to enter the middle class, a proposition implied by the American dream and enforced by prescriptive literature and social reformers (Reckner and Brighton 1999, Fitts 2001). However, the presumed rejection of their ethnic background, an implicit assumption of American middle-class culture, was contradictory to the reality that most immigrants faced when seeking work. The ethnic division of labor largely restricted cultural assimilation for immigrants in the labor market. Moreover, the ethnic division of labor was exacerbated by the development of patronage-based machine politics such as Tammany Hall, which not only ran the city government in the late nineteenth century, but also played a direct role in the lives of many Irish immigrants, including at least some of those who lived at 472 Pearl Street. One resident, tinsmith Timothy Lynch, is known to have repeatedly moved as much as six hundred dollars per month into and out of a savings account at the Emigrant Industrial Savings Bank. This figure is notable because the *New York Times* had established in 1853 that six hundred dollars was the minimum *annual* income required for a working family to survive in New York City. It is likely that Timothy Lynch was related to James Lynch, an alderman at Tammany Hall, and thus it is entirely possible that some of these funds were illicitly gained (Griggs 1999: 92). Other Five Points residents such as Thomas Wade and Patrick McCabe also received stable, well-paying municipal jobs from Tammany (Pitts 2001: 99–100). Notably, Tammany was known for doing political business in saloons as well as for its donations to Irish community organizations such as the Emigrant Society and the Ancient Order of the Hibernians, who used public spaces for fundraising and charity events like the annual Big Tim's Christmas party held in Chatham Square (Pitts 2001: 100). Public space, therefore, was dominated by an Irish identity in a way that, apparently, private space was not. During these moments in public space, and perhaps in these places and times alone, Irish immigrants were indeed ethnically "Irish." At home, however, in the private spaces of their family lives, they were not actively Irish except in personal choices symbolized by the use of "ethnic" condiments. Considering the hardships that their ethnicity caused, the choice to evade it at home seems entirely reasonable. I turn now to consider the construction of the middle-class home in working-class spaces in more depth.

Consumption and Respect

As noted above, the domestic material culture recovered archaeologically from Five Points in many ways reproduced dominant middle-class norms. Archaeologists and historians have shown that these norms of thrift, cleanliness, sobriety, and discipline were presented to Americans of the time through prescriptive etiquette literature (Fitts 1999, 2001, Reckner and Brighton 1999, Rosenberg 1971, Boyer 1978, Walters 1978, Stansell 1987, Kasson 1990). While this literature likely was not read by working-class immigrants, its messages guided reform efforts in working-class districts like Five Points carried out by institutions such as the Ladies' Home Missionary Society of the Methodist Episcopal Church and the Five Points House of Industry (Fitts 2001). Reform institutions professed Protestant values, and some embarked on active missionary efforts. These projects are now largely caricatured as blinded by the ideals of middle-class respectability that blamed immigrants themselves for their conditions. Citing laziness, a tendency toward alcoholism, and indifference to Protestant morals, many among the middle class ignored the material conditions and limited opportunities faced by the immigrant working class. Reformers' focus on the cultivation of respectability in an internal, authentic self, however, has not heretofore been seen as an application of capitalist subjectivity in the definition of social problems. Nor has the adoption of middle-class values by "reformed" persons been regarded as evidence of a strategic appropriation of capitalist-valued practices. Using archeological evidence from Five Points, I explore these issues in what follows.

The basic theme of working-class reform efforts was respectability. Yet respect is a relative social value, for it involves an external evaluation of one's actions. Respectable behavior thus socializes individual action, an important process that presumes that the individual stands apart from his or her society and therefore must be formally instructed on how to behave appropriately within it. In other words, seeking respect disciplines persons as individuals in the sense that they evaluate themselves in comparison with others, a process that enforces both the equivalence to and segregation of people from one another. In this way, respect embodies the capitalist subjectivity, regardless of whether it is defined by the behaviors promoted by middle-class reformers or through the construction of potential alternatives (see Reckner and Brighton 1999, Bourgois 1995).

Material culture was a focus of middle-class reformers, for they envisioned that proper etiquette at the dining table and in the parlor revealed internal qualities based in the recognition and respect of oneself and others. Furthermore, as respect was acquired through the proper use of mundane functional objects such as plates, utensils, teacups, service pieces, and decorative items like figurines, mirrors, and chromolithographs, all persons had the responsibility to own the requirements for respectable action. Also, respectability was not simply the result of owning matched sets of dishes, but, as Wall describes (1994), was acquired only through the ritualized actions surrounding their proper use. Thus, the material plates themselves were necessary, though in one sense, on their own, they were essentially useless. Still, their presence in the house alone suggested that their owners understood the rules of proper behavior, and they may in some cases have been purchased solely to send this message.

This construction of meaning in material culture forms the basis of the commodity in that the exchange-value of the self, indicated by the proper use of dishes or figurines, layers over and determines the use-value or function of these items for containing food or providing decoration. This practice also normalizes the abstraction of labor. As objects become primarily what they represent rather than what they do, their abstract associations (for example, the idea that matched sets of dishes represent a disciplined, sober self) become the focus of social desire and consumption. Similarly, inasmuch as persons regard themselves as owners of their labor, it is the abstraction of labor and the positive associations that may be affiliated with it that come to determine who people believe they are. Simply put, the competitive labor market that created contradictions within the meaning of ethnic identity discussed above also normalized abstraction as the basis of social experience. Ethnicity is such an abstraction, though it is layered over by another that is more substantial and necessary for capitalism: the abstraction of the self from society as an authentic individual. So, in order to be Irish or German one must first be an individual who is authenticated by a market for ethnicity in labor relations which calls for individuals of specific and distinct kinds.

While this is a complex argument, the evidence is direct. Archaeologist Robert Fitts summarizes the finds at Five Points in this way: "some, if not many, inhabitants . . . owned an extensive variety of goods, including many of the items used by the middle class as symbols of respectability . . . matching sets of Gothic-shaped ceramics, porcelain tea sets, and Staffordshire figurines were recovered in the 1991 excavations" (2001: 123). What is required to explain these findings are contextual data that illustrate the relative availability of these items in Five Points. Stephen Brighton explores market availability by investigating crockery advertisements in New York newspapers and comparing the value of ceramic assemblages from Five Points with those recovered in diverse, comparable contexts (2001). Newspapers, including those printed specifically for the Irish immigrant community, contained advertisements indicating that fashionable and respectable tablewares and teawares were readily available in Five Points shops. Brighton also presents evidence that secondhand objects could be acquired at neighborhood auctions, May Day yard sales, and junk shops. Using Miller's cost indices (1991), Brighton shows that the average value of ceramics recovered from the 472 Pearl Street tenement was comparable to that in middle-class New York sites and, more significantly, much higher than was normal for laborers and rural tenant farmers elsewhere in the country (2001: 20–21).

The adoption of middle-class values revealed in the archaeological remains at Five Points may be partly attributed to the availability of the materials required for practicing the rituals. However, when addressing the topic of capitalism, it is vital to avoid attributing "availability" to natural factors like the relative proximity of merchants to the sources of their products (that is, looking at New York as a port city with direct connections to English ceramic merchants). As any commercial loan officer will confirm, the more important factor for merchants is proximity to consumers and competitors. That there were as many as ten crockery dealers in Five Points suggests that there was sufficient demand for their products. What matters is that it was not the plates that were in demand, but the vital affiliations that the use of such plates provided to consumers. The fact that the value of plates in Five Points reaches the level of middle-class assemblages elsewhere in the city and surpasses those in other parts of the country shows that working people in New York were more pressed to develop their individuality. This is not a neutral cultural attribute, but a factor that results from the more advanced development of capitalism in mid-nineteenth-century New York than anywhere else in the United States at the time, as well as the more pronounced expectation that laboring people envision themselves abstractly through the eyes of capital.

Conclusion: Capitalism's Children

This argument would be not be convincing if we only imagined individual working persons submitting willingly to the dehumanizing expectations created by competition in the labor market. However, people, and perhaps laboring persons most especially, are not actually individuals in the sense that capitalism constructs them. All persons are relatively encumbered by real social relations of kin and community, in which people expect to be treated in customary ways that often appear irrational in the eyes of the market. The most obvious of these is the relationship between parents and children. With the dissolution of the home workplace, all working people became responsible for raising their children independently (Wall 1994). The significance of raising children cannot be overemphasized. In addition to children's importance in defining a family household, they are also incredible sources of physical, financial, and emotional stress. Given the multitude of difficulties attendant to procreation—from childbearing and birth itself to the costs of food, clothing, shelter, and health, to the responsibility of transmitting values—children are typically and rightfully the central focus of parental life. Their reproduction, in other words, is an extra burden on the already taxing efforts involved in reproducing the segregated self. Once living in a separate home was normalized, the multiple costs of childhood became tied to the commodity, for the sale of labor or other commodities is how social reproduction occurs in capitalist households. Childhood, therefore, underwent a radical transformation in this era, as people once imagined as "little workers" were removed form the workplace and became instead a symbolic representation of respectable domesticity and parenting (Fitts 2001, Baxter 2005). The modern relationship between parents and children, perhaps more than any other, reveals the substantial effect that the social division of labor within capitalism has had on American social life.

Before the industrial era, the conception of children as little workers was based on the idea that the family and community were organized directly by productive life. Parents were not exploiting their children as "free labor," for such a concept did not exist. Rather, they were reproducing the productive structures and social relations that organized society. While this may have produced a childhood framed more by work than play, it also resisted the abstraction of labor and the construction of work as peripheral to social and personal life that became normalized in capitalist households during the nineteenth century.

There are two categories of material culture related to childhood revealed in the archaeological remains from Five Points. One set consists of toys, including doll parts, a miniature cannon, a jack, glass and ceramic marbles, and a rubber ball which were recovered from a privy feature at 472 Pearl Street. The other set consists of children's tableware, such as a personalized cup and toy porcelain tea sets recovered from the same privy deposit (Griggs 1999: 95; Brighton 2001: 27). Together, these sets illustrate how modern childhood was imagined and how children were symbolized in working-class homes.

Griggs suggests that the presence of toys in tenement deposits indicates that "some children . . . may not have been required to work or scavenge to supplement the family income, but were allowed freedom to participate in childhood activities" (1999: 95). Within this assessment are two important points. Outsiders and reformers often highlighted the legions of unsupervised working-class children who, if they were not engaged in criminal behavior, were sorting through rubbish collecting recyclable and potentially valuable scraps of cloth and such. Toys contradicted this image, as they showed to children that at least some of their life was devoted to diversion and play. Freed from work, we can imagine these children frolicking, even if only in the crowded backyards and streets of Five Points. However, this freedom may be viewed alternatively as an increased burden that brought children into the fold of capitalist society. Implied in the idea of toys is a temporal element: that there is a given time for play. As opposed to the oppressive time of productive life doing wage-labor work, play takes place during "free time," when the authentic self is most capable of being revealed. Clearly, this perspective reverses the premise of how the self is produced. Rather than the socially constructed self, which emerges in the reproduction of the "natural" social relations of productive activity, the self envisioned here is an abstract projection of an imagined inward being that is the premise of the "spirit of capitalism." Toys thus work in two related ways. For children, they serve as material markers of *their* freedom, times when their real self is at hand, which may be contrasted with their unsatisfying working self, where, because of alienation and exploitation, they experience frustration rather than fulfillment. Related to this is the role of toys for parents. Inasmuch as parents provide their children with toys, they are enabling their children's freedom. Toys symbolize the capability of parents to protect their children from the amoral, impersonal marketplace. However, instead of creating a "natural" relationship, parents employ both commodified objects and time to construct childhood as a basic human experience revealed not through immaturity and dependence as much as through the fact that it will end with an adulthood defined by work and subjugation to the labor market.

In order to prepare children for this embedded eventuality, it was also the moral responsibility of parents to instill in their children the capitalist subjectivity required of individuals. Therefore, the personalized "John" cup (see Figure 4.6), which presumably marked the private ownership of this object by a young boy, disciplined him through material culture obtained in the market as to how he could conceptualize himself as an individual even within the realm of the family. The toy porcelain tea set would have performed the same disciplinary function among the presumably young girls who owned these commodities. From these children we can turn next to the generations that they and their cohort produced. These are the generations of the era of victorious capitalism.

5

Translating Survival into Success

The Archaeology of Victorious Capitalism

> Human actions cannot be explained fully as either the economically determined automata of an encroaching world system, or as idiosyncratic, and ultimately circumscribed, resistance to such a system. Rather, they constitute inherently, necessarily ambiguous material and ideological strategies for surviving the economic vicissitudes of later capitalism, and translating that survival into success.
>
> Margaret Purser, "Ex Occident Lux?"

This assessment, from one of the leading writers on the historical archaeology of the American West, describes the central problem in the study of capitalism in situations where it was the primary premise of social development. Up to this point, this book has discussed the emergence of capitalism from various precapitalist origins. Each chapter has advanced this emergence further along a continuum between noncapitalist and fully capitalist productive systems and social formations. Still, my discussions of the fur trade, the Georgian order, class formation, and urbanization have explained capitalist processes by showing how practices like individualism, private property, and commodity exchange realigned and dissolved long-lasting, "traditional" social and ideological systems. This chapter takes a different perspective by looking at advanced, or "victorious" (Weber 2003), capitalism. Rather than opposing capitalism to other ways of life, I consider in this chapter examples in which capitalism for the most part was not opposed. I do not mean to suggest that resistance to capitalism was not a part of early American industrialization or westward expansion and resource extraction. Resistance was in fact quite common, expressed in various, powerful ways, and at times successful (I explore several examples of resistance to capitalism in the following chapters). However, the forms of resistance that typify the situations described in this chapter were ones that have since been easily folded back into the capitalist trajectory. They were not struggles that shut down capitalism, but rather expressions that further solidified and naturalized capitalist social relations by "translating ... survival into success."

The principal impact of capitalism was the institutionalization of private property, most specifically that all persons owned, at the very least, their own labor. This abstraction of labor from its products to an existence *as* a product, or a commodity that may be possessed, had a variety of effects, the most pronounced of which concerned the nature of communities and the social construction of persons. Outside of capitalism, communities are produced by a common (though constantly negotiated) interest in survival and well-being defined by a mutual dependence of persons on one another. Communities in capitalism, by contrast, are aggregations of discrete individuals defined by attributes and interests that allow persons to find identity, but not necessarily affinity, with other persons. In capitalism, survival is not a given, it is an achievement, and persons are not social constructs, but abstract, self-interested individuals whose well-being is their private responsibility.

Archaeologist Margaret Purser helps to explain this process metaphorically by drawing interpretive meaning from a mended cast-metal bearing she found in a trash scatter in Paradise, Nevada (1999). The bearing was a component of equipment commonly used on early-twentieth-century ranches in the region. The interesting part was the mending substance, known as babbitt, "a soft-tin alloy used to mend and refit old, worn bearings" (Purser 1999: 116). Babbitt enabled persons to repair and continue using what were otherwise mass-produced goods that neither they nor others in their community made, but instead purchased from local and national retailers. The metaphor that comes from this substance, one which Purser in part borrows from Sinclair Lewis's 1922 novel *Babbitt*, is how mass-produced goods, which babbitt lengthened the usable life of, were themselves "a form of social babbitt" (Purser 1999: 117). With the rise in mass production and retail sales, social life in late-nineteenth-century American communities was radically redefined. The common productive focus of communities declined as work became an individual pursuit and responsibility. In place of a shared interest in labor and social reproduction, consumption became the primary basis of community belonging, in part because the purchase of materials and tools was necessary for any work to be done at all. In this way persons were discrete consumers, and their shared involvement in and dependence on the market was the way that they knew one another and formed a community. So this is the metaphor: communities in capitalism are the broken bearing, and babbitt, or the shared work of consumption, is the alloy used to seal, but not heal, the rupture. It was not the sense that persons were among one another, but, in fact, the feeling that they were not so interconnected, that had to be negotiated and then patched by a manufactured product (that is, babbitt, which is a not a naturally occurring and available resource, but an industrially produced commodity).

The babbitt metaphor also explains why survival is success in capitalism. Survival itself is a metaphor, as it stands for a primary foundation of capitalist practice. Capitalism accepts the basic notion of survival as cheating death, but it ties to this force those other persons whose competing self-interest causes us to face and then evade our ultimate fate. The definition of survival in capitalism posits that other individuals are a threat. We may extend this to see that because of this rupture within communities, individuals are each on their own, much less secure, and thus closer to death in capitalism than they would be in systems where communities are more integrated. Survival in capitalism at all, given how the cards are stacked against individuals, is indeed a success. This is why in almost every noncapitalist social formation, individual self-interest is strongly restrained (Diamond 1974, Patterson 1997). In capitalism, however, quite the opposite is true. As self-interest is taken for granted, the main concern is keeping competition free and fair. In this way, it can be said that those who failed had a fair and equal chance for success, thus their failure, their death, either metaphorical or literal, was their own fault.

This chapter explores the archaeology of victorious capitalism by examining how survival became interpreted as success. The particular focus is on the material practices of depersonalization and disembodiment that resulted from the commodification of labor. Owning their bodies, individuals sought ways to better maintain them for competitive use in the market. This interest is tied to various nineteenth-century movements promoting better hygiene, sanitation, health care, working conditions, and food for working people. The desire for better conditions created a market for the products and services that would improve quality of life, thereby naturalizing the capitalist foundations that led to this interest at the outset. This consumer market was in part appropriated by capitalists, as corporations in many cases took on the responsibility of providing for the housing and subsistence of their workers. This movement elaborated the commodification of the worker's body as corporations competed to provide better services, turning workers from producers, even at sites of production such as mills and mines, into consumers of their worksite. This shift from a focus on integration and maintenance to the competitive production and consumption of products for maintenance (including whom one would work for) is the basis of victorious capitalism. The long-term, material view of archaeology helps put this movement into stark relief.

Sanitation Reform, Class Distinction, and Bureaucracy

One of the most dramatic changes over the course of the nineteenth century relates to urban sanitation. In 1800, most American cities lacked any kind of sanitation services, including collection of night soil or garbage. In 1900, by contrast, garbage collection was among the most basic components of city services, while privies and other night-soil containers were largely outlawed and replaced by municipal water and sewage works. Similarly, private ownership and slaughter of animals also declined, as these activities were concentrated in specialized zones within the city or removed altogether to remote sites. The late-nineteenth-century private, urban yard was thus transformed from a site of productive household work to one of domestic leisure, storage, or disuse.

One cause for this shift was the threat of disease in rapidly growing cities. As greater numbers of people settled in cities, waste had fewer places to hide. The main concern with disease in the early nineteenth century centered around miasmas, or bad smells that were thought to cause disease (Crane 2000: 20, Melosi 2000). In order to control miasmas, many cities enacted ordinances defining and restricting the disposal of wastes such as animal carcasses and offal, night soil, vegetable matter, stagnant water, and so forth. Urban boards of health were also commonly established in the early nineteenth century to organize responses to outbreaks of diseases like yellow fever and cholera, which killed thousands during summertime epidemics. Certainly the spread of disease concerned everyone, but the advanced capitalist systems that came to organize American cities could not be dismantled to allow for reforms that could treat sanitation as a normal part of productive life. Rather, the overcrowding and unsanitary conditions that caused the spread of disease were themselves artifacts of capitalism, which demanded a large, competitive pool of working persons with nothing to sell but their labor. Moreover, as reproduction became increasingly an individual's private responsibility, workers created a market for affordable housing, leading to the subdivision of structures into low-rent boardinghouses and tenements. This caused unprecedented crowding. Such masses of workers also drove markets for basic consumer goods like food, utensils, and tools. This pattern was in part described in the previous chapter's discussion of the Five Points district in New York City.

Related to this process was a similar market for sanitation that emerged in two forms. First, some engaged in private sanitation work as scavengers or junk haulers collected waste or cleaned privies for a fee. In Washington, D.C., for example, scavengers were appointed by the mayor in 1820 for each ward and assigned to clean out private privies every two months at the rate of fifty cents a box. Scavengers were also permitted to sell night soil to farmers (Crane 2000: 21). In Lowell, Massachusetts, nearby farmers were hired directly to collect night soil from boardinghouse privies (Mrozowski et al. 1996).

The other aspect of sanitation was its formalization in the municipal bureaucracy. Accepted as a common problem, the spread of disease through unsanitary waste disposal called for rational, central control. Boards of health organized this effort, and, as they evolved from citizen panels to municipal health agencies, they became sources of full-time employment for bureaucratic officials of various sorts, working as directors, inspectors, physicians, nurses, and educators. While they performed vital services, these experts were unlikely to seriously consider alternatives to capitalism, since their careers required increasing amounts of training and specialization suited only for treating the problems capitalism caused. Their commitment to the general well-being of the population, that is, was also a commitment to the system that put that population at risk. It is worth remembering that a population of persons incapable of healing themselves is quite the opposite of a fit population, in the Darwinian sense of natural selection. Further, while social roles for healers are common in most cultures, the bureaucratic control of these resources by other experts is peculiar to capitalism. Evident in this system is the need to maintain bodies who may acquire health only through individual consumption.

Max Weber characterized this situation in *The Protestant Ethic* as the "iron cage" of bureaucracy. Once in place, a bureaucracy that manages public well-being becomes "practically unshatterable" (Weber 1970: 228). Too much is at stake, both in terms of the services which public health managers provide and their own personal investments in the training and specialization to which they have committed. The same holds true for those subject to this bureaucracy, as Weber points out,

> The ruled, for their part, cannot dispense with or replace the bureaucratic apparatus once it exists. Expert training, a functional specialization, and an attitude set for habitual and virtuoso-like mastery of single yet methodically integrated functions mean that the result of the bureaucracy being disabled will be "chaos." (1970: 228–29)

Personal well-being became a rational, calculable process based on the definition of persons in the terms of the market, or as equivalent, abstract individuals. This widely shared commitment to the need for bureaucratic management normalized impersonal, objective relations, and a mutual dependence on the bureaucratic system was internalized.

This may be related to the body within capitalism through the Marxian notion of the abstraction of labor. Divorcing persons from the products of their labor through abstraction led to the objectification of bodies as implements of work. The self was located, by contrast, in the unique, individual spirit that inhabited otherwise exchangeable bodies. In turn, persons adopted impersonal relations with their bodies—since, as individuals, they became disembodied from the social and material conditions that produced them—that mirrored their now-abstract relations with other persons and things. Finally, to help reconnect the self and the body, the market offered various forms of "babbitt" to seal the rupture in both potentially constructive (for example, hygienic products and sanitary environments) and destructive (for example, alcohol, tobacco, and opiates) ways.

This process is evident archaeologically in the way spaces and materials came under the gaze of the modern sanitation bureaucracy through two mechanisms. First, archaeology shows how private spaces were constructed to adhere to the prescriptions of modern sanitary practices.

Second, it reveals that persons illustrated their commitment to bureaucratic control by associating relative adherence to sanitary standards with the essential spirits that inhabit differing ethnic, racial, and class-affiliated bodies.

Domestic Sanitation in Nineteenth-Century Washington, D.C.

Tracking the deposition patterns for a wide array of urban interior (backyard) spaces in nineteenth-century Washington, D.C., archaeologist Brian Crane describes a tendency for yard scatter and features to contain a decreasing amount of unsanitary materials over time (2000). He relates these figures to various social factors, especially property ownership. In the early nineteenth century, the city removed night soil by hiring scavengers. After 1856, the city also contracted to collect household garbage (organic refuse), and after 1900 it began to collect rubbish (ashes and other inorganic refuse). Using this historical information as a backdrop, Crane tracks data patterns in densities of garbage and rubbish for a varied set of Washington households in order to record the adherence at particular sites to the new standards.

A clear distinction between households of different class standing is not evident in Crane's study until after 1856, when the city took control of the collection and deposition of organic refuse. After this date, a distinction between households is very clear, as the density of organic garbage (faunal remains) drops precipitously in the yards of the more well-off property owners and white-collar families, who seemed to adhere to city standards more strictly than their poorer, laborer neighbors. This finding matches with the dates when certain households gained a connection to city-provided water and thus initiated indoor plumbing (as opposed to outdoor privies). Higher-ranking households along one side of a downtown block were connected by 1859. Chamber pot fragments from these sites date to no later than 1862, indicating a rapid shift to the new technologies. By contrast, lower-ranking sites may not have been connected until the 1870s, and for one area chamber pot fragments date past 1900, showing a very slow adoption of the new technology, an observation that relates in part to the use of the area for boardinghouses.

A pattern of class distinction is also visible in Crane's findings on the relative density of rubbish, or inorganic refuse, which was not collected by the city until after 1900. In this case, upon the initial push to clean up their properties, the more well-off households appear to have removed all refuse, organic and inorganic, from their yards. This finding suggests that white-collar, property-owning households embraced not only the services of the municipal bureaucracy, but also the rhetoric that tied well-being and virtue to cleanliness and sanitation. Reports from the Washington Board of Health in the second half of the nineteenth century regularly commented that both African Americans and immigrant laborers were unaccustomed "to our climate, habits, or modes of living. Their manner of habitation and living, as well as occupation, peculiarly exposed them to the disease. The cholera bore down upon this class with great severity" (Washington Board of Health 1878, cited in Crane 2000: 23). Such beliefs, which tied supposedly inherent cultural and racial attributes to the potential for surviving (and communicating) disease, likely mobilized the upper-middle class to protect themselves from such negative influences and associations. Their effort to clear their yards of all refuse serves as a statement of affiliation to a certain "mode of living" marked off from others by wealth, class, race, ethnicity, and an internalization of the bureaucratic management of the social order. It was only through the rising trend of organizing urban society through abstract relations between natives and newcomers, the assimilated and the foreign, those suited to prosper and those destined to suffer, that neighbors on individual city blocks could see that vast distinctions in their likelihood for survival would not obviate their membership in one society. With the aid of bureaucracy, that is, the wealthy could isolate the poor as an inherently unsanitary group, then prime them for improvement at society's expense. The same process may be observed within the private spaces of early American industry. Archaeological research at the Boott Mills in Lowell, Massachusetts, illustrates parallels that diminish the distinctions between public and private bureaucratic management of human lives.

Uneven Improvement and Wonder in the Society at the Lowell Mills

In 1839, Reverend Abel Thomas of the Second Universalist Church offered the female operatives at the Lowell cotton mills the chance to converse about their diverse interests outside of work (Mrozowski 2006: 71). Asserting that manual labor "must in some measure unfit the individual for full development of mental power" (*Lowell Offering* Series 2, Vol. 1: iv), Reverend Thomas initiated fortnightly meetings, known as "improvement circles," for the mill operatives to balance their lives between manual and mental labor. These circles later developed into the *Lowell Offering*, a newspaper produced by Lowell's workers containing stories about their lives and intellectual interests. Emerging in the early years of Lowell's massive growth into an industrial manufacturing giant during the nineteenth century, these improvement circles capture the spirit of the covenant between the mill owners and the host communities that allowed the Lowell industrial system to come about. This covenant is typically described as the measures taken by the Lowell owners to assuage fears of manufacturing industry held by early-nineteenth-century New Englanders. Industry in Britain had earned a bad reputation in the United States for its association with child labor, poor work conditions, and unsettled urban populations. To convince New Englanders that industry was not entirely wicked, the factory owners at Lowell designed a system that appeared to control the forces of workplace degradation. The basis was "corporate paternalism," a system that put workers under the direct gaze of management and made them part of an insulated community constructed by and constituting the mill company. Improvement circles capture this community's ethos, in that Lowell's corporate structure proposed not only to turn a handsome profit, but to benefit the well-being of its workforce through modern techniques of management that would mirror the organization and cultivating spirit of American families. Improvement circles, worker newspapers, and similar efforts to exercise the mind and provide a balance to manual labor embodied this covenant. Ultimately, the success of this system of surveillance and control enabled the success of Lowell, which was interpreted during its rise as the "wonder of its age" (Mrozowski 2006: 72).

Given the assertion of paternalism, the local fear of industrial ills should be paired with a fear of the "wonderful" new systems of commercial organization and management epitomized by the Lowell mill owners. The mills were created by a group known to historians as the Boston Associates (see Mrozowski 2006: 67). Organized as a joint-stock company that combined investments from some of the region's wealthiest families into one enterprise, the Boston Associates controlled substantial capital to back their commercial interests in ways hardly known before. In addition, by establishing a corporate model, mill owners, like their investors, were not directly involved in the day-to-day operation of the mills. Instead, they hired a vast number of representatives, agents, managers, and overseers to ensure a competent workforce, a timely production of quality goods, and sizable profits. While agents were touted as defenders of worker well-being, their position was simultaneously a mechanism for replacing the commitments that Lowell's largely female workforce had to their families with commitments to the modernization effort of Lowell's corporate structure, a process by which corporate capitalism inserted itself into the framework of American society at large. Writing in the *Lowell Offering*, many of the operatives described their happiness with a community that cultivated their education and gave them the wages necessary to afford small luxuries (Mrozowski 2006: 71).

Considering evidence of what archaeologist Stephen Mrozowski calls the "representational space of the Lowell Mills complex" (2006: 74), we can see how the corporation modeled a social order in material form. We can also recognize in these constructions how the abstractions of corporate and bureaucratic reform came to control the lives of workers in the beginning stages of victorious capitalism, leaving little space for alternatives, even as the conditions at Lowell's mills fell far below what had been promised in the project's early years.

Perhaps the most powerful expression of corporate capitalism lies in the creation of planned industrial communities, of which Lowell was the first large, successful one. Revealed in an integrated network of factory buildings, worker housing, roads, canals, and so forth, an abstract, ideal, and whole community was built for the sake of production and profit. This abstraction of the community reveals an underlying and novel notion of great importance to understanding how capitalism came to control so much of everyday life in the United States during the nineteenth century. This is the idea that a community or "society" may be considered an entity unto itself rather than simply the aggregate of people and relations within a place or region. Archaeologist Sarah Tarlow attributes the emergence of this idea in part to the theoretical framework of capitalism embodied in Adam Smith's famous work, *The Wealth of Nations* (Tarlow 2007). To articulate his conception of the capitalist political economy, Smith described society as a "mechanistic whole . . . such that changes to any one part of the system can have effects elsewhere, ultimately in the whole economic and moral health of the nation" (Tarlow 2007: 22–3). Subsuming distinct individuals and parts of social life under such an abstract, integrated whole enabled conceptions that communities could be invented from scratch, a process that disarticulated production from existing networks of kinship, property, and other relations and commitments that

Figure 5.1. An 1876 bird's-eye view of the Lowell Manufacturing District (courtesy Center for Lowell History, University of Massachusetts, Lowell).

had long run counter to self-serving capitalist development. A planned community provided producers control over all resources related to it, putting them in charge of not only the mills, but virtually the entire social formation that constituted their operation.

Charged with building a society from scratch, mill owners at Lowell elaborated a landscape for their system of production and hierarchical authority that stretched from the excavated canals that supplied power to the mills to the vast factory buildings to the residential housing built for workers and management (see Figure 5.1). The production system—which was based in the integration of capital costs, including natural water power, mechanical production, and manual and managerial labor—was mirrored by the construction of mill communities, whereby operatives, skilled workers, and managers were spatially segregated from one another yet integrated as employees within a hierarchy of authority. This system is best illustrated in the housing built for the different ranks of employees.

In designing the factory complexes, precise plans were drawn up and executed for the varied worker housing (see Figure 5.2). Such renderings established owner authority over not only the operative's work and home life, but its very conception, in that the plans commissioned by the owners dictated the actual material spaces workers ultimately engaged with.

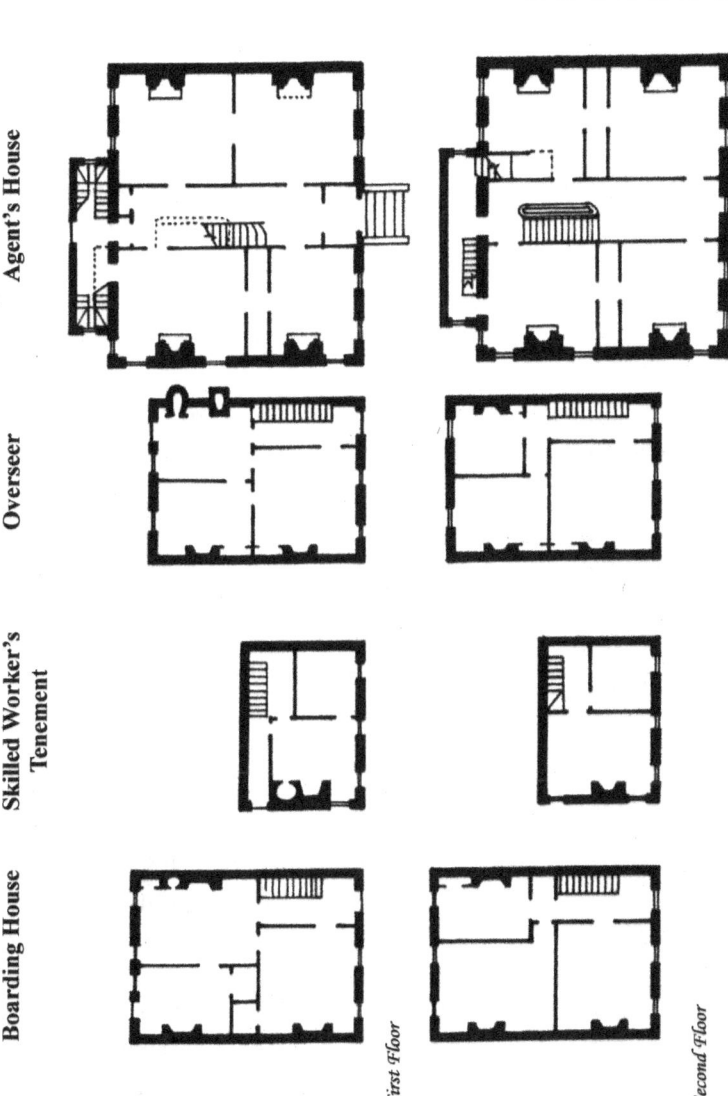

Figure 5.2. Diverse housing plans for mill employees at Lowell (drawing by Ross Rava after Mrozowski 2006: 76).

Mrozowski argues that such planning was aimed at establishing social control, such that "the Boston Associates made conscious choices at the outset to construct a space where worker housing and class difference were set in stone" (2006: 74). In the very material form of the mill buildings and corporate landscape, social difference was reflected consistently throughout the system and, by extension, effectively naturalized.

Among the best evidence of this constructed, systematic approach is the archaeological record of change at Lowell as the mills faced increasing competition and began to decline toward the end of the nineteenth century. This record shows that the survival of the system was deemed more important than that of its constituents in terms of the application of capital. Apparently, the constructed society required its material appearance to be intact if it were to be reproduced through time, despite the struggle of its operatives to even survive.

Two principal categories of archaeological evidence stand out from the record at Lowell: the use of yard space and the company's sanitation efforts. Archaeological research at Lowell collected data from four locations related to worker housing: a Boott Mills boardinghouse and a tenement unit, both of which housed mill operatives; the Lawrence Company overseer's block, which housed low-level managers; and the Kirk Street agent's house which was home to the Boott Mills' principal manager. During the first decade of mill operation, backyards at both the boarding and tenement structures contained a well, a privy, brick-lined drainage features, small ornamental plantings, and posts for clothesline supports. Botanical data suggest that the yards were mostly barren of ground cover. Such a clean and functional yard would have symbolized the well-maintained workforce that mill owners promoted under their care. By the late nineteenth century, these yards had undergone a dramatic decline in quality, a pattern indicative of the mill's larger decline, but one that stands in contrast to the findings from higher-status worker housing at the other sites.

Late-nineteenth-century deposits at the boardinghouse and tenement sites show that the overall rubbish density had increased dramatically from earlier levels, and botanical analysis shows an increase in weeds. The picture painted is of unkempt yards that were largely abandoned except for the vital functions they served for obtaining water and disposing of waste, issues that demand close consideration in light of a decline in sanitation. Faunal deposit analysis shows an increase in rat bones, and rodent-gnawed bones were found throughout the backyard, including its drainage features, suggesting a space colonized almost entirely by vermin, the drains clogged by their waste. Archaeology also verifies the continued use of boardinghouse privies until after 1900, despite earlier calls for their elimination and clear evidence of contaminated drinking water. The most disturbing finds are the extremely dangerous levels of lead found in soils surrounding drainage features and within privies. Likely from paint and pipes, these high lead levels (quite lethal in the long term) were clearly a component of everyday life for the later mill operatives.

The Lawrence Mills overseer's block contrasts in important ways with the worker's housing sites at Boott Mills. Overseers occupied single-family, attached dwellings. They had backyards that originally contained wooden sheds, later replaced by brick structures added onto kitchen ells. Backyards also show improvements made in the form of new waste- and water-management systems. These improvements date after 1880, meaning the new underground pipe network and water closets may have been a response to municipal board of health orders. However, this is also the time when evidence from the boardinghouse and tenement sites shows a dramatic deterioration in sanitation there. These investments clearly indicate that the mill owners were carefully selecting who and what they valued within the company community. Notably, lead levels from the overseer's house are comparable to those from the operative's housing, suggesting that the corporation's investment in quality and environmental control had its limits.

The Kirk Street agent's house at Boott Mills was occupied by two elite employee families. The Bartletts lived there from 1846 to 1861, along with a number of servants. They were succeeded by the family and servants of Frank Battle, the company agent, who lived there until 1889. Archaeological work at the agent's house shows that the site went through a significant transformation when the Battle family moved in. Botanical and faunal evidence indicate that the Bartletts kept well-manicured, grass-covered front and side yards. Their backyard, however, was a site of frequent animal butchery and a place for refuse and weeds. When the Battles moved in, the entire yard was covered over with a fresh layer of sod that showed no sign of regular refuse accumulation after planting. The front and side yards were also landscaped such that a clean layer of loam was deposited to raise the ground surface prior to laying in the new lawn. This landscaping and cleanup clearly marks an effort on behalf of the company to establish a sense of newness for the arriving agent's family. Notably, lead levels at the agent's homesite were significantly lower than at the other excavated sites, and there were no rodent bones recovered at all.

By eliminating a backyard working area, the agent's homesite also came to epitomize the growing class difference between manual and mental, or blue- and white-collar, laborers in the late nineteenth century. The homes of white-collar, mental laborers were to be associated with sanitary, clean, and manicured spaces for leisure instead of work. While even the early female mill operatives were engaged in mental stimulation through improvement circles, later generations of owners, involved during the time of the mills' decline, reserved such stimulation for its managers. This may be seen as an investment in their status and authority that the Boston Associates hoped would be returned in better and more profitable management of the mills.

Such distinctions in both the architecture and environmental quality of the different sites excavated at Lowell show the distinctions that the corporate system built different employees' status. However, the archaeological record of change reinforces that the highest value in the corporate community was placed on those most closely connected to the generation of profit, rather than the assuring of the community's overall well-being. Such changes also reflect growing class distinctions, a prominent component of the original fears held by the mills' resistant rural neighbors. Industry's inherently antirepublican nature had been made clear in British factories. However, at Lowell, obvious class distinction based in quite divergent interests in the well-being of the corporation emerged only after the system was put into place, when the question of whether the Lowell mills should have been built was long past relevance. The questions that did emerge thus appear to be about how to strengthen corporate management so as to assure that class distinctions did not evolve into class conflict. Additionally, by the time the mills began to decline, the owners' commitments had tied up large sums of their personal capital, too much for them to leave the mills' operation to those interested in worker well-being at the expense of profits.

The result is that, through the construction and reproduction of the mills at Lowell, we can see how the powerful systems that capitalism imagines and constructs can come to control the lives of those who support them. The system is based on an integrated and deeply invested mechanism that emerges from an *abstract* conceptual origin of the social relations of production. This can be a society, a business, and/or other communities that engage with one another for the sake of production and profit. What occurs most often is that the lived reality fails to match the abstract plan, and adjustments are required. Typically, these adjustments are skewed toward the preservation and enhancement of capital, without which the structures already in place—the factories, employee communities, and contracted agreements with suppliers and retail merchants—would suffer. At Lowell this is evident in the unequal corporate investments in the quality of life of different employees. Yet even at Lowell, the adjustments continued, ultimately causing the mills to be largely abandoned by 1920 as companies relocated to the Southern states, which promised cheaper labor and related capital costs. Interestingly, these Southern mills have recently (in 2007) closed as owning companies respond to the same offers from governments and investors in South America. As Mrozowski describes (2007), this movement of capital leaves a great deal in its wake. For one, working-class populations left behind suffer from the loss of corporate structures that provided at the very least jobs, if not the principal base for building communities. Even more, the remaining society, which was in part constructed for the benefit of capitalist investors, is stuck with a host of problems to contend with, such as an underemployed workforce and environmental issues like high lead levels and industrial brownfields—issues that were undoubtedly caused by the corporations, but for which they do not claim responsibility without lengthy litigation. Examining additional archaeological examples of the spread of victorious capitalism—a victory claimed in the present without regard for past conditions or future consequences—elaborates.

Bodies of Work and Capital in the Mythic West

This section considers the capitalist organization of a regionally formed way of life that constituted an important base for sustaining capital, enhancing investment, and, not infrequently, presenting to the American population there and elsewhere the forces required to reproduce capitalism despite resistance. The region in question is the American West, from the Rocky Mountains to the Pacific Ocean. My discussion focuses on the archaeology of extractive industries, which collected the raw materials and resources required for industrial production, and in their organization established certain social forms and practices that demonstrated how capitalist social relations can structure even the most profound aspects of production and reproduction. In mining and work camps, model company towns, and satellite settlements, the basis of communities was often a single kind of work—funded and supplied by outside capital—that produced goods for outside markets. As a result of this trend, a great number of places in the West were without local control over resources or even the direction of future development. Accordingly, archaeology shows that persons in these settings focused on pleasuring as well as damaging their bodies, a process that may have satisfied an urge for belonging snubbed by limited incomes and absent material structures that would have enabled community development. In the following, I discuss the work of several archaeologists to describe these places and demonstrate how this process of worker alienation successfully served the interests of capitalists, despite signs of resistance and even rebellion.

Following Randall McGuire and Paul Reckner (2002), we should consider the historic nineteenth- and early-twentieth-century American West as an underdeveloped periphery of the northeastern, industrial, capitalist core. A periphery indicates two particular aspects for understanding social life. First, peripheries are defined by extraction not only of natural resources, but also labor value (McGuire and Reckner 2002: 47). Thus, the value of work for all persons conforms as much as possible to its value in the market as a capital cost. In practice, this meant that unskilled labor was prized above skilled labor, and that severely limited investment in infrastructure and services left settlements underdeveloped, making them unappealing to residents interested in creating lasting communities. Work was designed to consume as much of life as possible, leaving little space for developing autonomous social relations and communities outside of capitalism. Second, the core-periphery approach allows us to consider the West as a regional whole. It was not just isolated places that exhibited capitalist underdevelopment, for the entire West was constructed this way. This meant that the experience of space and place, a powerful functional resource and limitation in social life, was undertaken by people in the region uniformly, such that laborers in Arizona or Colorado worked and lived in ways quite similar to those in Montana or California. Despite variations in industry, ethnicity, and certainly local history, the West appears to have been experienced as a place with a predominant, if not a single, way of life—an idiosyncrasy geared to support outside capitalist interests.

To explain this assertion I refer first to a historical ethnographic study by William Douglass of the creation of the community at Tonopah, Nevada, in the early twentieth century (1998). Tonopah was settled after the discovery of silver there in 1900. Along with the establishment of Goldfield thirty miles away, this lode constituted "one of the three or four most important mining booms in the history of the American West" (Douglass 1998: 104). Contrasting with images of the mining camp as "a collection of strangers, rather than a community of kinsmen, friends, and neighbors" (1998: 100), Tonopah illustrates the regional and supra-regional bases of both mining towns and the mechanisms that structured these communities. The Tonopah deposit was discovered by Jim Butler, a California-born, lifelong miner. Strapped for cash, Butler financed the mining through arrangements with friends and a local merchant from his then-current home in Belmont, Nevada. From this base, a community of over one thousand people formed in the first several months, drawn mostly from surrounding towns and through existing social networks. Ultimately, Tonopah grew to house more than eight thousand people. The point is that Tonopah was not a collection of strangers, but one of already-related miners and merchants. The integrated character of this community across the region is notable, since the construction of Tonopah involved the destruction of other towns. To build it, structural materials from surrounding towns such as Belmont, Silver Peak, and Sodaville were "cannibalized" (Douglass 1998: 104), as people abandoned one town to build another. The same holds true for businesses that first set up satellite shops and then moved their enterprises entirely to Tonopah. Populations in towns even further away in Nevada, California, and Colorado also dwindled. Nearby agricultural ranching enterprises were similarly affected as small homesteaders left for the mines, allowing larger landowners and mining entrepreneurs to increase the size of their holdings. Finally, the community's diverse ethnicities represented long historical trends of ethnic group movements, which tended to follow prospects for work and wealth from town to Western town. For example, the Italian population at Tonopah came from Delamar, Nevada, and had previously moved from Eureka, Nevada, after booms in these places passed during the late nineteenth century.

This movement of people, materials, relations, and local capital through existing relationships describes what Douglass calls "a community without a locus" (1998: 106), meaning the people and relationships of a community existed, but its place was not necessarily determined. Such "industrial cowboys" were primed to move and abandon their homes and even property for new opportunities (Emmons 1994: 449, in Hardesty 1998: 84). This system was clearly based on the great potential opportunity for not only work, but also wealth and success that the West presented. Left undeveloped, however, was the chance for those doing the work to accumulate resources for their own security and toward ends designed by themselves in their own ultimate interest. While Jim Butler likely left Tonopah in a better financial condition than he was in when he discovered the silver, this was in part because he and his colleagues sold their claim in 1901 to Philadelphia-based investors, who financed the mine's intensive and ultimately complete extraction. This feat was accomplished rapidly, as both Tonopah and Goldfield were in decline by 1910.

Viewed from the perspective of the core-periphery system, the transient, regional, Western mining community described by Douglass is an appropriate response by those in the West to life in an underdeveloped periphery. Why, in this context, would anyone choose to risk their well-being and fortune by settling in one place? And what could be more useful and appealing to outside investors than a large and integrated population of laborers without resources who were prepared to relocate at any time? Yet such a situation strips persons of locality and local control, as they are reliant solely on the ownership of their laboring bodies and the relations they have with others for connecting to labor markets. Transience of this sort also prohibits ownership of other resources, most notably real property, and commitments to its development in place, both of which would challenge the freedoms enjoyed by outside capitalistic investment. Understanding the community in this way allows for a productive examination of how laboring bodies themselves became a focus of attention. Without other resources, Western workers turned on their bodies as sources of pleasure as well as sites for making claims on their behalf within the system. Placing the emphasis on bodies, however, reproduced capitalistic expectations that laborers agree to their standing within the system as those who own their commodified labor, an understanding, that is, that their well-being was tied solely to their physical health and productive capacity. It is perhaps this tenuous situation of extreme alienation that helps to explain why workers in the American West "proved to be the most radical, militant, and class conscious of working people" (Dubosky 1985: 16, in Hardesty 1998: 84).

Company Towns and Work Camps

One mechanism that helped to influence the dynamics of the working community in the West was the creation of model company towns owned and built by extractive companies for their workforces. In many respects these towns adopted structures of order and a management of space put into place in the enterprises at Lowell, except in Western company towns, the entire settlement was owned by the corporation, rather than just a segment of it, as was the case at Lowell. For example, the well-documented town of McGill, Nevada, built by the Nevada Consolidated Copper Company in 1909, was stratified into three sections: "High [status] company officials lived in an exclusive area called The Circle; middle-management and skilled workers in Middle Town; and unskilled workers in the neighborhoods of Lower Town" (Hardesty 1998: 88). These sections were complemented by ethnic sections known as Greek Town, Austrian Town, and Jap Town (McGill Ghost Town 2008). At McGill, even the names of neighborhoods reflected the employees' relative social standing in the company's organizational structure. This pattern was elaborated across the region as different settlements specialized and were hierarchically ranked and connected through a network of extraction, milling, redistribution, residential, and transportation efforts, all constructed under a widespread umbrella controlled by a single or a few companies.

Model company towns and regional networks imposed an abstract order over what was otherwise viewed as an untamed Western region and population. Often, towns were platted out in a grid of streets and properties, further emphasizing the authority of the company over the natural world. Companies also controlled negative influences that might undermine the town's communities by prohibiting gambling and prostitution and frowning on other behaviors and even businesses not deemed "necessary" (Goddard 2002: 89). The point was to create a social order "derived from labor routine, isolation, and company-imposed rules or policies" (Gardener 1992: 4, in Hardesty 1998: 88).

Such conditions were found even in temporary work camps built to house laborers on pipeline, dam construction, and similar short-term, mobile labor projects (Van Bueren 2002, Maniery 2002). Thad Van Bueren's study of the 1912–13 Alabama Gates camp, situated along the Los Angeles aqueduct in Inyo County, California (2002), shows a stratified and orderly community of supervisor cabins, canvas worker bunkhouses, and service structures (see Figure 5.3). The distribution of alcohol-related artifacts at the site suggests that workers were prohibited from drinking at the camp, while supervisors were not (Maniery 2002), although workers appear to have been free to drink in local saloons. Notably, worker tent sites had a high rate of association with smoking artifacts, indicating that smoking was permitted at the site and that tobacco was likely used to mitigate the effects of the hard manual labor and the isolation of the work. The supervisors' cabins point to another mechanism by which class difference was conveyed. Remains of a purse latch, ceramic tablewares, and landscaping in cabin yards indicate that the occupants were married couples. Combined with the alcohol and smoking data, married supervisors clearly illustrated to the single, male, unskilled workforce the benefits that came with following the company's rules.

Besides speaking to workers about the benefits of playing by the rules, married supervisors may also have been advertisements of the civilizing moral and social benefits that industrial work brought to the region. Such illustrations likely satisfied some social critics, but they also spoke to current and potential investors, who would have seen happy employees as a sign of good management. A similar conclusion was reached by William Gillespie and Mary Farrell based on patterns of worker and supervisor housing at two mining camps in Arizona (2002). At a camp run by the Santa Rita Company, housing for supervisors was substantially sturdier than workers' tent platforms, which were constructed at a distance. In contrast, at the Exposed Reef Mine, differences in quality and spacing between the housing for supervisors and workers were not evident. This variation in status display matches other differences. At Exposed Reef, the primary equipment requiring investment was the mill and a cyanide plant. At Santa Rita, there was no mill or heavy construction involved; rather, the most impressive structures were the headquarters, including the supervisors' housing. Thus, the greatest effort and investment were put into "the showpiece of each operation . . . as a kind of advertising, symbols meant to convey solid investments and high optimism" (Gillespie and Farrell 2002: 66). Combined with the authority to impose order on the landscape, the ability to produce at least an appearance of being a good investment certainly influenced what and how sites were created, and therefore the actual spaces workers and their supervisors occupied.

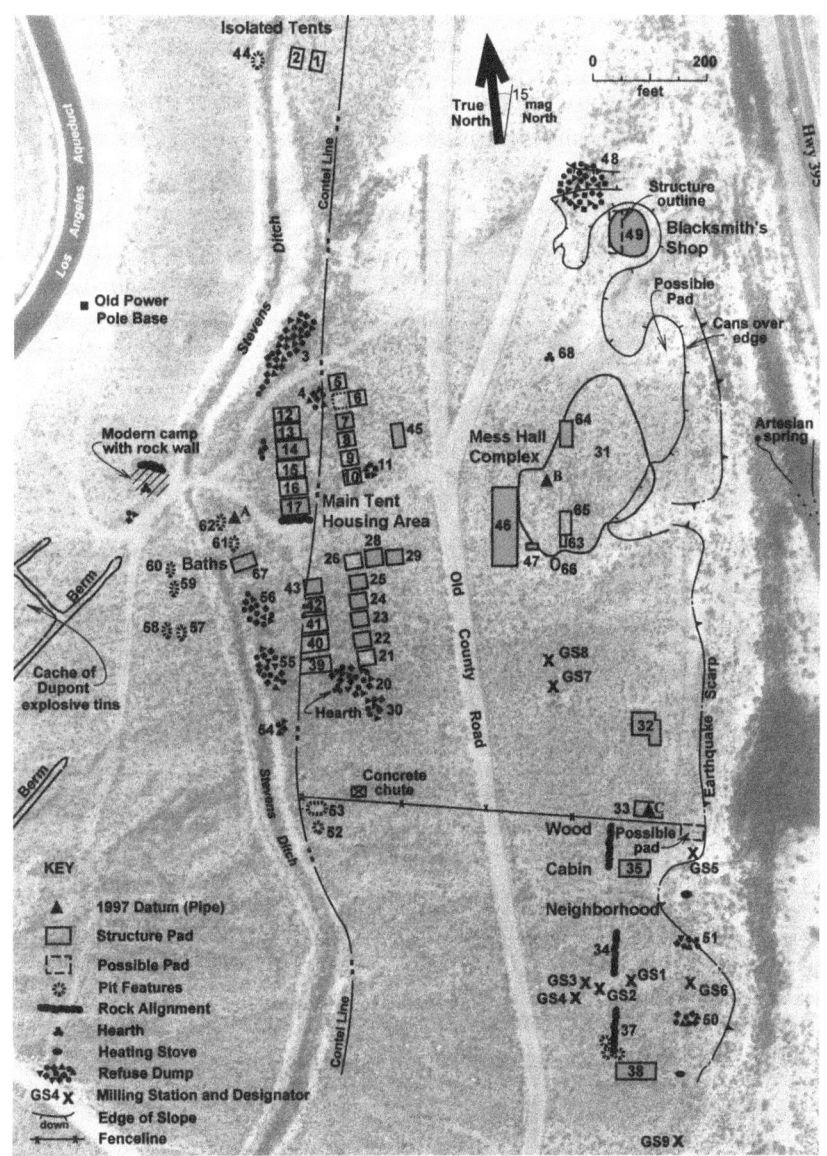

Figure 5.3. Layout of Alabama Gates labor camp (after Van Bueren 2002: Figure 4, Drawing by Kendall Schinke).

Satellite Towns

Against this backdrop of abstract ordered space and discipline, another site type studied by archaeologists stands out. Satellite towns were marginal settlements that sprung up alongside company towns. Their position beside company towns was both a physical and figurative reality. For example, Steptoe City was located adjacent to the company town of McGill (Goddard 2002), and Reipetown was located near the company towns of Kimberly and Ruth (Hardesty 1998). Satellite towns were also adjacent in a figurative sense. They were characterized by the very activities prohibited in company towns, such as gambling, prostitution, saloons, and at times, union radicalism, violence, and lawlessness. Archaeology at these sites has produced several interesting findings about how these communities varied from the company mainstream, yet were intimately a part of it as well.

At Steptoe City, next to McGill, Nevada, the architecture was uniformly of very low quality, consisting often of recycled materials. Unlike McGill, the settlement lacked electricity, running water, telephones, paved streets, and garbage collection. Richard Goddard suggests that this lack of quality and services may have been part of a strategy employed by some Steptoe residents (2002: 90–91). While census records show a high turnover rate, there were some long-term residents of Steptoe who chose to stay rather than "advance" by moving to McGill. Goddard suggests that one purpose of marginal settlements like Steptoe City was to provide a space between traditional rural and modern urban ways of life, allowing those who could not abide by company authority a place to remain connected to others and, in fact, alive. Goddard identifies some of these settlers as nonconformists and eccentrics who were attracted by cheap housing and, therefore, the possibility of making a life without sacrificing their ideals.

Reipetown, discussed by Don Hardesty (1998), presents similar findings based on excavated materials. The most notable finding is that, while nearby company towns were marked by clear status differences in housing related to company position, households in Reipetown showed no evident social distinctions by status or even ethnicity. Besides "a couple pieces of Japanese ceramic tableware there were no artifact markers of ethnicity" (Hardesty 1998: 92), despite the documented presence of Greeks, Slavs, Italians, Mexicans, and Japanese in the town. More distinguished was the overall variety of house form and organization, suggesting a much more individualized and circumstantial process of development. Excavated remains show a wide variety of domestic and wild foods as well as exotics such as fig, raspberry, and grape seeds.

At both Steptoe City and Reipetown, two business types stand out as typical of and important to satellite towns. The first were bars and saloons, which offered company employees opportunities and settings for drinking, smoking, socializing, and entertainment. A 1908 account indicated eleven bars in Reipetown, a figure that likely grew as the town peaked in the years before 1920 (Hardesty 1998: 90). Liquor is often regarded as an attraction for working people as it provides release, recreation, and, for many, a way to cope with the hard work and alienation presented by wage labor. That drinking was an important function of satellite towns shows one way these settlements were part of the larger, mainstream society next door. While drinking to forget social and personal troubles is common, it is not an acceptable means for handling these issues in public settings. Displacing the locations for such activities to spaces outside of company town limits embodied the same displacement asked of those struggling to stay within the company's society despite the damaging effects it had on their capacity for fulfillment and success. Drunkenness, even by company town residents, did not take place in the company town, a factor likely embraced in the promotion of the company's positive effects on its workers and the larger regional landscape they were constructing.

A second business typical of satellite towns was the brothel. Alexy Simmons notes that prostitution was part and parcel of mining towns in the American West as well as New Zealand (1998). In many cases, brothels operated unconcealed, standing alongside other main street businesses such as general stores, saloons, and transport companies. Servicing the largely male workforce of the region, brothels offered sexual services and female companionship and were, predictably, quite successful in satellite towns. Simmons importantly observes the role, as with foodstuffs, of exotics in satellite settlements. In many instances, prostitutes were classified as exotic because of their racial status as octoroon, quadroon, mulatto, or Japanese women. In other cases, records show that qualities of Frenchness were desired, leading Anglo-American prostitutes to adopt French names and accents. These attributes once again helped to simultaneously mark off and connect satellites with central towns.

Important to understanding prostitution in this context is that women were, for the most part, in control of their services. This personal authority was far from the mainstream norm, in which middle-class, Victorian-era women were expected to be subservient to and dependent on the authority of fathers, husbands, and men in general. Prostitutes thus not only served male sexual needs and desires, but also extracted from the system a living as independent women. In this way, brothels may be seen as a hidden part of the mainstream company society. For one, the services provided by brothels should be seen as paired with saloons, for they both offered their patrons a form of release and recreation in a setting that allowed the company town to remain distinct and thus an acceptable symbol of the owning company. Second, brothels revealed that the company towns provided a moral alternative to the free market in vice, where fragile women fell daily to the extreme demands of survival presented to those who opted out of the mainstream.

This argument works both ways. Goddard concludes that satellite towns "existed because they filled the gap between the ideal and the real. They provided whatever was necessary for human existence that was not provided for by the structured community. They represented the failure of the social and economic system to fulfill its promise" (2002: 92). This statement captures the atmosphere of concern, if not fear, that likely underlaid a great deal of daily life in the historic American Western periphery during the early twentieth century. Company towns and work camps offered employees the security of order and a wage. They also required conformity to company rules and authority. At the edge of this society, so it was presented, was the threat of non-survival, a threat that breaking the rules materialized. The West was a generally harsh climate with few settlements, so to lose a job was to put oneself in a truly desperate situation. At these interstices between the order of the company and the disorder of the wilderness, satellite towns emerged.

But satellite towns did little to promote lasting alternatives. Having the least in terms of capital and power, their function was to soothe the wounds caused by a system based in worker isolation and exploitation with barely adequate shelter, alcohol, and prostitution. Hardesty notes that in Reipetown, expected signs of status, class, and ethnic difference did not materialize (1998: 90). This may be taken to reflect the harsh reality of the situation in satellite towns, and further, the way satellite towns embodied the dynamics of the region as a periphery. In this context, even seemingly given distinctions such as ethnicity are revealed to have costs to those who hold them. Lacking resources, workers in the industrial American West were stripped down to simply their bodies—mechanisms for extracting ore, digging canals and ditches, cutting timber, and hauling loads. The maintenance of these bodies was a capital cost, but given a surplus of labor and the few alternatives for actually surviving in the region, it was a cost that those closest to the margins had to assume for themselves.

Satellite towns served marginal people by allowing laborers to change for themselves their baseline requirements. Low-cost housing, easy access to bodily pleasures, and affiliation with company towns and work enabled them to change their standing from one who relied entirely on the company to one who, at their own expense, sought to build relations with power in part on their own terms. With alcohol and other vices, laborers themselves mended—as with babbitt—their bodies and psyches so that they could return to the mines for another day. The main impact of satellite towns, therefore, was their role in forging a basis of belonging that forced one to choose conformity or deviance, a choice that made life either the product of the capitalistic company system or one framed in terms where loss of life was the responsibility of those individuals who opted out, not the system itself.

Therefore, we may conclude that the American West, as McGuire and Reckner describe (2002), was neither the mythic world of gunslinging cowboys and Indians nor one of prospectors and homesteaders. It was, instead, an underdeveloped periphery built in the interest and design of outside capital investment with the use of undervalued, hard, manual wage labor. So, as McGuire and Reckner also describe, at the root of the West was class struggle, but this struggle was not solely of labor against capital in the abstract. It was also a struggle against the isolation enforced on persons by a system based on the extremes of alienation that oftentimes prized the individual over the collective, creating a situation where the West's not-so-mythic gun violence was as often as not cases of alienated laborers murdering each other (see Hardesty 1998: 94).

"The Stuff of Conundrum": Consumption in Paradise

Frederick Charles Buckingham Sr., a long-time resident of the remote town of Paradise, Nevada, described to archaeologist Margaret Purser how the community had traditionally organized around the death and burial of one of its members. Speaking about his grandfather's store, Buckingham noted, "They carried everything to make a casket, see? They had casket hinges, and the name plates, the handles, and all the material to cover the casket both inside and outside" (Purser 1991: 110). With these materials, a local carpenter would assemble the casket during the night. While a local rancher supplied ice to preserve the body, neighbors would take care of it, then a spring wagon, perhaps borrowed from someone, would transport it to the church. Six pallbearers would later carry the casket to the gravesite as another person tolled the church bell. Considering that all those involved were local, a person's death in nineteenth-century Paradise was in many ways a community-wide affair.

Aspects of this process are not unusual. A person's burial typically requires the help of many family members, friends, and acquaintances, as well as services provided by commercial businesses. Notable in this memory, however, is how the organization of people and services blurred the place of commerce in the community, at least as we recognize it now. Specifically, while local merchants supplied nonlocal materials like the hardware, it was local carpenters who completed the casket, who, along with the other locals who donated the ice and their time to help with the burial, considered their responsibilities to the local community a top priority.

Purser's research on the Paradise community indicates that this snapshot event marks the earlier of two phases in the community's history, phases that may be distinguished by the invasion of industrial capitalism and consumer culture around the turn of the twentieth century. A probate record from 1904, for example, shows that another Paradise resident purchased a ready-made casket from an undertaker in Winnemucca, a larger town on the railroad line forty miles away. By this time, many tradesmen who performed assembly and maintenance services for the community, like the carpenters in this story, had left Paradise for Winnemucca or elsewhere. In their place, and in part a cause of their emigration, were directly available, finished products from stores in Paradise, Winnemucca, or even from the Montgomery Ward or Sears catalogs that required no local assembly at all.

As it considers the impact on community relations, Purser's approach to understanding these changes yields one of the best examples of the archaeology of capitalism. Communities like Paradise underwent profound changes as they connected with and managed the invasions of industrial capitalism, especially regarding the associated culture of consumption. As she remarks, "the people of industrializing societies increasingly exchanged any direct access to technological knowledge or productive capacity for the more relative, socially contingent controls of selective acquisition and consumer choice" (Purser 1991: 105). The growing distance between production and consumption did not simply involve negotiating new market patterns, but also negotiating new relationships with the very people who may have formerly helped to bury one's mother or father. Communities and neighbors were no longer connected by maintenance relations—that is, favors or commercial services provided to one another that assisted each person or family in completing their work. With the invasion of capitalism, communities were challenged at their core as good neighbors increasingly became defined more by good fences than connections and relationships.

This process is summarized for the American West by historian Richard White (1991: 242): "what westerners produced they did not consume, what they consumed they did not produce" (in Purser 1999: 120). Against this generality, Purser argues that archaeology provides specific community and personal histories of how new relationships with production and consumption created new ways of life in capitalism. Her approach also describes a powerful way to handle the volume of materials that came with industrial mass production. Purser situates industrial materials in a framework where consumption itself was not a passive activity, but one among the complex strategies employed by large-scale producers as well local individuals to adjust to the transformative circumstances engendered by economies of scale. As these transformations are related to, if not determinant of, the value of labor, Purser helps shift the analysis from artifacts to understanding the community's structure, so that we can understand why different households would embrace mass production. Not discounting individual artifacts or artifact types, this approach considers first the systems that assemblages as a whole represent, and therefore asks: What sort of household strategies within and perhaps against capitalism are revealed?

An example is the assemblages collected from two sites in Paradise (Purser 1999: 125–31). The earlier of the two is from the 1870s homestead cabin of John and Ida Merchant. Materials recovered suggest that the Merchants were comfortable and connected with the market of consumer goods, for they left behind fragments from wine, liquor, and soda bottles, sardine cans, a Lea and Perrins' Worcestershire sauce bottle, hand-painted china, pressed glass dishes, and an iron cookstove manufactured in Chicago. Standing out from this set is the lack of any non-can metal except for

Figure 5.4. The Reinhart Ranch, Paradise, Nevada (photograph by Margaret Purser).

a broken pitchfork and a cookstove fragment. While metal objects most certainly constituted part of the living assemblage of the Merchants' material world in the form of nails, farm tools, and cooking equipment, these objects likely left with the Merchants and perhaps reentered the community as recycled materials.

The second site is the 1920s Reinhart Ranch (see Figure 5.4), the location where the babbitt-mended bearing discussed in the beginning of this chapter was discovered. The occupants of the site were the members of the Mendiola family, Basque immigrants who lived there as tenants. Compared to the Merchant home, the diversity of materials is vast, though the level of comfort seems comparable. There were more name-brand bottled products, and ceramics were plain, but more numerous. Some goods indicate efforts at home improvement, like broken doorknobs and paint buckets, while other goods indicate potentially special purchases such as fancy women's shoes, polychrome printed china, a painted glass lamp, and a toy rubber ball. Also, the Reinhart Ranch had an abundance of metal, many scraps showing that they had been "reworked by hand to serve small, expedient tasks around the ranch" (Purser 1999: 28). This factor suggests that when the Mendiolas moved away, they did not need to bring potentially recyclable or reusable materials with them.

These two cases show that over the span of a generation in Paradise, mass-produced artifacts grew in number as families like the Mendiolas took a greater interest in the commercial market than those like the Merchants. The specific finds also show how the Mendiolas, as relatively poor people, negotiated this connection. Among the assemblage are artifacts—especially the reworked metal fragments and replaced doorknobs—that indicate their self-provisioning of maintenance labor. By this point, there was no blacksmith in Paradise, for they had already left along with other tradesmen as the market for their work dwindled. Homeowners in turn had to perform the curation and maintenance of their tools and homes. For the Mendiolas, this meant that they needed to fashion their own tools out of waste metals. But part of the story is the availability of waste metals by virtue of the growing number of mass-produced goods, which limited demand for reuse and recycling. One wonders if the Mendiolas acquired waste metals from their wealthier neighbors, who were more frequently disposing of and replacing aging and broken products. Certainly, the babbitt-mended bearing represents this activity of self-repair, and again, the availability of babbitt from local stores reflects this shift from community-based to self-provided maintenance.

Purser argues that this is evidence of growing isolation between households. Without ties formed through shared work, such as trade, barter, and maintenance relations, households within the community drifted apart, each becoming increasingly independent and individually responsible for their reproduction. For one, households and their members were more directly connected with national mass producers and retailers, creating less demand for local community resources. In addition, as households separated, they became competitive, since opportunities for income and work were increasingly framed through an abstract labor market rather than through skills and other concrete, mutual interests. The only real basis of their community was their shared interest in individual responsibility.

It is here that Purser's babbitt metaphor is best deployed. She tracks evidence of adjustments made in the community by showing how households embraced their isolation, despite attendant costs to their well-being. Many houses were redesigned by adding porches, subdividing rooms, and adding and enlarging kitchens and cellars. Some homeowners also built barns, wagon sheds, and garages to meet their new, independent, working needs, while others fenced off their lots, thereby separating themselves from the larger social space in town. Public spaces like hotels and merchant shops were also subdivided and restricted. While these spaces had previously been de facto common spaces where community members met to do business and socialize, they now became for the use of paying customers only.

Purser argues that these transformations served as babbitt for the broken community. In many ways, house additions and specialized spaces were rational and functional, providing independent households with necessary areas for self-production. However, the separation of work spaces like kitchens and garages within but apart from the home, or of parlors and porches as semipublic spaces for separating family and communal space, were little more than rationalizations of the isolation that constructed the family as an independent body within society despite the insecurities and extra burdens this created. Among the highest costs, though, were not just the renovations and expenses of recreating the home, but the concomitant psychological costs to individuals and families involved in hiding whatever struggles and failings they were experiencing in the effort to appear successfully independent. These would have included both renovations to the space and architecture and equally important renovations and maintenance of bodies themselves. This helps to explain the archaeological finding at the Reinhart Ranch of fancy shoes, likely purchased by a woman from the relatively poor Mendiola family. It also helps to explain their printed china and painted glass lamp, as well as why a tenant family would paint their house and replace the doorknobs, making improvements to a property that belonged to someone else. These improvements may be seen as ways that the Mendiolas created and adorned their private family space. Given the isolation of families and their growing connection only through a shared experience of consumer culture, improvements like these allowed the Mendiolas and their neighbors, as well as the many thousands of others indoctrinated into capitalism and consumer culture during this era, to find ways to communicate. Yet, we have to include that among those being spoken to by the Mendiolas were the Mendiolas themselves: that through the purchase and use of consumer products, people were in part saying to themselves that despite their isolation, insecurity, and the costs thus incurred, they were nevertheless able to understand and meet the standards of the middle class. We should reflect on that inasmuch as this is true—that the Mendiolas and their peers, through consumption, were managing the alienation of their own labor from themselves, such that they were purchasing for their bodies goods that would mend but not heal, as babbitt does, the ruptures that capitalist exploitation caused.

Conclusion: Archaeology and Victorious Capitalism

James Symonds captures the spirit of industrial capitalism described in this chapter in an unusual way (2005). He proposes, "If Marx were alive today . . . how delicious it might seem to him that the modern-day bourgeoisie is earnestly engaged in an activity that maps the decline and failure of its own capitalist forebears, and moreover seeks to . . . [pay] *homage* to the generations of workers that struggled to create the modern world" (Symonds 2005: 33). His point is that our access as archaeologists to sites of past capitalist industry is an important part of their story. We are not digging active industrial sites, but sites long ago abandoned and, for many, forgotten. Our excavation accentuates their status now as failures, and symbolizes the costs of industrial capitalism. Mrozowski explores this at Lowell by relating current struggles to past capital relocation and social and environmental degradation. The same story, in different terms, is also found at virtually every other site discussed in this chapter. The California mining camps were planned to be abandoned. Paradise, McGill, and Steptoe City are ghost towns. Reipetown is now a trash dump. Even the sites discussed by Crane were excavated as part of a development project to build a sports arena in Washington, D.C., which ultimately obliterated these sites (2000). Loss and the threat of loss appear inherent in industrial capitalism (Gonzalez-Ruibal 2008). Having no regard for persons, the lack of regard for place within capitalism is not surprising. Nevertheless, capitalist decline and abandonment is a part of the story we need to record, if for no other reason than that it is from this part of the story that archaeological research emerges.

The story of decline is that while capitalists lose investments, laborers lose their livelihood, if not their lives, and while businesses lose profits, communities are almost irrecoverably fractured. For Marx and Weber, capitalism earned victory in the construction of a society based in the creation of profit rather than community. Weber described developing corporate and governmental bureaucracy as an iron cage, in the sense that that the middle-class managers not directly benefiting from corporate profit find themselves nevertheless operating on capital's behalf and against the interests of labor. A question that arises is: If and how does archaeology, a preeminent middle-class profession, fit into this victory march? For some, archaeology's engagements are eye-opening insights into dynamic social processes hidden by capitalism's self-produced history (that is, they comprise resistance to it). These works suggest archaeology can escape from and even help to break open the iron cage. For others, archaeology is more like babbitt in the service of capital, sealing the ruptures it causes by simultaneously presenting for consumption the progress of modern society as well as modernity's very ability to apparently surpass its own limitations, an agenda to which archaeological research contributes. Considering these possibilities is the focus of the final chapters of this book.

6

Communities Outside Capitalism

Archaeologies of Resistance

> It is no surprise to learn that technical systems of various kinds are deeply interwoven in the conditions of modern politics.
>
> Langdon Winner, *Do Artifacts Have Politics?*

This volume has so far tracked American capitalism in a temporal fashion from the beginnings of European colonialism to the maturation of American industrial capitalism in the early twentieth century. Throughout, my aim has been to coalesce a variety of archaeological studies around the emergence of a culture of individualism, exploitative labor relations, and the commodification of all parts of human life. I am quite sure the story thus far depicts a capitalism that bulldozed its way through American society, either picking up or mowing under those persons and communities it encountered along the way. No one seems to have escaped. I have chosen this organization to underline the powerful forces that must be associated with capitalism. As I stated in the introduction, capitalism is extremely personal. It places people in a position where they must consider and balance their own well-being against that of their community, including members of their own family. It also places capitalists in positions of authority over not only production and the making of personal profit, but, through the commodification of labor, over the well-being of persons who are essentially reduced to components of their profit-making system. Capitalism, in other words, produces its own community, and with that, a consciousness that serves only the very few, who jealously protect their ownership of the means of production. Within the capitalist community, the question is not whether capitalism is a fair or responsible system, but how one is to survive *given* the conditions capitalism creates.

Working within capitalism can be rewarding and even potentially equalizing for individuals, but it is not without significant costs. In capitalism, the basis of wealth does not necessarily lie in inheritance (though that provides clear advantages). Rather, power and authority derive from the ownership of vital resources; however, with human labor situated at the core of these resources, the very notion of human life is reconstructed such that capitalist communities claim to consist of a coalition of willing individuals rather than individuals who are the social product of communities. It may be said that success in the capitalist community is ultimately "anticultural," as community and other cultural affiliations are seemingly the result of individual preference rather than conditions for understanding the diversity of experience and consciousness that constitutes the basis of identities and the meanings of social action. The point is that the community within capitalism is a falsehood, for it proposes that objective, individualized labor relations reflect a natural state of human affairs rather than the exploitative and unequal conditions that the majority must negotiate in order to participate and survive.

It is likely that few of those who encountered capitalism willingly bought into its social constructions entirely. Capitalism has always engendered a social negotiation in which individuals, families, and communities resist their dissolution and reconstruction as commodities. The historical textures of American social history reflect this process. Even apologists for capitalism recognize resistance in the power of labor unions, the expansion of civil rights and the franchise to women and minorities, and even the tolerance of a critical and independent academy. These are usually portrayed as signs of the willingness and capacity of capitalism to accept change and reform. However, resistance to capitalism comes in different registers. Open rebellion and revolution lie at one end of the spectrum of resistant activities. Many examples can be found in American history, and the study of collective actions, rebellions, and strikes is starting to be a focus of diverse archaeological studies in the United States (Saitta 2007, McGuire 2008, Shackel 2000, 2003, Epperson 1999). At the other end of the spectrum, resistance may be found in what James Scott has famously termed "hidden transcripts" (1990). These include malingering, foot-dragging, joking, and other activities by which laborers assert authority over their own humanity and thus their power to either enable or subvert the productive process. These hidden activities at times also involved covert acts of destruction that decreased industrial output and profits. In the following, I discuss an archaeological study by Michael Nassaney and Marjorie Abel of industrial waste from New England's nineteenth-century cutlery factories as an example of this form of resistance (1993, 2000).

Additional powerful evidence of resistance to capitalism derives from other hidden spaces crafted during the course of American history. More emancipatory than negotiatory, these involve cases where the degrading, anticultural effects of capitalism were sidestepped by forming alternative communities both outside the dominant authority and directly critical of it. Domestic reform movements led by urban middle-class women, for example, encouraged the development of a critical female consciousness. Described by Suzanne Spencer-Wood, these efforts aimed to involve female domestic labor in the market in order to build a society less founded on exploitative labor relations, whether at home or at work. The failure of this movement reveals the nature of social authority in capitalist society. Similarly, exclusive utopian societies that formed soon after the American Revolution offered their members an existence insulated from the contingencies and threats of capitalist social life. Utopias were based in communalism, a social process consciously at odds with American capitalist individualism. While utopias more often that not failed, several Shaker communities survived for generations. David Starbuck's archaeology at Shaker communities illustrates that Shaker ideology and practice sustained an adherence to communalism, but also shows that this adherence involved consistent negotiation with the surrounding capitalist market.

A final example, discussed in the following chapter, is of a *culture* of resistance that emerged within African diaspora communities. African and African American resistance was not necessarily aimed directly at capitalism, but at racism and enslavement. Still, the nature of racial slavery in early America is so closely tied to the exploitation of labor at the root of capitalism, that I urge us to see African diaspora communities in active dialogue with the supporting capitalist premises of other, more direct, forms of oppression. Examining a variety of expressions associated with an archaeologically recovered African American material culture, I connect material practices of African diaspora communities to a long and complex struggle to overcome the exclusion of people of color from America's mainstream capitalist society on the basis of race. Archaeology is vital to the effort to record resistance and the development of a critical consciousness in American history. In contrast to the documented histories of these communities, archaeology provides important alternative information. Most successful subversive efforts employed by these groups were intentionally hidden behind a fabricated façade of conformity. It is this surface expression—or what Scott calls the "public transcripts" (1990)—that makes up most of what is found in the archives. Archaeology provides a necessary complementary record, where the hidden activities that constituted subversion and the construction of communities outside capitalism may be found. As Nassaney and Abel propose, "artifacts have politics" (1993: 247), and, in fact, the relative level of politics they contained may be an important basis for evaluating historic America's many examples of resistance to capitalism.

This chapter therefore considers how the culture of capitalism was criticized and rejected through the development of diverse alternative forms of consciousness that were embedded in the spaces and artifacts of community life. In each case, the spirit of capitalism was laid bare as those who struggled to survive its contingencies created alternatives and built new relationships and communities—arguably the most powerful resource for challenging capitalism—that bolstered their critical positions. My aim is to show that, for some people, this effort sustained a temporary success that mitigated their immediate struggles, while for others, their constructed alternatives produced longer-lasting movements that have made significant impacts on the effort to challenge American capitalism, efforts that have proved and should continue to prove useful to those still challenging America's capitalist hegemony.

Hidden Transcripts, Deskilling, and Mountains of Waste

Among the most profound signs of capitalist development are the industrial factory systems built to increase and rationalize production. I explored the construction of factories at Lowell, Massachusetts, in the previous chapter as an example of this. An important theory behind industrial capitalism at these sites was the material assertion of the interchangeability of workers as laboring bodies in lieu of concern for their individual personhood and histories. One of the most powerful mechanisms in this process was the deskilling of labor. Deskilling transformed artisans into workers, such that laborers lost control over the workspace and its products (Shackel 1993). Replaced by machines and assembly-line production techniques, skilled labor became unnecessary. As John Stuart

Mill commented in 1848, workers "should not be required or encouraged to think for themselves, or give to their own reflection or forecast an influential voice in the determination of their destiny" (cited in Nassaney and Abel 2000: 258). In other words, workers should have no agency, nor even a history, that would suggest a working-class identity.

Nassaney and Abel emphasize that the lesson from these processes runs against trends established in standard histories of industrialism (1993, 2000). Rather than placing the technological innovation at the start of the explanation—that is, arguing that because of new inventions, production was streamlined and labor reorganized—they argue that we need to ask why new innovations were sought out. They suggest that the political relations that emerged with industrial capitalist growth show the reorganization of production was driven less by technological innovation than "the efforts of capitalists to control workers" (Nassaney and Abel 1993: 254). In opposition to the assumption that mass production produced cheaper products, in some industries mass production actually translated into more expensive goods. Paired with lower wages for deskilled work, this factor shows that it was profits and the control of labor that drove industrial growth and technological innovation rather than the reverse.

The question is whether these industrial politics can be read from the concrete relations that formed between workers and owners in the factories. Archaeology is an important tool here, for as much as these relations were formed around the production of things for the market, artifacts found at factory sites should bear marks of the relationships built to produce them. In other words, industrial materials themselves were sites of social negotiation and therefore were indeed "artifacts with politics" (Nassaney and Abel 1993: 247).

Nassaney and Abel have explored the implications of these politics in an archaeological study of the nineteenth-century cutlery industry in the Connecticut River Valley in Massachusetts, focusing on the Turner Falls factory, which was built by the John Russell Cutlery Company in 1870 (1993, 2000). The Russell factory was built in the current fashion, espousing many aspects of scientific management, particularly a careful design that managed the flow of production from raw material to finished product in a streamlined and systematic way (see Figure 6.1). Included in this architectural sequence was a formalization of deskilled labor, in which workers carried out only a single task that was to be repeated throughout

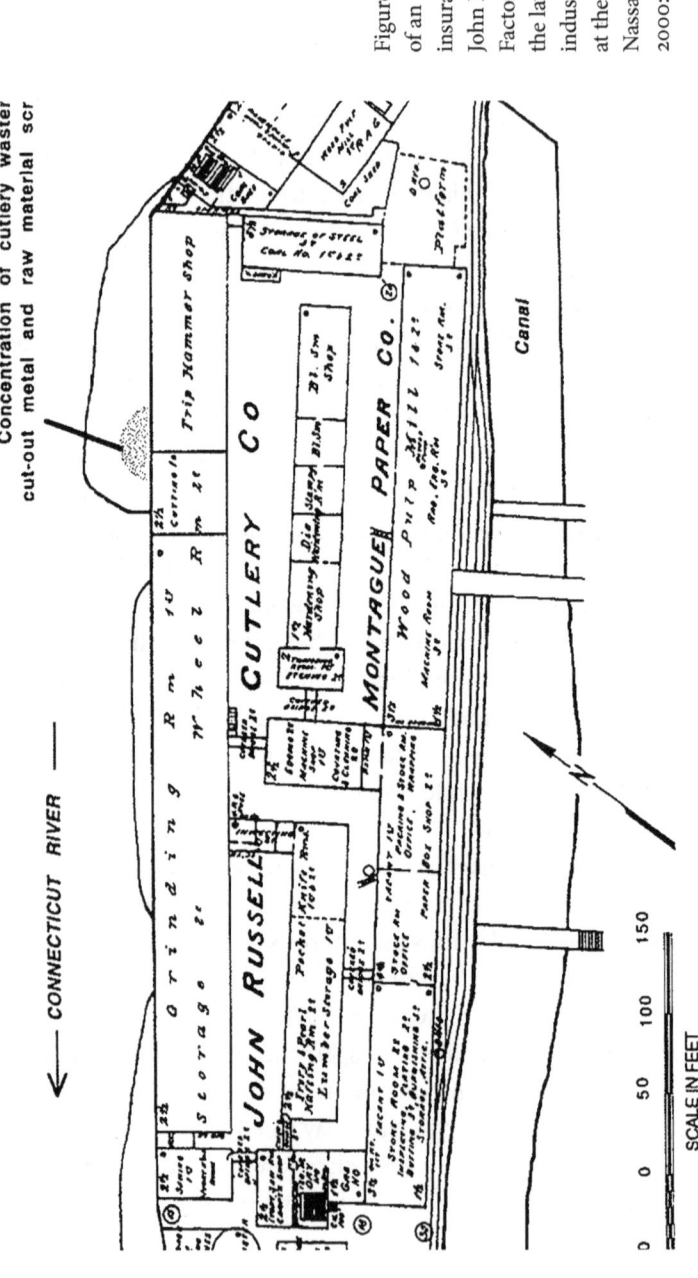

Figure 6.1. Detail of an 1884 Sanborn insurance map of the John Russell Cutlery Factory showing the layout of the industrial process at the factory (after Nassaney and Abel 2000: 248).

the day, such as grinding or polishing blades (see Figure 6.2). This system would have fostered a need for a negotiated response from workers, but records of these negotiations are sparse. Following Scott (1990), Nassaney and Abel suggest a technique highly appropriate for archaeology:

> The acceptance or rejection of the conditions created by management is often expressed in subtle ways that may go unnoticed by shop foremen and unrecorded in written documents. Acceptance or consent can be seen as a "public transcript" in which workers enact expected roles.... This contrasts with an alternate, yet parallel, "hidden transcript" which consists of a challenge to ideological hegemony constructed by workers—a dissident political culture, for instance—that takes the form of daily conversations, jokes, and songs. (Nassaney and Abel 1993: 251)

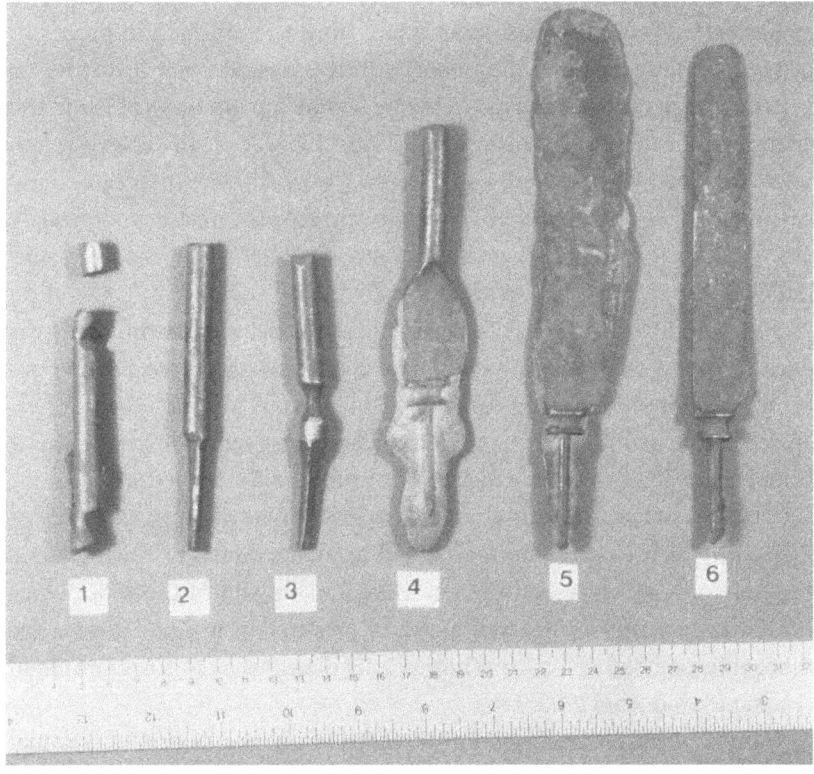

Figure 6.2. Wasters (*left*) and knife blades (*right*) in varied stages of production recovered from surface collection surveys of the Russell Cutlery site (photograph courtesy of Michael Nassaney).

It is from the record of the concrete rather than idealized relationships of industrial capitalism that the influence of worker resistance to capitalist domination can be discovered, and archaeology is an important tool for documenting the remains of these negotiated relations that still exist.

Some of the most important findings relate to the "work to rule" system employed at the Russell Company factory. Work to rule obviated any form of skilled knowledge by deferring to written manuals that established rules for machine speed and output. Disregarding workers' previous experience and knowledge allowed companies to hire anyone who promised obedience. However, a lack of knowledge about machinery and the demand to "work to rule" ultimately produced "mountains of scrap" in the form of industrial wastes and discards due to mistakes (Nassaney and Abel 1993: 253). A shoreline archaeological surface survey at the Russell factory site recovered over two hundred such objects from an area of approximately one hundred square meters: "Most of the objects collected in the field represent either scrap metal from the production processes or wasters. Furthermore, the majority of the wasters were discarded in the early stages of production . . . before significant amounts of labor and energy were expended" (Nassaney and Abel 1993: 265). To explore meanings associated with these discards, former workers were interviewed, revealing that "in order to avoid having to correct manufacturing mistakes, objects were 'thrown out the window, into the river'" (Nassaney and Abel 1993: 265).

This activity is a hidden transcript of resistance. Similar findings have been recorded at Lowell Mills in the form of drinking on the job and unkempt yards in the company housing (Mrozowski et al. 1996). Another example is a buried stash of manufactured artifacts recovered at the Rhode Island State Prison in Providence (Garman 2005). Buried and hidden activities in fact may be considered a necessary part of capitalist development, in which workers were expected to match demands for increased pace of work at what seemed the unpredictable will of the mill owner. Waste was actually considered a cost of production in that "it assuaged more intense conflict . . . or other serious disruptions to the work flow" (Nassaney and Abel 1993: 269).

Industrial wastes are therefore a record of the negotiation of domination and resistance in early American factories. Additional information from documentary sources adds important layers of meaning that deepen the impact of worker resistance on the nature of industrial capitalism.

Payroll books from a comparable cutlery factory in Northampton, Massachusetts, suggest that workers came from a limited set of families and were relatives and neighbors as well as coworkers. Such outside-of-work relationships in the factory created a "shop floor culture" and were another important way for workers to resist their exploitation and isolation. "Workers and, maybe even supervisors, would look the other way as mistakes were thrown out the window by relatives, friends, or household members" (Nassaney and Abel 1993: 266). These relations likely lie behind Russell's observation that American men were "too free and independent" as workers, and that immigrants, presumably because they were less networked, were better suited for the job (Nassaney and Abel 2000: 256).

Another example of worker resistance may be found in the activities of women who headed domestic areas at factory housing sites like those at the Russell Company. Even though the housing was owned by the factory and adopted the same rigid rationalizations of space or order promoted by scientific labor management, women broke the boundaries imposed on them in several ways. They developed ties among households to support their families, and they took in boarders and used the back lot space for gardening and raising domestic animals to supplement the family resources and income (Nassaney and Abel 2000: 266). These activities took advantage of the spaces left open to women at home to deconstruct the home-work divide imagined by industrial reformers. In this process, women produced relationships, resources, and income that made their families' lives of labor possible.

Considering this varied evidence as a set of hidden transcripts of worker resistance allows us to document a variety of ways in which the negotiation of the capitalist transformation was brought about on behalf of workers *by workers themselves*. This evidence turns the Industrial Revolution from a brief period of capitalist innovation and change into a longer process of negotiation by which a minority came to control an increasing percentage of the overall means of production in America. In no instance, however, were capitalists ever capable of acting alone. Their dependence on labor could not be resolved. This fact supported the various acts of worker resistance identified by Nassaney and Abel. However, the durability of these hidden transcripts must also be considered. What impact did creating waste, and thus increasing the cost of production for the capitalists, bring about? It certainly seems to have crafted a more manageable workplace for laborers, but as Nassaney and Abel suggest, this was a cost that capitalists could absorb and may even have preferred, given that contented workers produce better results. Another main finding, derived from interviews with former workers, describes this hegemonic process: "One proud retiree . . . stated that there were no spoiled items at the cutlery because he and his co-workers were skilled craftsmen" (Nassaney and Abel 1993: 265). Given that most factory workers were unskilled, this man's memory likely derives from the lessons he learned by negotiating with his supervisors regarding how the factory community publicly considered the value of his work. This proud assertion that he *did not resist* suggests that this negotiation served capitalists like Russell quite well.

Making the Whole World Homelike: Cooperative Housekeeping and Domestic Reform

In chapter 4, I detailed Diana Wall's research on how early American urban settings became marked by a separation of the home from workspaces, resulting in the creation of highly separate, gendered social spheres. A basic contrast was presented: male spaces of work were defined by the competition, amorality, and individualism of the market; female spaces were domestic, morally rich abodes that offered refuge for all family members from the ill effects of urban life, all under the watchful and caring eye of the household wife and mother. This arrangement is presented by many scholars as the result of male agency combined with female accommodation, such that women gained status and security only in exchange for independence and community. Archaeologist Suzanne Spencer-Wood also describes separate female and male spheres as being private and public realms—the home was considered a private, domestic retreat from the public space of the street, the market, and most of the primary arenas of political power (1996, 1999, 2004). Spencer-Wood highlights how this arrangement undermined women's self-reliance, as the definition of the public sphere did not just separate men and women, but confined women to their homes, where they were isolated from political society except through the voices of fathers and husbands.

American domestic reform movements, which included attempts to develop housekeeping cooperatives led by women, challenged this situation. These efforts publicly exposed the inequality of the sexes and helped to redesign the gendered public-private dichotomy of the American landscape. They simultaneously laid bare the fact that capitalist labor relations served as the model for household relations, a space that was otherwise promoted as a private refuge from the ill effects of urban capitalist culture. Domestic reformers espoused many of the same tenets as the utopian communities discussed below, drawing on a combination of Enlightenment and Christian beliefs that supported a radical social equality and the possibility of effecting change from within. The main goal of domestic reform was not simply the improvement of women, but the transformation of society in favor of the values relegated by capitalism to the women's sphere. To "make the world homelike" was thus to change the focus of production from individual, private gain to a more inclusive form of community growth (Frances Willard, cited in Spencer-Wood 1999: 172).

Common Tea and Secular Community

A clear example of this movement as discovered in the archaeological record comes from Diana Wall's research on the diversity of middle-class women in early New York. As part of a larger study of ceramics recovered from early-nineteenth-century, middle-class homes in the city, Wall identified a distinction between the households of homeowners, who drew from the higher-ranking professions such as medicine and law, and those of suburban tenants, who drew from middle-ranking professions such as clerks and shopkeepers. The principal difference in the archaeological assemblages of these types of households was in the teaware ceramics. Tea service was a public event, with tea being served at home by household-leading women to invited guests in the late afternoon. In contrast, dinner service was intended for the family, and thus treated as a private affair. Wall posits that teawares should indicate the method and meaning of social interaction between households and their neighbors. Teas were also class-based affairs, in that guests tended to represent people of a household's same or higher social standing.

Teawares from higher-ranking, upper-middle-class households indicate a more serious investment in the tea ritual. For example, at the Robson household, a doctor's family on Washington Square South, teawares were found in a variety of types. They included Gothic paneled wares that matched the white granite dinnerwares, as well as higher quality and more costly painted, printed, and molded ceramics and porcelains (see Figure 6.3). The variety of teawares suggests that tea sets may have been regularly replaced through time, indicating an effort by Eliza Robson to stay current with popular fashions. We may also read from this evidence

Figure 6.3. Teacups from Greenwich Village, New York. *Top*: Hand-painted, floral porcelain teacups from 50 Washington Square South, an upper-middle-class doctor's household. *Bottom*: White granite, Gothic paneled teacups recovered from the 25 Barrow Street site, a lower-middle-class rental building (photographs courtesy of Diana diZerega Wall).

that better-off households invested in distinguishing themselves from their neighbors and peers, while simultaneously consolidating their class authority as a group through patterns of conspicuous consumption. This assessment stands in contrast to findings from tenant households only a few blocks away.

Located in the West Village, the households at 25 Barrow Street consisted of several renting families that lived there during the 1860s and 1870s. Census records and city directories indicate that the occupants included lower-middle-class families of small-business owners and clerks (Wall 1991: 72–3). The majority of the Barrow Street teawares consisted of white granite, Gothic, paneled types that matched the household's dinnerwares (see Figure 6.3). This stylistic continuity between tea- and tablewares may suggest not simply thrift, but also that the competitive nature of keeping abreast of current fashion was not highly valued by these households. As Wall states:

> when they entertained their friends at afternoon tea, the meal had a different meaning. Instead of trying to impress and compete with their friends for family status . . . [they] perhaps only invited over those equated with family and community into their homes for any meal at all. The paneled cups and saucers . . . may have served to elicit the almost sacred values of community and mutual help—values that could be very useful from those at the lower end of the middle-class spectrum—among the women who were gathering together for tea. (1991: 79)

The conclusion here is that, through a shared experience, made real and understood by the social ritual of tea and its artifacts, women heads of renting households built an important community support network outside the relations of capitalism.

This network underlies an important critique of the capitalist organization of labor that largely constructed the spaces for building communities in early New York and similar American urban centers. Rather than embracing modes of individual and independent household distinction, lower-middle-class women—who bore relatively more of the struggle to survive the capitalist assault on community solidarity than their wealthier neighbors—found a means not only to bolster their well-being, but to do so through an opening in the system that allowed them to break with their isolation from the centers of production, their husbands, and their neighbors. Being "women at home" did not mean that they were solely dependent on their husbands. Rather, this position inculcated a consciousness that allowed women to create a separate and critical community within and against capitalism. It was a community that rejected not only the second-class status of women, but that of the entire home domain. Changing the value relationship between work and home is the basis of the broader domestic reform movement whose more overt expressions have been tracked by Suzanne Spencer-Wood.

Cooperative Critiques of Capitalism

The domestic reform movement in Europe and the United States emerged in the nineteenth century among many educated middle- and higher-status women. The premise of the movement was simple: first, reformers asserted that the isolation of women in their homes was exploitative because women were held at a lower status than men, who, as the public representatives, were given ultimate authority over their households. Reformers sought to create equity between men and women by asserting that women should control the domestic sphere and expand its influence onto broader society. Reformers argued strategically that women were better suited for this work, by virtue of their natural talents for mothering and housekeeping, which included "conscientiousness, accuracy, efficiency, tact, taste, and prudence" (Spencer-Wood 2004: 143).

Extending from this conception, reformers secondly pushed against societal norms of gendered public-private distinctions. They sought to transform society by blurring household-community distinctions, producing communities not of several households, but of "the community-as-household" (Spencer-Wood 1999: 170). Their goal was to develop new forms of "cooperative housekeeping," in which several families worked together to meet their mutual needs, redefining the meaning of some of American society's core institutions along the way.

This relocation of the family into the public sphere had impacts on many arenas that can produce archaeological evidence. Among the most pronounced was a complication of the early capitalist urban landscape's transition, from one dominated by either public or private spaces, to one with spaces that reflected the blurring of norms advocated by domestic and other reformers. In New York's Five Points section, for example, several very large buildings dedicated to social reform and improvement were built. These institutional homes served the neighborhood by providing temporary housing, meals, and training in employable skills. The Five Points Mission House was a four-story, ten-bay-wide structure on Park Street, and the Five Points House of Industry was a huge, six-story structure on Worth Street (Fitts 2001: 119). These large, multipurpose buildings changed the residential landscape of narrow, two-, three-, and four-story tenements that had marked the neighborhood in earlier periods. Spencer-Wood has recorded similar landscape changes made by domestic reformers in Massachusetts. In Boston, she recorded over one hundred and twenty sites of domestic reform created between 1860 and 1925 (Spencer-Wood 1996, 1999: 181). These included childcare cooperatives, kindergartens, kitchen gardens, playgrounds, and public cooperative kitchens such as the New England Public Kitchen, which opened in Boston in 1890, as well as neighborhood cooperatives that provided multiple services.

Among the latter was the Cambridge Cooperative Housekeeping Society (CCHS), initiated by Melusina Fay Pierce in 1869 (Spencer-Wood 2004). Pierce drew from her own published critical theorizing, in which she explained that women's loss of status was due to their association with unpaid domestic labor, which left them dependent on the income of men to survive. The purpose of the CCHS was to reinstate female authority in the public sphere by demanding that domestic work be paid a decent wage. Pierce's strategy was to establish a local multifamily cooperative for laundry and food. Families paid to be members of the CCHS, and in return they had their laundry done and, in the original plan, benefitted financially from the CCHS's ability to buy in bulk. Also embedded in the CCHS was a process for building cross-class female alliances between the middle-class managers of the cooperative and the laborers who worked there for wages. With the support of multiple families, the workplace was nicer and the wages higher than most other options presented to working-class women.

Domestic reformers also proposed changes to the way private spaces in the household should be arranged. Some of these changes have since been widely adopted and are now normal parts of modern American households. Among the most important was the "raising of the kitchen" from the basement to the main floor of the house (Spencer-Wood 1999: 182). The model Spencer-Wood highlights comes from Beecher and Stowe's *The American Woman's Home*, published in 1869. Beecher and Stowe illustrate a raised kitchen with a highly rational organization of space and material to allow orderly work to be displayed from a kitchen positioned at the center of the household (see Figures 6.4). A more radical proposal from domestic reformers, aiming in the other direction, was the construction of houses *without* kitchens at all. These homes used a communal kitchen shared by several families. Such structures are recorded to have been built in Yelping Hill, Connecticut, and planned bungalow communities with a central kitchen, sewing room, laundry room, and communal play area were designed in California. It is notable that while these California bungalow communities were never built, a mirror of them, with communal eating and bathing facilities, was constructed at California's many early-twentieth-century work camps briefly described in chapter 5.

While certain domestic reform efforts took root, like the raised, central kitchens, many other aspects failed to be developed or sustained. One of these was the CCHS itself, which folded after just two years in 1871. The documentary record of the CCHS is detailed enough so that we can know the problem was, in Pierce's words, "husband-power" (Spencer-Wood 2004: 148). Speaking about the abolitionist husband of one member, Pierce reported:

> "What!" exclaimed this apostle of freedom for negroes, "my wife 'cooperate' to make other men comfortable? No indeed!"—Now was that not the crack of the slave-driver's whip, though, the master this time is not a Southern planter, nor the slave a colored brother? (In Spencer-Wood 2004: 149)

Clearly, the efforts of domestic reformers were seen by some as an attack on American principles so close to the core of society that their success would undermine it, or at least its ability to serve those middle-class and elite men who most benefitted from it. Even in Cambridge, where CCHS members came from liberal, academic, and professional families, men were unwilling to let their households suffer any change, even with evidence of the likely long-term benefits. Such changes, we may surmise, threatened the security of the household as it was envisioned by men who were now long accustomed to seeing their market competitors eagerly await any misstep in order that they might gain advantage. Ultimately, Pierce was forced to conclude that women in the CCHS were "not free agents" (in Spencer-Wood 2004: 151), and, lacking independence, that cooperative housekeeping would never succeed.

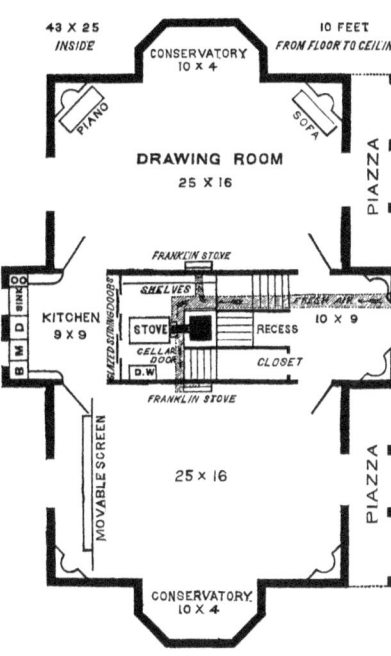

Figure 6.4. Elevation and plan of a "Christian House" and a design for "a rational kitchen," from Beecher and Stowe's *The American Woman's Home*, 1869 (images courtesy of the Harriet Beecher Stowe Center, Hartford, Connecticut).

One aspect of the domestic reform movement that did find footing emerged from a cult of "home religion." Taking the separation of home from work to an extreme, some reformers promoted the sacredness of the feminine home as a force to run counter to the amorality of masculine public space. Beecher and Stowe designed a "Christian" cruciform house plan (see Figure 6.4), as well as a Christian cooperative neighborhood. "Christianity" also found expression in a variety of Gothic forms, such as the white-paneled ceramics discussed in chapter 4, as well as architectural elements such as archways, windows, niches, and rooflines in Gothic-inspired domestic structures (Spencer-Wood 1996: 418–9). This symbolism built an association between domesticity, sacredness, purity, and nature. Smaller-scale evidence of this religiosity has been found in a large number of sites in the form of flowerpots and floral-decorated ceramics that literally brought the beauty of nature into the home and placed it under the authority of the wife and mother.

This sacred basis of the feminine identity stands in contrast to other domestic reformers' demands for an essentially secular and public recognition of institutional sexism. However, it is probably true that many reformers felt the same frustrations as Pierce as they confronted a lack of material support for social change from their husbands and fathers. The embrace of home religion was one that cost much less than wholesale social change, yet it was still an effort that promoted and distinguished women on their own terms. Substantial limitations nevertheless remained. Specifically, the embrace of Christianity failed to sustain the alternative consciousness outside of reformers themselves. While Christianity offered a space for social criticism, in that reformers appealed to specific Christian teachings that called for cooperative work and communal sharing of resources, the mainstream Protestant foundations of the reformers' Christianity could neither sustain nor promote significant social change. At the root of this problem was a continuation of the separation of work from domestic life, which formed the base of a successful capitalist culture in the United States. Turning next to examine the evidence of a critical consciousness in the emergence of Shaker religion and culture, I will illustrate how the archaeology of ideology and religion demonstrates the material basis of the successful formation of communities outside of capitalism, where such distinctions between work, home, and belief were resisted and re-signified.

The Living Building: American Communal Utopias

Almost immediately after independence from Britain, several small groups took to the American countryside in an attempt to create from the supposedly raw materials of the virgin wilderness what they believed to be its highest potential: model communal utopias. Closed to nonmembers, American utopian communities strove to realize the ideals of freedom, democracy, and an equitable community. Many utopias were in fact created after a serious financial panic in 1837, and thus may be seen as direct social critiques of capitalism. While the overall population of the utopias was never more than a tiny percentage of the nation, their existence was widely known and is essential to understanding broader trends in nineteenth-century American culture. Utopias also provide a perspective on how the effects of capitalism were negotiated and potentially controlled when isolated from other community-building forces. The root of this negotiation may be seen in the emphasis on the communitarian basis of reform, which had a clearly emancipatory agenda. Utopias were to be "new beginnings." They claimed to embody the very ideals that modern people had envisioned in biblical millenarianism and the human-centered philosophy of the Enlightenment. Perfection, they thought, could indeed be realized in a way that was fair for entire communities, who, if they separated themselves from the masses, could construct heavens on earth (Holloway 1966, French and French 1975, Hayden 1976).

The history of utopias in the United States, however, consists mostly of failures. Proposals and designs by reformers such as Robert Owen and Charles Fourier promised opportunities for cooperative communities during the first half of the nineteenth century. The Owenite plan for a commonly owned community at New Harmony, Indiana, was implemented starting in 1825. Over one thousand people responded to his invitation to create a self-sufficient community of craftsmen and farmers. Only two years later, after craft shops failed to be built or an adequate food supply generated, Owen sold off the New Harmony property in individual parcels. The experiment was deemed a failure. Fourier believed that model communities should be built through the support of shareholders, who may or may not be residents. Larger shareholders would be exempt from work, while smaller shareholders worked to support them, and profits would be divided among shareholders by their level of investment.

Founded in 1843 near Red Bank, New Jersey, the North American Phalanx was the first and most successful Fourierist community. It focused on the production of agricultural crops for sale in the market. However, after ten years, the spirit of the community began to wane, and after their mill and shops burned in 1854, they reportedly "had no will to continue" (Holloway 1966: 151). The failure of those who followed Fourier was in part a result of their loss of initial enthusiasm and attention. Esteemed visitors like Ralph Waldo Emerson and Henry Thoreau stopped coming after the first years, and new members created divisiveness. However, it is generally accepted now that the fact that none of the community members "seemed prepared to tolerate a check to his will or abide by group decision" ultimately quelled the general interest in a long-term commitment to this utopia (McWilliams 1973: 241, in French and French 1975: 70).

Shaker Communal Villages

Given this history of failed utopias, the success of Shaker communities at not only creating lasting ones, but also at replicating them in many different locations, is astounding and worth considering in some detail. Fortunately, David Starbuck (2004), has undertaken more than two decades of archaeological research at Canterbury Shaker Village in New Hampshire, a study that provides necessary information for reflecting on Shaker community success and materiality within the context of capitalism.

Shakers in the United States were originally led by "mother" Ann Lee, who converted while in England after losing four children at or before birth and declaring that "sexual intercourse was the cause of all the world's evil" (Hayden 1976: 65). She came to the United States to build a Shaker utopia. Founded on the principles of chastity, community access to goods, confession of sins, and separation from the world, twenty-five Shaker communities were established in the Northeast and Midwest United States between 1780 and 1826 (Hayden 1976: 65). Shakers were a millenarian sect, believing that the Second Coming of Jesus Christ was not a future event, but was ongoing and embodied by their communities. This self-promoting understanding offered a powerful basis to Shaker existence that may be discovered in virtually all of Shaker life, including their utopian architecture, landscape, craftwork, and other material culture. Their commitment to a distinct religious understanding as well as the orderly communal life that their understanding required are important reasons why the Shakers were the most successful of the American utopian groups.

Architectural historian Delores Hayden describes a unity in form to Shaker landscapes and buildings that bounds community and belief: "The physical process of designing new settlements—the communitarian goal—was fully integrated with Shaker religion. Members found environmental design the only activity broad enough in scope to accommodate their aspiration to turn the earth into heaven" (Hayden 1976: 66). This awareness of the significance of human constructions and material activities, set within a powerful ideological context, presents a radical departure from material meanings generated within capitalism. Instead of objects as sources for the separation of persons from one another, Shaker things, being communally produced and consumed, bound Shaker communities together—in spite of the fact that these objects and productive processes in part served to separate the Shakers from the "world's people." Archaeological evidence describes this separate productive life as essential to Shaker economic well-being, in addition to serving as a basis of their social and ideological identity.

Perhaps the most basic evidence of Shaker community-building efforts was the communal residence. At Hancock, Massachusetts, the Church Family dwelling was designed to house one hundred members, who were divided by sex into different sleeping areas. Common dining and meeting rooms served all members (Hayden 1976: 81). Similar structures were built at most Shaker villages, including one for the Church Family at Canterbury, New Hampshire (Starbuck 2004: 17). At both the Hancock and Canterbury villages, the communal dwellings were large, three-and-a-half-story structures that clearly varied from the smaller, single-family homes that dominated the American landscape at the time. Similar distinctions in architecture are found throughout Shaker villages, which were populated by large three- and four-story structures that served as offices, meeting houses, barns, shops, laundries, and infirmaries for entire settlements (see Figure 6.5).

Archaeology at Canterbury Village also discovered the detail and determination involved in Shaker planning in the form of an extensive waterworks that supported eight interconnected millponds that in turn powered over a dozen mills for various industrial activities (Starbuck 2004: 24–5). Many of these, especially the wood mills, supplied both Shaker

Figure 6.5. An 1857 woodcut from *Harper's* depicting the landscape at Canterbury Village, New Hampshire, and showing the multistory residential structures (after Starbuck 2004: 16).

needs and commercial enterprises that profited from the sale of products to outside neighbors. The amazing feature of this Canterbury system was that it was created without any preexisting bodies of water, and therefore involved extensive ditching, damming, and, most of all, planning. Running from north to south, the flow of water over a 2,800-meter length gradually declined over fifty meters in elevation (see Figure 6.6). This waterworks afforded the community a steady and powerful energy source that provided them materials for their own use and for sale to their neighbors. Also, the system certainly required constant upkeep in order to preserve the races, dams, and silt levels in the ponds. Given that this work was undertaken communally, the water system was likely a principal focus of the group's consciousness regarding the continuing viability of their settlement.

Shaker distinctions from the mainstream may also be found in the smaller scale of personal space, an arena where the "commitment mechanisms" devised by Shakers are especially pronounced (Hayden 1976: 68). Hayden describes an enforcement of orthogonal rules aimed at minimizing unnecessary labor, such as the provision of food for every two to four

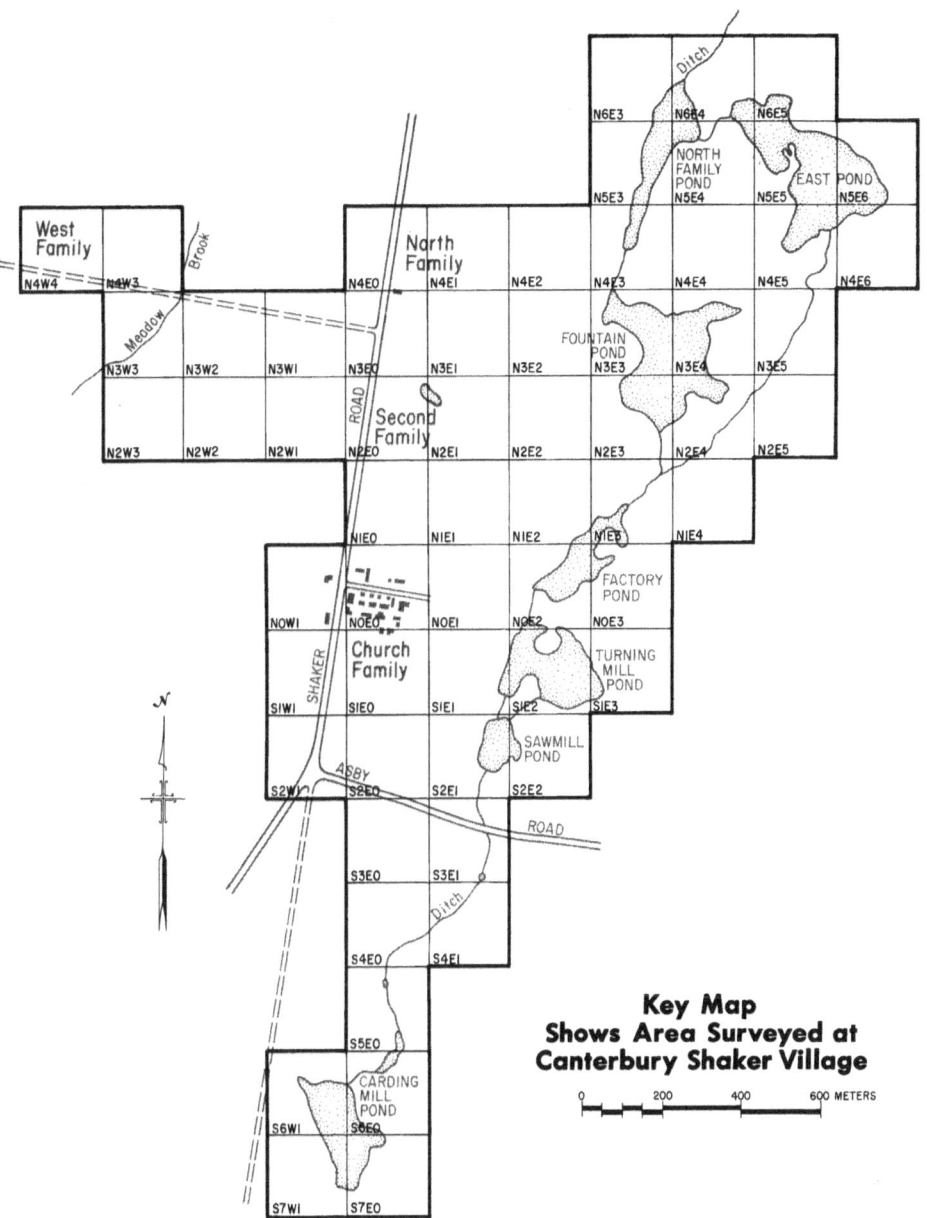

Figure 6.6. Archaeological survey map of Canterbury Shaker Village showing the extensive pond and channel system for powering mills (plan by David Starbuck).

persons to discourage diagonal reaching or the cutting of bread and meat into squares. Paths through the villages were kept at right angles to eliminate diagonal wandering. Such strict spatial flow was accentuated by the separation of men and women into segregated dwelling rooms, spaces within the meeting halls, and work activities. Segregation of individuals was also prized, as evidenced by their individually tailored clothing and shoes, and by the common use of individual, straight-back chairs that hung from individual pegs on the house walls. In short, these objects reveal an embrace of individualism, but without the concomitant emphasis on competition, "a synthesis quite at odds with modern bureaucratic control and anonymity" (Hayden 1976: 71).

Shaker utopias diverged from the world's people in ways that would have been familiar and rewarding to nineteenth-century Americans seeking alternatives to the culture of capitalism. However, minimizing competition required additional measures that outlined the substantial commitments demanded by adherence to Shaker ideology. According to Hayden, Shaker villages paired earthly space with heavenly space to produce a closed system where "all physical resources were a sacred trust, part of a total physical system for redemption" (Hayden 1976: 76). This meant that the unity between building and landscape revealed the unity between humanity and God and between body and spirit: a unity found in their sense of themselves as a "living building" and expressed in the open embrace of the imaginary during Shaker rituals.

The source of the sect's name, Shaker rituals often involved ecstatic, body-shaking expressions of religiosity. They also involved dances that allowed men and women to engage one another in formal interactions that broke from their otherwise strict sexual segregation. Rituals involved pantomime, the donning of imaginary clothes, and the presence of imaginary visitors such as Indians, devils, and even George Washington (Hayden 1976: 71). This mass, communal imagination also speaks to a powerful rejection of capitalist empirical rationality, which prized rational individualism over an embrace of the irrational made possible only by a shared sense and experience of the imaginary. Playing with the material and immaterial further merged the earthly and the divine in Shaker experience: "the Hancock people, dressed in imaginary golden robes, approached a fenced enclosure containing an imaginary fountain, bathed in imaginary tubs, and partook of an imaginary feast of exotic fruits gathered from imaginary gardens and orchards" (from an 1848 observation cited in Hayden 1976: 100). Perhaps this may now appear quaint, if not deranged, yet such open displays of belief and fantasy—oftentimes in the presence of nonmembers—established for Shakers a sense of belonging formed through relationships they built with one another and their common millenarian faith.

Shaker Archaeology

David Starbuck's long-term archaeological investigation at Canterbury Village in New Hampshire sheds additional light on Shaker life. This research illuminates some of what lies behind the formal public façade produced by both the Shakers themselves and most of those who have written about them. Embedded in this literature is a bias against the Shakers, a characterization of them as a people without history. Their ways of life are idealized as based in an unyielding commitment to isolation, high-standing morals, and obedience to Shaker law and practices. This literature, as Starbuck suggests (2004: 9), has served the "Shaker myth" well, assisting those who benefit from it due to their connections to the Shaker tourist trade or because they seek to identify alternatives to the culture of capitalism (also see Van Bueren 2006).

Archaeology at Canterbury has discovered this missing history, and it allows us to contextualize the Shakers and, therefore, to better understand their way of life *within* the context of capitalism. Two main findings from Starbuck's work stand out. For one, Shaker isolation and self-sufficiency cannot be supported. Second, material aspects of everyday life in Canterbury Village do little to support the notion of strict obedience to Shaker laws.

Documentary evidence shows that the Shaker community at Canterbury was integrated to a certain degree with its surrounding neighbors. Shaker shops, mills, and craftsmen provided high-quality goods and services that their neighbors prized. This work certainly boosted the Shakers' income and helped validate their individual commitments as they learned that their products were considered to be of such high quality. Excavations at one production site, the Second Family blacksmith shop, turned up an unexpected finding. Rather than simply directing a site for providing the community and its neighbors with valued products and services, the master at this shop was involved in the market for clay tobacco pipes. From the northeast corner of the structure, archaeologists recovered over three thousand waster fragments from over four hundred redware clay

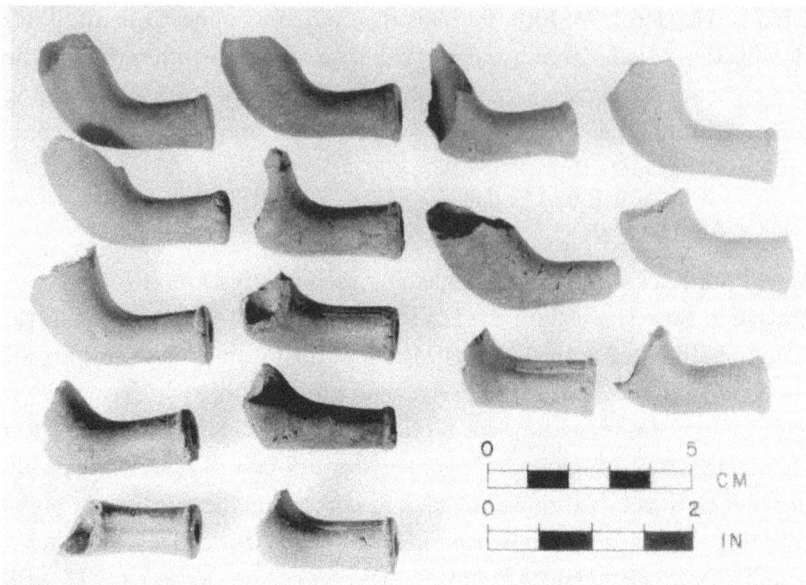

Figure 6.7. Fragments of redware tobacco pipes from the Second Family blacksmith shop, Canterbury Shaker Village (photograph by David Starbuck).

pipes (Starbuck 2004: 72–3) (see Figure 6.7). Shaker law forbade smoking after 1845, so this find likely predates the mandate, but the quantity of pipes demonstrates Shaker involvement in the open market for profitable goods. This finding is replicated by discoveries at several other Shaker sites, such as that at Pleasant Hill, Kentucky, where Shaker pipes were stamped with the village's name as a form of advertising (McBride 2005). These findings suggest a new idea about the Shakers: that their long-term success may be a result not only of their isolation and commitment, but also of the way in which their separation and communal living afforded them a strategic advantage in negotiating the free market. Having tight control over the means of production, especially the management of the community's labor, Shaker villages housed productive industrial enterprises that competed with those of the world's people quite successfully. A likely conclusion is that, as compared to the Owenites and other utopian failures, the Shakers were able to employ a communal ideology, often called the "we-spirit," in support of the demands for maintaining their separation *through* an engagement with the market, rather than solely as a justification for their isolation from it.

Archaeology at Canterbury Village supports this connection in another way. Excavations from a handful of large trash dumps revealed that Shakers were avid consumers, and, notably, that they purchased the same sorts of material items that would be expected in any late-nineteenth-century, rural, American homestead. This list includes common but unexpected luxury and adornment items that stand in contrast to the popular image of Shakers as austere. Starbuck concludes that the evidence suggests Canterbury Shakers "evolved into middle-class consumers" (2004: 64).

Thousands of artifacts from a large artifact dump, called Hog Heaven because of its original association with a hog house, tell this story (the following draws from Starbuck 2004: 56–64). As eating pork was also banned by Shakers in 1845, this dump is presumed to postdate this period and to have been used into the beginning of the twentieth century. The artifacts recovered included ceramic dishes, bottles, and jars, glass bottles, toothbrushes, shoes, marbles, household fixtures, and dozens of personal items. Among the latter were shoe blacking, a Mrs. Allen's Hair Restorer bottle, combs, perfume bottles, an intertwined-hearts pin, thimbles, cufflinks, a sterling silver spoon, and a set of miniature, decorative, brass scallop shells. Unlike the popular Gothic ceramics that were favored by middle-class families on the Eastern Seaboard, Shaker ceramics were highly decorated, transfer-printed whiteware and gilt-edged Meaken ironstone, a type available in the Sears Roebuck catalog. There were also a number of wine bottles and a wide array of patent medicines, which were often consumed for the alcohol they contained.

On the whole, these findings show that the Shakers were regularly involved with the consumer market of the world's people. They likely purchased goods wholesale and perhaps also retail, and maybe even hid some personal adornments under exterior clothing to create an individual identity underneath their outward uniformity. Nevertheless, the pattern here speaks to another form of accommodation that may have been important in supporting the long-term survival of Shaker communities. Starbuck's analysis suggests that these findings relate to later years at Canterbury, a period in Shaker history when "the somber image of the early years was gradually replaced by a less rigid lifestyle" (2004: 85). Being able to change, while maintaining their core beliefs and outward practices, certainly helped Shaker communities endure and recruit new members.

Starbuck's conclusion explains the following: instead of adhering to fixed rules unyieldingly—the sense we get from reading Shaker laws as well as from the non-Shakers who desire the Shaker myth to be true—the Shakers, as these dumps establish, engaged in a different history uncovered by archaeology. Drinking alcohol, wearing perfume and jewelry, and cherishing luxury goods are not signs of "Shakers behaving badly" (Powell 2000), but of the way the people who adopted Shaker life maintained the viability of their community given the conditions in which they lived. As Starbuck says, "Archaeology . . . is helping to give the Shakers back their humanity, as opposed to the overly sanitized portrait imposed upon them" (2004: 86). All Shakers have a history, and it is one that is less distinct from the world's people than most think. However, given our interest here in understanding capitalism, Shaker history is also an example of how a communal ideology successfully promoted a community for the sake of production within the market. The question left to consider is whether there is evidence that shows how people may have developed communities in America that stood against the market as the basis for developing individual and group identities. To examine this possibility I turn to the archaeology of African America in the next chapter, examining a community-building process that stands out among those who resisted the effects of commodification within capitalism. Rather than negotiating from a position within the social discourse of capitalism, as in the examples above, it can be argued that the making of African America illustrates a resistance to exploitation by persons distinctly removed from mainstream social life by virtue of typical capitalist constructions of race, labor, and citizenship.

7

The Archaeology of Race and African American Resistance

> This past, this endless struggle to achieve and reveal and confirm human identity, human authority, yet contains, for all its horror, something very beautiful.
>
> James Baldwin, *The Fire Next Time*

Perhaps the most powerful examples of exclusion in American history are the multitude of ways that the dominant society has defined membership by race (DuBois 1994, Orser 2007). Despite the historic variability of the category (for example, see Roediger 1991, 2005, Ignatiev 1995, Jacobsen 1998, 2006, Guglielmo 2003), racially defined nonwhites have been consistently shifted to the margins of American society, no matter their origin. Native Americans, African Americans, Hispanic Americans, Asian Americans, and the wide array of "provisional" or "probationary" whites (Jacobsen 1998), such as Irish, Eastern European, and Southern European Americans, have faced similar, unjust challenges in their attempts to participate in civic society and obtain its promised material well-being and opportunity (Orser 2007, Voss 2008). However, because of a history of race-based slavery, the case of African Americans stands out. Without diminishing past and ongoing struggles of other minorities in the United States, the qualities of slavery demand that African American history and archaeology be considered a distinct topic in a book on capitalism. The basis of this distinction is the fact that in the modern enslavement of people of African descent, the exploitation and commoditization that defines capitalist labor relations was taken to an extreme. Modern enslavement was not the result of retribution or capture (Patterson 1982, Davis 1966, 2006), but was instead a radical debasement by which the humanity of the enslaved person was disregarded in assessing their capacity to labor and the manner in which their work could be translated into the production of value for its true owner—the master—in the market. The root of this system was racism, or the belief that because of inherent and inheritable attributes, some persons are naturally superior to others. Racism has enabled segregation, violence, and a willful disregard for many segments of the American population—especially African Americans—since its founding. In modern slavery, the principal variant of this belief established that people of African descent were savage, heathen, and incapable of surviving in, let alone producing, civilization. They were therefore best served by a system that restricted their freedom and put them in the service of civilized whites.

While this racist ideology is seriously flawed and has been challenged since its inception, antiblack racism still has firm roots in contemporary society (Jordan 1968, Fields 1990, Frederickson 1987, Holt 2000, Ford 2008, Wise 2008). It has been the goal of many archaeologists studying the African diaspora in the United States to develop a counter-hegemonic account that challenges and disarms racist assumptions about the history and culture of people of African descent (Singleton 1995, LaRoche and Blakey 1997, Wilkie 2000, Franklin 2001, Franklin and McKee 2004, Mack and Blakey 2004, Orser 2007, Mullins 2008). This work has recorded a wide array of practices that captive Africans and their descendents developed to assert their humanity and resist both enslavement and the sustained inequalities that came with emancipation. My goal here is to contextualize some of these findings within the capitalist constructions of labor and personhood. I show how African diaspora archaeology presents evidence critiquing both white supremacy and, especially, the capitalist system that provided theoretical and practical knowledge for establishing racism as a matter of fact in modern life.

I primarily consider evidence of race as an ideological hegemony, drawing from Barnett and Silverman (1979), who show that dominant cultures order social life by explaining how and why experience may be separated into distinct phenomenal categories.[1] Racism stands out among such categories for its especially cogent assertion that persons may be ordered by unalterable, inherited biological characteristics that establish America's social statuses. Accordingly, critical scholarship seeks to identify how the categories of race and racism organize social action by producing and

---

1   The following discussion is adapted from Matthews, Leone, and Jordan 2002

reproducing the dominant cultural hegemony (Gramsci 1971, Roseberry 1989, Fields 1990). In this sense, domination is not only informed by and responsive to cultural categorizations of an elite, it is also an inherent aspect of most tools to which the nonelite have access. The result, therefore, is often that resistance produces only a very limited effect, and often no substantial structural change. In contrast, successful strategies of resistance are those that acknowledge the dominant order, but are informed by and respond to a critical, alternative, cultural sensibility. Successful resistance is based on understanding the deeply situated powers that organize and categorize social life and the production of meaning, then seizing opportunities to craft alternatives that emerge through ruptures or interstices of the dominant system.

Notably, archaeology is one of the best methods available for recovering these strategies. For one, material culture, unlike dominant linguistic and related discursive modes, has the unique ability to contain and sustain necessary ambiguities (Gundaker 1998, Howson 1990, Mullins 1999, Voss 2008). Things, that is, can take on a variety of meanings, sometimes meanings that are themselves contradictory except in that they reflect applications to objects made by groups from different, if not opposing, sectors of society (Leone 2005). Howson (1990), as well as Perry and Paynter (1999), emphasize the multivalence of material culture, meaning that the same object may hold very different meanings in, for example, European or captive African hands. Second, archaeology has the opportunity to look at and contextualize expressions of resistance found at the level of assemblages. Successful resistance is not to be found in the simple objects that people make and use. Rather, it is found in the way objects are ordered and related, reflecting the adherence by oppressed people to a system altogether different from, if not also critical of, the dominant majority. African diaspora archaeology is flush with evidence that captive Africans and African Americans developed and embraced such alternatives. I discuss a few examples in the following.

The Complexities of Colonoware

Discovered and identified as early as the 1930s, the remains of low-fired, handmade pots crafted from local clays are a common find at American archaeological sites, especially plantation slave quarter sites associated with captive Africans who lived in the Chesapeake and Southern colonies. While these pots were originally thought to be made by Native Americans who produced them for trade, Leland Ferguson argues that the vessels were produced and used by captive Africans themselves (1980, 1992, 1999). Ferguson proposed renaming these vessels from colono-Indian ware (Noel-Hume 1962), to simply colonoware, so that pots made by both African and Native American hands could be considered a product of these groups' engagement with colonization. Since Ferguson's identification of the African American origins of many of these pots, a trait that he rightly argues should have been obvious all along, archaeologists have turned up tens of thousands of colonoware sherds from plantation sites dating to the seventeenth and eighteenth centuries. Patterns in these findings show that vessels produced by captive Africans describe a powerful history of making a life and community under the conditions of forced migration, enslavement, and racial violence. This is especially evident when colonoware vessels are contextualized in the race-making dynamics of colonial America.

James Deetz shows that the archaeological record of late-seventeenth-century Virginia plantations is marked by an increase in locally made colonoware vessels and a reduction in the average number of rooms per house (1994). The smaller houses are said to reflect a resolution of social tensions between masters and their white indentured servants, achieved through the construction of separate houses for them, which reduced overall house size (also see Epperson 1999, 2001). However, this argument overlooks another important component of late-seventeenth-century colonial society in the Chesapeake. Outlined by Morgan (1975) and Jordan (1979), the period after 1660 saw the rise to prominence of the first generation of native-born, property owning white men. Rather than accumulating capital through servitude, as did many of their fathers, these men inherited it. So, even as the demands of white indentured labor challenged the consolidation of an elite hegemony, a new generation of masters were in a position to subvert the challenge through the replacement of white labor with more expensive enslaved Africans. This pattern was widely accepted, resulting in a rapid growth in the population of people of African descent in the Chesapeake between 1680 and 1720 (Kulikoff 1986). This strategy not only resolved a crisis in labor, but also redefined the social order by creating a foundational distinction defined simultaneously by race *and* class. The greater number of colonoware vessels during this period is therefore evidence of such a transformation, since within the new slave-based system of production, colonoware vessels identify the emergence of a racially framed social distinction that segregated blacks and whites both

Figure 7.1. Vessel on right is a Virginia-made colonoware copy in the style of the delft English-made vessel on the left (courtesy of the Colonial Williamsburg Foundation, image # 1959-DW-0703-8).

physically and—as the labor force was enslaved and marked by race—categorically as well (Epperson 1990, 1999, 2001).

The racist culture that subsequently emerged illustrates a reconsolidation of the dominant cultural order in response to a rupture in the system brought about by a tremor of unrest in the labor force. Nevertheless, this was only the first of a series of ruptures relevant to the emergence of African America. A subsequent development may be identified in the vessel forms of Virginia's colonoware pots. Africans in Virginia were subjected to white domination longer and under different conditions than in other Southern colonies, and Virginia's colonoware vessels were often made in forms resembling those from Europe (see Figure 7.1). The presence or absence of these "copy" vessels is usually attributed to the level of interaction among whites, blacks, and Native Americans (for example, see Ferguson 1992, Deetz 1994, Mouer et al. 1999). The story goes that the greater the number of "copy" vessels, the more intensive and long-term the "contact" between people of different racial and ethnic backgrounds was. This thinking, however, reduces the dynamic complexities of colonialism to a problematic factor of the relative acquaintance of consumers with producer populations. The production of colonoware vessels may in fact have been part of a contentious and ongoing cultural process of domination and resistance. Rather than simply reproducing familiar forms, Africans in Virginia were likely attempting to assert a position *within* mainstream society and to challenge the racial foundations of slavery that produced their supposed exclusion. It was certainly clear to enslaved Africans that Europeans were a different sort of people, based both on their constructed superior status and their different cultural habits. For captive Africans to try to be more like their masters—an assertion powerfully embodied by the production and use of similar vessel styles, styles that were indeed different from those that African-born persons would have known—may have been a way to acquire some of the substance and practice of what Europeans were and thereby close the gap that both differentiated and subordinated Africans in colonial American society. From the dominant perspective, however, this practice identified yet another rupture within the system and produced new reactions that further removed blacks from the white-dominated society, such as the invention of the segregated slave quarter and other institutional racist practices that further alienated captive people from the products of their labor and the society in which they lived.

Autonomy Through Critique: A Culture of Resistance in African American Religion

A dominant thread in African diaspora archaeology asserts that the archaeological record is valuable for the unique information it provides about the persistence, resilience, and syncretic survival of African cultural practices in the African American diaspora. The implication is that by maintaining African culture and belief, captive people and their descendents established an autonomous position that supported their communities and secured their identities despite the dehumanization, oppression, and violence of enslavement and racism. Autonomy may in fact have been the ultimate goal for Maroons and other American self-emancipated and free black communities (see Deetz 1996, Leone et al. 2005, LaRoche 2004, Geismar 1982, Weik 2004, 2007), but the survival of African beliefs is not sufficient evidence to establish that autonomy was either realized or even a desired end for the many held captive or confined to living in similarly white-dominated contexts like towns and cities. In fact, it is far more reasonable in these integrated settings that cultural critique, or the active negotiation and rejection of racist oppression, would have been a more successful resistance strategy. Considering material evidence of African American religious expressions in these settings, I believe archaeologists have defined many activities, artifacts, and features of African American historical material culture that assert a powerful critique of the underlying principles of the dominant order, an order that relied on capitalist theorizations of materiality, labor, and personhood to establish white supremacy in the face of a diverse social world.

The first part of this argument draws from compelling studies that establish that black and white colonial communities overlapped and interacted more than they diverged (for example, see Sobel 1987). In material culture studies, this understanding is pronounced by Dell Upton (1988, 1990), who shows that early Virginia landscapes bear the marks of and intersections between both white and black community structures. Upton opposes these landscapes as articulated and informal constructions of space. The white gentry, backed by the resources and authority of the colonial state, created a far-reaching landscape in which their "houses, churches, courthouses, and other public structures, as well as the roads and ways which linked them, were conceived as an articulated spatial network" (Upton, 1990: 72). It seemed as if, over the whole of space, whites established a consistent order that marked their dominion. Nevertheless, within this network, certain spaces were occupied and controlled by enslaved Africans, and accordingly reflected their agency. Near to and inside their houses, around plantation service buildings, and in the fields, woods, and waterways, numerous spaces were under African control. Whites rarely ventured into these spaces, other than to visit the quarters and barns in order to reassert their authority through expressions of oppression and violence, including whippings and rape. Especially in the interstitial spaces between plantations, captive people found the resources to undermine the control of the articulated white landscape. Albert Raboteau records, for example, that African Americans often had "a private praying ground, located in thickets, woods, bushes, or at a particular tree" where they could go to engage the spirits (Raboteau 1995: 154, also see Gundaker 1998, Edwards 1998). Exploring the material remains of activities that occurred in these African spaces allows us to understand how the enslaved constructed a sense of belonging in their own communities, and especially the ways in which these communities developed around conceptualizations that criticized the racist foundations of the larger plantation dominion.

The current archaeological depiction of African American religious expression has cited artifacts representative of a presumably African-derived spiritualism, in which forces assumed to be static by the dominant white ideology were instead taken to be quite active. Here I refer to

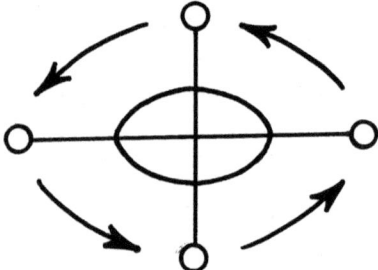

Figure 7.2. Incised colonoware bowl alongside a stylized image of the Bakongo cosmogram. The marked vessel is a representation of the cosmogram used in an African-derived boundary-crossing ritual (photograph by Leland Ferguson; drawing by Ross Rava after Thompson 1983: 109).

interpretations of 'X' marks on colonoware vessels and architecture, root cellars/subfloor pits, beads, crystals, coins, nails, animal bones, crab claws, turtle shells, mirrors, marine shells (especially cowries), rings, gaming pieces, charms (such as *figas*), as well as carefully selected and reworked glass, stone, and ceramic sherds (for example, see Blakey and Rankin-Hill 2004, Brown and Cooper 1990, Brown 1994, 2001, Chan 2007, Coplin and Matthews 2007, Emerson 1999, Fenell 2007, Ferguson 1992, 1999, Jones 2000, Leone 2005, Leone and Fry 1999, Leone et al. 2005, Logan et al. 1992, McKee 1992, Orser 1994, 1998, Perry et al. 2006, Russell 1997, Samford 2007, Singleton 1995, Stine et al. 1996, Wilkie 1995, 1997, 2000, Woodruff et al. 2007, Yentsch 1992, Young 1997).

Taken as a whole, these many examples comment on a general process of transcending boundaries in both material and ideological senses (Franklin and McKee 2004). For example, Ferguson suggests that incised

'X' marks on colonoware vessels reproduce a Bakongo cosmogram (1992, 1999) (see Figure 7.2). Many of the marked vessels were found by divers in rivers adjacent to large plantations, suggesting that their use involved ritually pushing these vessels across the boundary between land and water, which in Bakongo belief is interpreted as moving from the material world of the living to the spiritual world of the ancestors. Stine et al. similarly show that blue beads are commonly associated with African American sites (1996). They suggest that the color blue, which represented the sky and thus heaven, was used by African Americans in different media, such as house paint and decorative beads, to ward off ghosts and malevolent spirits. Yet another example comes from caches of materials unearthed in spaces formerly occupied by captive African people, which often included crystals and other reflective stones, glass, and ceramics, pierced coins, discs, and buttons, bent pins and nails, beads, doll parts, and other materials (see Figure 7.3) (see discussions in Brown 2001, Leone 2005). These caches are interpreted as spirit bundles, or *minkisi*, that were placed in the ground or in enclosed spaces, especially near such spiritually charged liminal areas as hearths, doors, stairs, pipes, and northeast corners. *Minkisi* were placed to protect the living from powerful spirits that may have been directed by others to cause harm. Mark Leone argues that *minkisi* were also used "to keep dangerous, burdensome, people away and in their place. It was not passive; it was aggressively about wishes to kill, drive crazy, and cause sickness and harm" (2005: 231). He concludes that *minkisi* were a form of symbolic violence reflecting an effort by captive people to control the actions of their masters, if not do them outright harm.

Piercing boundaries was thought to allow communication between separate worlds and extended the control of living people into the spirit realm of the ancestors. The most common interpretation of these efforts argues that these are examples of the unique development of African American culture during slavery as a creolized, African-derived society (Mintz and Price 1992, Gundaker 1998). Seeking to regain the control over their lives denied them by slavery, so such an argument goes, captive people embraced their heritage of African spirituality. To date, however, there has been too little emphasis on the American context, for most scholars have described these practices as continuations and permutations of African traditions (Holloway 1990). Reconnecting these practices to the African American destabilization of institutional racism is vital.

186 · The Archaeology of American Capitalism

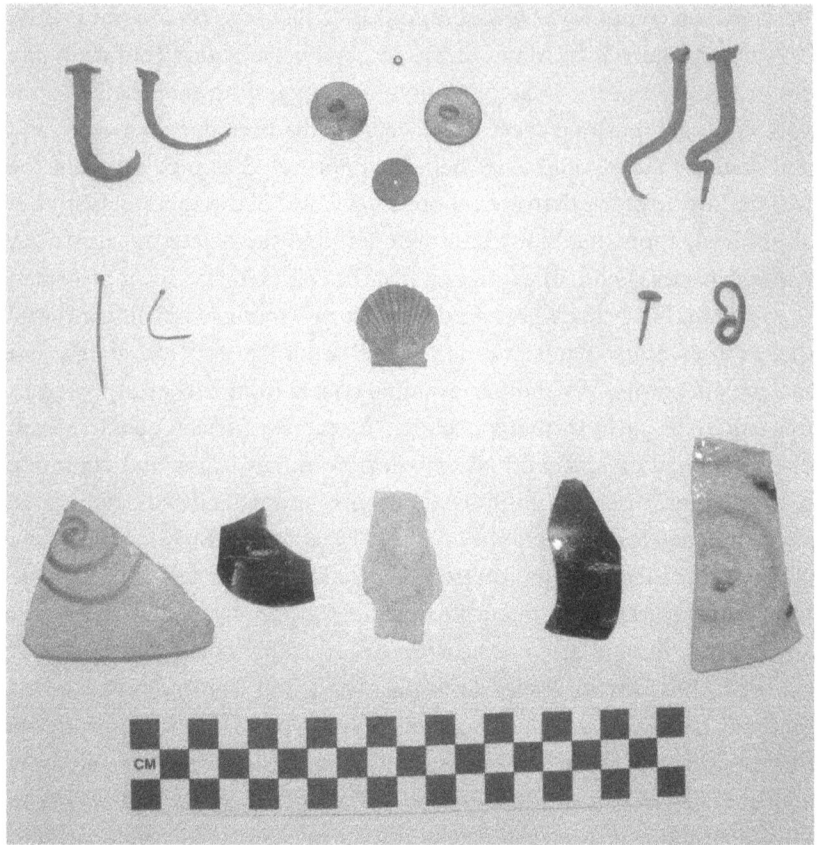

Figure 7.3. Artifacts constituting a *minkisi* bundle recovered from a cache found under the floor at the top of the basement staircase at the Latting's Hundred site in Huntington, New York (courtesy of Reginald Metcalf, photograph by Jenna Coplin).

The boundaries crossed were constructed in an African American belief system that spiritually animated physical features of the environment such as land and water. On the one hand, then, these practices describe a distinct cultural order, one that whites commonly asserted was filled with superstition and fear (Wilkie 1995: 140). However, these same physical features also acted, albeit in different and often unrecognized ways, to organize and determine the dominant white cultural order. Land, water, color, coins, stones, nails, shells, and bowls functioned as mute commodities in capitalist culture. Their purpose was found in use and the exchange value they held in the market. Any other enhanced meanings or enchantments were—through a cultural separation of the material from the spiritual—rejected, condensed, or lost. The meanings applied to these objects by African Americans, however, provide evidence that more than their utilitarian or exchange values were at play and, in their association with symbolic and spiritual power, that these meanings disturbed the dominant discourse and, by extension, arguably challenged the hegemony of the capitalist order.

The same signification process applies even more substantially to captive Africans themselves, who, being enslaved, were commodified human beings. Captive people faced a powerful contradiction between their existence as persons and members of communities and their existence as commodities or objects that were comparable and severable from all others. This contradiction was obviously felt every day inasmuch as captive people were aware that at any time they might be sold, sundering their ties with home, family, friends, and familiar settings and communities.

Challenging a growing pattern of commodification, or the stripping of any meaning from objects beyond their exchange value in American culture, the practice of animating persons and objects with spiritual power formed a community of believers who together stood against the premise of their enslavement. In these practices, captive people asserted their personhood, and they animated and re-signified the spaces and objects that lay at the root of the capitalist construction of reality. If a property is embodied by sprits, then it is not solely a real estate investment; if a bowl can carry the wishes of the living to the spirits of the dead, then it is not merely a product for the market; if a nail can be bent to reflect the order of the cosmos, then it is not simply a tool for fastening boards; if a person can construct reality, then he or she is not just a laboring body. Such significations certainly did not stop capitalism, but they did establish for African diaspora communities—those most debased by capitalism's social construction of reality—that the system of their oppression rested on arbitrary and challengeable categorizations.

Crossing boundaries by venturing into forests and waterways and animating supposedly static objects like earth, plants, water, and the sky ultimately accomplished two things. It established that the difference resulting from racism could be the creation of both black and white agency, in the sense that it was the creativity of Africans in America who found ways to practice sustainable alternatives to dominant sensibilities. Having failed in any attempt to be like their masters, I argue that Africans in America sought to be increasingly *unlike* them, and therefore they challenged the claims to commonality and the universality of humanity that served as a key foundation to the white domination of a racist and capitalist society. If Africans were categorically different and incomparable *on their own terms*, then white supremacist arguments about their inferiority were invalidated. Second, these activities, as they challenged the separations of the white cultural order, critiqued and undermined the forces which established and relied on those separations. Turning everyday commodities into fetishes that could protect as well as do harm at the very least destabilized assumptions that otherwise made racism and the capitalist exploitation of labor seem natural and inevitable.

Conversion and the Archaeology of African American Christianity

An examination of African American religion is not complete without a consideration of Christianity, the faith that the vast majority of the African diaspora population in the United States came to embrace and continues to practice. Historical archaeologists have spent very little effort thus far researching the history and culture of African American Christianity. With no exceptions that I know of, descriptions of artifacts with Christian associations are accepted either as products of assimilated Christian converts or as evidence of syncretic Afro-Christian practices that deployed Christian artifacts in African-based contexts. An example of the former is found in Orser's consideration of an African American man buried in New Orleans around 1800, who was found with a rosary and two silver Christian medallions (1994: 38). This individual also had modified teeth: "purposefully notched first mandibular incisors." The dental modification is interpreted as evidence that the person was African-born, while the rosary is interpreted to mean that "he had accepted Christianity." Lacking in this assessment is a contextual appreciation for the malleability of Catholicism in African American contexts. Various African American religions across the hemisphere, such as Santería, Candomblé, and vodou—a religion known to be practiced in New Orleans—employ Christian symbolism to express belief. For example, in vodou, African spirits and gods were disguised as Catholic saints, allowing believers to appear Christian while preserving the African traditions of the orisha (Anderson 2005). There is no way to know for sure whether the man with the rosary practiced

Christianity, vodou, or even something else. But it is important not to simply interpret the recovery of Christian objects as a sign of Christian assimilation.

Still, when done hastily, the interpretation of Christian artifacts as syncretic is also problematic. Wilkie, for example, suggests that finding "a nativity scene porcelain figure head, a brass rosary medal, and a brass Christ's head medal" in the late-nineteenth-century assemblage of Silvia Freeman, an African American servant at Oakley Plantation in Louisiana, is "not surprising when one considers the similarities between these medals and traditional African charms" (1995: 142). This pattern of explaining findings in the United States in relation to Africa is obviously tempting for archaeologists (see Ferguson 1992, Emerson 1999, Leone 2005, as well as my own discussion above), and it is often supported by compelling evidence. However, we need also to be careful not to do a historical disservice to those who may very well have embraced Christianity fully, even to the extent of debasing African practices. We need not see, in other words, that African American conversion to Christianity is evidence of a negative process of assimilation or acculturation. Why is it that African Americans must maintain their African heritage in order to be recognized as resisting slavery and racism? Might not their conversion to the religion of their masters, especially given its tenets of forgiveness, salvation, redemption, and equality before Christ, be a powerful critique of those who oppressed, condemned, and despised Africans because of their supposedly unredeemable state?

One such voice that is now under archaeological investigation is the captive African Jupiter Hammon (Coplin and Matthews 2007). Hammon, born in 1711 and owned by the Lloyd family on Long Island, New York, lived in a manner atypical for a slave. Despite being enslaved, he was educated, learned to read and write, and managed at least some of his own business affairs as well as some of those of the Lloyd family (Ransom 1970, O'Neale 1993). Hammon was also one of the first captive Africans to be published (see Figure 7.4). His known writings consist of four poems and three works of prose that speak to other captive Africans and clearly and openly challenge the injustices of slavery. It is likely that these texts were widely known in the region, as Hammon is thought to have been a preacher and had his work published in Long Island, New York City, and Hartford, Connecticut. Hammon's writings are devoutly Christian. It is

AN
Evening THOUGHT.

SALVATION BY *CHRIST*,

WITH

PENETENTIAL CRIES:

Composed by Jupiter Hammon, a Negro belonging to Mr Lloyd, of Queen's-Village, on Long-Island, the 25th of December, 1760.

SALVATION comes by Jesus Christ alone,
    The only Son of God;
Redemption now to every one,
    That love his holy Word.
Dear Jesus we would fly to Thee,
    And leave off every Sin,
Thy tender Mercy well agree;
    Salvation from our King.
Salvation comes now from the Lord,
    Our victorious King;
His holy Name be well ador'd,
    Salvation surely bring.
Dear Jesus give thy Spirit now,
    Thy Grace to every Nation,
That han't the Lord to whom we bow,
    The Author of Salvation.
Dear Jesus unto Thee we cry,
    Give us thy Preparation;
Turn not away thy tender Eye;
    We seek thy true Salvation.
Salvation comes from God we know,
    The true and only One;
It's well agreed and certain true,
    He gave his only Son.
Lord hear our penetential Cry:
    Salvation from above;
It is the Lord that doth supply,
    With his Redeeming Love.
Dear Jesus by thy precious Blood,
    The World Redemption have:
Salvation comes now from the Lord,
    He being thy captive Slave.
Dear Jesus let the Nations cry,
    And all the People say,
Salvation comes from Christ on high,
    Haste on Tribunal Day.
We cry as Sinners to the Lord,
    Salvation to obtain;
It is firmly fixt his holy Word,
    Ye shall not cry in vain.
Dear Jesus unto Thee we cry,
    And make our Lamentation:
O let our Prayers ascend on high;
    We felt thy Salvation.

Lord turn our dark benighted Souls;
    Give us a true Motion,
And let the Hearts of all the World,
    Make Christ their Salvation.
Ten Thousand Angels cry to Thee,
    Yea louder than the Ocean.
Thou art the Lord, we plainly see;
    Thou art the true Salvation.
Now is the Day, excepted Time;
    The Day of Salvation;
Increase your Faith, do not repine:
    Awake ye evtry Nation.
Lord unto whom now shall we go,
    Or seek a safe Abode;
Thou hast the Word Salvation too
    The only Son of God.
Ho! every one that hunger hath,
    Or pineth after me,
Salvation be thy leading Staff,
    To set the Sinner free.
Dear Jesus unto Thee we fly;
    Depart, depart from Sin,
Salvation doth at length supply,
    The Glory of our King.
Come ye Blessed of the Lord,
    Salvation gently given;
O turn your Hearts, accept the Word,
    Your Souls are fit for Heaven.
Dear Jesus we now turn to Thee,
    Salvation to obtain;
Our Hearts and Souls do meet again,
    To magnify thy Name.
Come holy Spirit, Heavenly Dove,
    The Object of our Care;
Salvation doth increase our Love;
    Our Hearts hath felt thy fear.
Now Glory be to God on High,
    Salvation high and low;
And thus the Soul on Christ rely,
    To Heaven surely go.
Come Blessed Jesus, Heavenly Dove,
    Accept Repentance here;
Salvation give, with tender Love;
    Let us with Angels share.

F I N I S.

Figure 7.4. *An evening thought: Salvation By Christ, with penitential cries*, a poem by Jupiter Hammon, December 25, 1760, original broadside printing (courtesy of the New York Historical Society Broadsides SY1760 no. 2).

generally accepted that he was influenced by the messages of Great Awakening preachers who came to Long Island during his young adulthood in the 1730s and 1740s. These Evangelicals spoke about conversion in shining terms, and they promised essentially all that one can imagine captive people longed for: salvation, redemption, forgiveness, and the validation of a personal faith that did not require an intermediary such as a priest, pope, or master for believers to receive the gifts of God.

Hammon's writings consistently refer to conversion as a route to freedom. Becoming "new creatures," being born again, and being saved are regularly referenced, and he makes note that with conversion captive people, "black as we are, despised as we be" (in Ransom 1970: 99), are presented with an opportunity to undo the system of their oppression. As he wrote in "An Evening's Improvement," "if we are slaves, it is by the permission of God; if we are free, it must be by the power of the Most High God," and also, citing John 8:36 in *A Winter Piece*, "if the Son therefore shall make you free, ye shall be free indeed." In these and many other passages he counsels his enslaved "brethren" that they may replace their unjust master's authority and its "daily physical, psychological, and emotional attacks against one's dignity as a person" with the redeeming authority and love of Jesus Christ (Raboteau 1995: 157). This strategy clearly undermines the master's authority by employing the very Christian hierarchy and belief system that masters supposedly adhered to and often perverted to justify the enslavement of African people.

Historian Albert Raboteau argues that conversion should be set among the basic characteristics of black religion outlined by W.E.B. DuBois (1995: 152–65). In his chapter "Of the Faith of Our Fathers" in *The Souls of Black Folk*, DuBois identified "the preacher, the sorrow songs, and the 'frenzy' or ecstasy" (Dubois 1994, in Raboteau 1995: 152). None of these aspects of the American black church are possible without conversion. However, conversion is not simply an acceptance of faith or a change of behavior, it is "*metanoia*, a change of heart, a transformation in consciousness" (Raboteau 1995: 152). Conversion, furthermore, is an experience involving visions, exuberance, speaking in tongues, and other afflictions that are interpreted usually as the gift of God.

Two points explain how conversion was an anticapitalist act of resistance. First, the conversion experience is the basis of a community of believers. Church membership often required conversion. Revivals and "experience meetings" allowed members to share their stories, which are marked by the following common theme: prior to conversion, the convert admits, they were devoted to the kind of earthly temptations with which Satan attempted to lure Christ. Being touched by God, receiving his gift, converts became unified with Christ. Conversion, therefore, is based in a very personal history and, inasmuch as this was a community of believers, a social history as well. It was a history by which the debased experience of slavery and racism could be, in a sense, instantly overcome through engagement with supportive, communal experiences quite at odds with the alienated individualism espoused by capitalist culture. The second point is that the freedom which Hammon and so many others discussed was considered a gift. It was not something that could be purchased or acquired through direct exchange. It came as the result of sacrifice and an understanding of the mutuality of experience, and it came with an expectation of reciprocity that ultimately bound communities together and persons to God. The thematic of the gift works directly against the priority of the commodity in capitalist culture, which is assessed solely by its value in the market, a value that may be abstracted from the social relations and histories that brought the object about and imbued it with meaning. By contrast, gifts are essentially embodiments of these very relationships and histories (Hyde 1983, Matthews 2001).

DuBois recognized this gift and its political implications. He concludes his most famous work, *The Souls of Black Folk*, with a discussion highlighting the three gifts of African Americans to the United States, including the gift of story and song, the gift of sweat and brawn, and the gift of the Spirit. The third is described this way:

> out of the nation's heart we have called all that was best to throttle and subdue all that was worst; fire and blood, prayer and sacrifice, have billowed over this people, and they have found peace only in the altars of the God of Right. Nor has our gift of the Spirit been merely passive. Actively we have woven ourselves with the very warp and woof of this nation,—we fought their battles, shared their sorrow, mingled our blood with theirs, and generation after generation have pleaded with a headstrong, careless people to despise not Justice, Mercy, and Truth, lest the nation be smitten with a curse. (1994: 187)

These gifts, especially that of African American spiritual fortitude in the face of extreme racist violence and oppression, embodied the essence of the United States: "Would America be America without her Negro people?" (DuBois 1994: 187).

How may this understanding of the gift of the Spirit be applied in archaeology? Since I do not know of any archaeological studies of African American Christianity, I turn to Raboteau to provide an example from James Baldwin's novel *Go Tell It on the Mountain* to suggest what we might look for. Told to clean the living room in his Pentecostal family's home, John Grimes, the novel's teenage protagonist, discovers an arrangement of objects on the mirrored mantelpiece which "held, in brave confusion, photographs, greeting cards, flowered mottoes, two silver candlesticks that held no candles, and a green serpent poised to strike" (cited in Raboteau 1995: 158). These materials reveal and contextualize a history. Greeting cards identify friends and events, photographs show the people as they are, and mottoes present the words of belief. It is the candlesticks and the serpent, however, that clarify the image. Candlesticks provide light, while the serpent threatens death, or, more specifically, the denial of "who we are" that only comes from the light of knowing our history and that we have survived it. Raboteau cites a powerful passage from another of Baldwin's works, *The Fire Next Time*, to explain: "people who cannot suffer can never grow up, can never discover who they are. That man who is forced each day to snatch his manhood, his identity, out of the fire of human cruelty that rages to destroy it knows . . . something about himself and human life that no school on earth—and, indeed, no church—can teach. He achieves his own authority, and that is unshakable" (1995: 165). The strict opposition of salvation and the serpent expresses this philosophy in material symbols, leaving no room for ambivalence. The philosophy is based on a strict commitment to the victory and loss that characterized the lives of those who struggled and overcame.

In this perspective, it takes the persistent presence of the danger of the serpent, set in opposition to a community's consciousness of its history, for a marginal population to survive and produce the persons and resources they need to continue. I think archaeologists can find these remains. The candlesticks are already material, and the serpent is depicted here as a statue, but it is also possible that we will find various other types of symbolic artifacts once we carefully analyze African American–produced assemblages for patterns of opposition that derive from antiracist and anticapitalist theorizations of the African American social world. While this process requires patience and conjecture, it is vital that we undertake it, for "America has much to learn from the experience of her black citizens" (Baldwin, cited in Raboteau 1995: 164), a history that can offer great beauty but which requires archaeological study to be fully recovered.

8

Archaeology and Ethics within and against Capitalism

> If we understand ethical practice to involve, in its deepest sense, a thoroughgoing notion of social accountability, then the central requirement for an ethical archaeology in the postcolony becomes clear. That is, to think through the relation between archaeology and society in all of the complexity and detail demanded by its context, and to develop forms of practice adequate to the conceptualization. Not "to give the past back to the people," "to tell the full story," "to bring the bones to life," but more modestly: to give the discipline an adequate conception of its own history; to not stand in the way of public negotiations around heritage, access and social accountability; to agree to revisit unexamined notions of science and society; to acknowledge the validity of rival claims to the sanctity and significance of the remains of the dead; to agree to give up a little after having benefited from so much.
>
> Nick Shepard, "What Does It Mean 'To Give the Past Back to the People'? Archaeology and Ethics in the Postcolony"

To conclude this study, I want to explore some of the relationships between capitalism and the practice of archaeology as a way of knowing about and living in the modern world. I focus on ethics in the sense that I explore the ways in which archaeology, the knowledge it produces, and the interests and livelihoods it supports are integrated with capitalist social relations. This chapter brings assumptions about archaeology's political and economic position into a critical light and suggests ways to change current practice so that archaeologists may be more aware of the networks of ideas and power that sustain our industry. This inquiry forms the principal base of critical archaeology (for example, see Leone et al. 1987, 1995,

Leone 2005, Shanks and Tilley 1987, Handsman and Leone 1989, Pinksy and Wylie 1989, Matthews et al. 2002, Hamilakis and Duke 2007, McGuire 2008), which seeks to better understand how archaeology serves those who engage with it and how the community for archaeology may be expanded so as to provide its benefits to those typically excluded.

I begin with a brief history of archaeology set within the culture of capitalism. Following Bruce Trigger's masterful work (1989), I situate archaeology as both a middle-class profession and a middle-class passion. In many ways, archaeology embodies the ethos of the capitalist bourgeoisie, as it highlights human-driven progress and potential and the universal experience of humankind. Archaeology may also be related to core aspects of the capitalist construction of reality, especially its basis in rational, empirical knowledge and the elaboration of natural law. These processes in particular enabled modern persons to identify ancient monuments and artifacts as resources comparable in many ways to minerals, water, and other "natural" products of the land (Hamilakis 2007).

I expand on Trigger's work by associating the emergence of professional archaeology with other trends in American history in the middle and late nineteenth century. Among the most important was the development of "expert" authority in the modern age. Experts could speak on subjects for the benefit of all humankind, yet as often as not this talent was used for the benefit of particular persons or groups, who themselves sought to represent the rest. Concurrently, American commercial capitalism developed a space for pursuits like archaeology through the construction of a nonprofit sector. This structure should be tied to the main underlying principle in archaeology's history: the idea of Culture (with a capital 'C') as that form of expression that embodies the spirit or genius of a people (Levine 1988). This elite or high Culture serves as an important point of reference for capitalism, for the sense of Culture that emerged in the late nineteenth century was not restricted to religious or political spaces such as churches, religion, capitol buildings, or state power. Rather, Culture was to be found in open spaces and in places where skills and artwork may be put to use outside of the market, yet it was also in large part defined by the market as those items and practices that surpass gross commodification. These spaces include museums, art galleries, concert halls, university campuses, and archaeological sites, and may be assembled as places where moderns may engage with Culture without also having to engage with persons (Bennett 1995). This distinction between Culture and everyday life epitomizes the capitalistic construction of a segregated personhood that results from the alienation of labor and the individuation of experience.

To illustrate this process in a concrete way, I refer to archaeological studies that consider the development of elite Culture to be evident in the construction of heritage sites for tourism and the creation of public memory. While examples of such sites abound in the Americas, archaeologists have only recently started to engage with the construction of heritage as a material or archaeological phenomenon (Shackel 2000, 2003, Matthews 2002, Holtorf 2005, 2007). Considering research on heritage tourism in Las Vegas, Nevada, and Annapolis, Maryland, I explore how this work elicits a deeper understanding of archaeology's role in creating experiences and validating elite Culture in the modern world. I also consider examples where such validation failed to emerge. I highlight in particular the contentious encounter at the New York African Burial Ground site in order to forge an understanding that disputes over heritage can simultaneously embody past and present injustices (LaRoche and Blakey 1997). I argue that archaeology and heritage rely on stifling social constructions that in the end serve capitalism well by fixing persons and groups into objective categories based on factors like race and ethnicity, rather than allowing for social fluidity and diversity. In this area especially, which is often housed under the umbrella of public archaeology, the need for a critical examination of ethical practice is most clear. Drawing from the continuing discourse at the New York African Burial Ground, I show why heritage cannot be packaged for sale. If we are to produce histories that are equally about the capitalist contexts of their original production and our present understanding, then we need to examine not only what happened in the past, but why and for what purposes people, including ourselves, want to know about this today. The result, I caution, should not be novel forms of market research, but rather multi-sited, ethnographically informed understandings of how American historical archaeology can break the long-term cycles of alienation and desperation that capitalism has engendered in American society (Marcus 1998, Castaneda and Matthews 2008). I conclude that the answers rely on our own integration with history as both professionals and persons.

A History of Archaeology within Capitalism

A variety of useful histories of archaeology have been written to date (for example, see Willey and Sabloff 1993, Trigger 1989, Fagan 2005, Patterson 1995, Shanks 1996, Kehoe 1998). Many of these histories, however, do not embrace the critical traditions of history-writing about disciplines as seen in anthropology, for instance, which aims to understand not only how present conditions came to be, but also the problematic origins and legacies of colonialism, capitalism, ethnocentrism, and sexism in current practice (for example, see Asad 1973, Handler 2000, Baker 1998, Stocking 1992, Castaneda 1996, and compare Kehoe 1998, Trigger 1989, Patterson 1997). Histories of archaeology typically offer an objective account of the discipline's past or a celebration of the triumph of rational, scientific authority over uncritical antiquarianism, collecting, and related self-interested constructions. The overarching trajectory is of an archaeology that began as a form of random collecting and grew into a field driven by the pursuit of increasingly systematic interpretations of past human life and events. Today's archaeology, that is, supposedly epitomizes the values of the dominant society in the modern world, which encourages empirical investigations that produce truth rather than myth, and fact rather than feeling (Feder 2007). Histories like these fail to consider archaeology's relationship with the diverse and developing contexts of politics, social theory, and nation-building which, since the nineteenth century, have brought about these modern values and arguably produce the dominant form of archaeology we know today. No study, furthermore, has made an explicit attempt to connect archaeology to the emergence of capitalism itself. I briefly initiate this discussion here.

While histories of archaeology frequently document the practice of collecting and excavating ancient remains by societies beginning in the sixth century B.C.E. (Fagan 2005: 5), these digs are largely credited as efforts to glorify those who sponsored them. The purpose of these early archaeologies was to collect ancient objects, satisfy curiosity, and proclaim either a continuity with or a break from preceding cultures. Yet, as Fagan declares, such people could "hardly be called ... archaeologist[s]" (2005: 5). Citing now widely bemused, mistaken interpretations, we learn for example that "Herodotus was no scholar and no archaeologist. He was a sucker for even the most outrageous tales, solemnly proclaiming that the pharaoh Khufu sold his daughter into prostitution to pay for the building of the Great Pyramid" (Fagan 2005: 5). Obviously, no real archaeologist would ever suggest such a thing. However, this statement appeals to a set of values that Fagan presumes to be universal, but which are in fact quite arbitrary and context-dependent. We need not accept that the pharaoh sold his daughter to consider that perhaps this was a story told to Herodotus by an Egyptian informant who may very well have believed it to be true. Why this belief would have been accepted is an interesting and important question, and certainly one that cannot be addressed if the story is appropriated for the glorification of current archaeological science.

The turning point in most histories of archaeology is the Enlightenment era, when select antiquarians decided to do more than simply collect ancient objects. Documenting where objects were found, making illustrations, and comparing objects with one another to identify patterns, some early researchers eventually began to build histories of ancient and prehistoric people through their material remains. Among the most powerful influences on the development of archaeology was the discovery of Pompeii and Herculaneum in the early eighteenth century, which brought to light entire ancient cities buried by volcanic flows. The discoveries from these sites provided material for one of the first accepted scholarly works in archaeology: Winckelmann's *History of Art in Antiquity*, which contained "systematic descriptions of Greek and Roman art" (Fagan 2005: 14). It is notable that this systematic approach was also embraced by the capitalist merchant class, who employed it to rationalize production and exchange in an effort to seize control of the means of production from the landed elite (Leone 1988).

Bruce Trigger also accepts systematic documentation as the root of archaeology, but he situates this process within a shift in intellectual traditions as literate Europeans moved from a dogmatic, medieval Christianity to an Enlightenment-era humanistic paradigm. Approaches to the past in the medieval Christian tradition followed a set of basic principles. "The world was of recent, supernatural origin . . . the physical world was in a state of degeneration. . . . Humanity was created by God. . . . It was believed to be natural for standards of human conduct to degenerate. . . . The history of the world was interpreted as a series of unique events. . . . Medieval scholars were [not] conscious of historical changes in material culture" (Trigger 1989: 31–4). The medieval worldview was one of divine origin and plan, a process in which human beings were entirely subject to external forces that reflected patterns, at best, only in the evidence of their fall from grace.

The rise of humanistic Enlightenment philosophy brought about a wholesale change in the literate European approach to the past. Stasis and degradation were replaced with the optimistic notion of progress. At root in this change was evidence revealed in the scientific revolutions brought about by Galileo, Newton, and others. These findings stood out not only because of their applications, but also because they were based in the empirical observation of the natural world and ultimately determined that nature was orderly, knowable, and universal. History too was to be revealed through empirical evidence, but only so long as it was accepted that human beings themselves, rather than God, controlled their destiny, and that human beings were seen as being in a constant state of development or evolution. The key to Enlightenment history was a set of basic proposals:

> 1. Psychic unity. All human groups were believed to possess essentially the same kind and level of intelligence and to share the same basic emotions. . . . 2. Cultural progress as the dominant feature of human history. . . . 3. Progress characterizes not only technological development but all aspects of human life. . . . 4. Progress perfects human nature, not by changing it but by progressively eliminating ignorance, passion, and superstition. . . . 5. Progress results from the exercise of rational thought to improve the human condition. In this fashion human beings gradually acquired greater ability to control their environment, which in turn generated the wealth and leisure needed to support the creation of more complex societies and the development of a more profound and objective understanding of humanity and the universe. (Trigger 1989: 57–58)

It is among these latter pursuits that Trigger places archaeology.

Following Trigger, we can see how archaeology would be a middle-class passion. It embodied a commitment to empiricism and progress both in the story it told of human historical development and in the manner that it employed the same suite of rational, objective practices that justified the wealth and leisure of the middle class. Trigger also suggests that archaeology is a middle-class pursuit. Its theoretical and methodological commitment to empiricism, its search for universal laws of nature and humanity, and even its romantic organization of a psychic human unity add up to the experiential norm of the capitalist middle class (Blumin 1989, Bledstein and Johnston 2001). Situated between the capitalist owners of the means of production and the working class who have only their labor to sell, the middle class became distinguished by the faculties acquired in higher education, where they learned theories and applications in administration, marketing, communication, and technology aimed at improving systems of production. The principal difference, therefore, between working- and middle-class persons is engagement in manual versus mental labor, a point emphasized by Max Weber in his critical descriptions of the modern state bureaucracy (Weber 1970).

Mental labor is prized among the middle class in capitalism because it abstractly conceptualizes society and humanity in an operational way. The practices of detailing broad patterns of social behavior, identifying variation at the level of the group rather than the individual, and, most powerfully, considering persons interchangeable because of a presumed human universality afforded the middle class great authority in their service to the capitalist elite. Historian Dipesh Chakrabarty argues that in capitalist society, the "labor of abstracting" is the defining practice of the middle class, for whom "the abstraction . . . becomes true in practice" (2000: 54). Sociologist Derek Sayer complements this thought with his notion of the "violence of abstraction" (1987). Sayer argues that middle-class conceptualizations are not neutral assessments, but mechanisms by which concrete persons and unique relations become categorized as types. Categories then replace reality as they are used to organize persons and validate experiences regardless of the meanings taken from those experiences by persons themselves.

While archaeologists do not typically use abstract sociological constructions to analyze modern societies (compare Buchli and Lucas 2001, McAtackney et al. 2007), their method and theory draw from the same sources that typically do. Archaeology, therefore, often projects modern middle-class abstractions and categories of experience and meaning onto past people and ways of life. The notion here is that archaeology is not only a middle-class passion and pursuit, but is essentially an embodiment of the practical theoretical constructions of capitalism itself. The history of archaeology is thus, in one way, a history of capitalism as well.

Notably, this leaves open an important and useful space for critical reflection on and analysis of the contrast between history and archaeology.

While the history of archaeology may relate to the story of capitalism, an *archaeology* of archaeology may be able to achieve a different result. If all that we claim about archaeology—especially historical archaeology—as a source for making alternative histories is true (Schmidt and Patterson 1995), then archaeological research itself, as a method for recovering unconscious, routine, material practice and undocumented social actions, should provide new insight into how archaeology as a discipline need not be solely an expression of capitalism. This, however, requires various considerations.

First, we need to reflect more on how archaeology functions as a middle-class pursuit. Examining the contexts and constructions of expert authority within capitalist culture shows how archaeologists play into this role. Turning then to applications of expert authority, by archaeologists and non-archaeologists alike, in the arena of heritage tourism, we can critically evaluate one prominent location for archaeology within the capitalist market. Finally, examination of emergent failures in archaeologically constructed heritage tourism yields a sense of how to reconceive of archaeology through a different ethical framework, one that works as much against capitalism as it operates from within it.

Archaeology and Public Culture

An underlying premise of the modern social sciences is that there are spaces in modern society where people from varied communities, circumstances, and interests come together to actually form a society. Modern society, that which birthed modern archaeology, may be conceived of as a special sort largely created in urban settings and in the particular space defined as public culture. Historian Thomas Bender defines public culture as an articulation of the capitalist market with persistent forms of social conflict (2002). In the social spaces created by the free market, spaces supposedly open to everyone, there remain significant conflicts over how these spaces are to be structured and controlled. In other words, for Bender, while everyone desires access to public culture, they also seek to control it.

Bender identifies several important effects of these contests that have a bearing on the history of archaeology. For one, the principle of the market engenders "a pattern of economic and cultural exchanges among strangers" (Bender 2002: 58). Second, the market/public cultural nexus produces a "constant movement between local cultures and public culture" that belies an underlying liminality to modern life that is not "a special or periodic condition, but rather an ordinary one" (Bender 2002: 60). These observations suggest that participation in public culture requires a frequent suspension of one's local identity and the adoption of a *public* persona, a process that mirrors the capitalist alienation of one's labor from oneself in the construction of social identity. For Bender, this process supported the coexistence in New York and other early American cities of quite distinct and diverse local communities, despite the homogenizing effects of urban capitalism. However, a reading of the material forms that embody the processes of cultural development in urban America suggests that the duality of diversity and homogeneity was typically less harmonious than usually presented, and that the construction of public culture was an effective means for rationalizing capitalist social life despite the anticultural tendencies of market-based relations.

From an archaeological perspective, evidence of this process lies in several public cultural spaces that emerged in the late nineteenth century, including parks, museums, concert halls, and universities. While diverse, each of these spaces enabled urban residents to adhere to the expectation of civic participation by demonstrating the appropriate use of the spaces of public culture. One of the grandest artifacts of nineteenth-century public culture is New York's Central Park (see Figure 8.1). According to Frederick Law Olmsted, the park's designer as well as a prolific recorder of American social life, Central Park "brought closely together, poor and rich, young and old, Jew and Gentile . . . [who expressed] evident glee in the prospect of coming together, all classes largely represented . . . each individual adding by his mere presence to the pleasure of all others" (in Bender 2002: 63). The park's success lay in the exclusion of "much of the dynamic of city life, particularly the commercial and competitive qualities of life in the city, while bringing citizens together in a kind of protected space" (Bender 2002: 63). Central Park, as an artifact, allowed people to separate themselves from the city without necessarily rejecting its alienating effects on their lives. In fact, because of the promise of the park, many late-nineteenth-century Americans praised the capitalist system that created it (Rosenzweig and Blackmar 1992). This, of course, may be read in quite the opposite way. It was only through the park and other spaces of public culture that persons who were alienated by the capitalist system could rationalize their continuing participation in it. In the park, even the

Figure 8.1. Bird's-eye view of Central Park by John Bachman, 1863 (The Lionel Pincus and Princess Firyal Map Division, The New York Public Library, Astor, Lenox, and Tilden Foundations).

most estranged people could find a sense of belonging. However, this feeling of belonging came at the cost of the physical and emotional journey away from home required to reach the park, a journey that also necessitated an inhabitation of the liminal state of their public persona. Those who sought to evade this expectation were deemed "disorderly" and only proved to the majority that private interests had no place in public life (Rosenzweig and Blackmar 1992). It may be said that this is essentially the same process by which in archaeology we must engage with our subjects in public cultural spaces and through our shared public personae.

Cultural Authority

Bender outlines a history of cultural authority in nineteenth-century America in three stages. The first was an era of generalized elites, men who led the political, economic, and cultural aspects of given communities. As an example of this, he describes the case of DeWitt Clinton in New York, who as mayor also promoted education, science, literature, and the arts. This blurring of interests and talents revealed a sense that leadership was endowed to those naturally most capable. A second phase coincides with the instability of the 1830s and Jacksonian politics, when diverse populations lost respect for a unified authority and embraced the spirit of democracy. Bender cites, as an example, P. T. Barnum's American Museum, which openly encouraged visitors to judge for themselves the validity of his claims about exhibits of a mermaid, a dog-faced boy, and a bearded woman. Moreover, these exhibits were displayed with an eclectic mix of fine art, with paintings and sculpture adjacent to natural history dioramas and live animals. The basis of Barnum's work was less to educate than to entertain and make money, both of which he did quite well.

It was evidence of such an extreme disorder, what Bender describes as "a promiscuous collection of all kinds of objects without any apparent logic of arrangement" (2002: 75), that brought about a third permutation in American cultural authority. It was during this last phase that city leaders sponsored the construction of Central Park and similar public cultural spaces in the city. Authority in this stage was again restricted to the elite, though it was an elite defined by their affiliation with Culture. Authority was to be located in those most capable of assessing value, a talent not acquired through wealth or political power alone, but from earned social distinction (Bourdieu 1984). These "best men" established that Culture was not for everyone, but was reserved only for those who could appropriately evaluate the inherent qualities of art, music, literature, theater, and so forth. They declared this in their own publications, such as an 1867 *Harper's* editorial, which established that "certain things are not disputable. Homer, Shakespeare, Dante, Raphael, Michael Angelo, Handel, Beethoven, Mozart, they are towering facts like the Alps or the Himalayas. They are the heaven-kissing peaks, and are universally acknowledged. It is not conceivable that the judgment of mankind upon those names will ever be reversed" (in Levine 1988: 146).

Stepping away from an authority based in wealth and political power, Cultural elites asserted that their intentions were honorable and for the benefit of all. This was the theory behind Central Park. It was a space available for everyone, but one that embodied the values of the Cultural elite, who expected park users to adopt these values in order to successfully understand and experience its intended effects. The same was true of New York's Metropolitan Museum of Art and American Museum of Natural History, which bookend Central Park's east and west sides. These institutions were distinguished from Barnum's cacophony by their systematized approach to art, natural science, and public cultural space. They allowed visitors not only to view displays, but also to learn the rationale behind their organization. Here especially we can see the parallel with the distinctions that historians of archaeology have made between antiquarian collectors and scientific archaeologists.

Perhaps the most powerful aspect of these institutions, including Central Park, was a promotion of the common good through private efforts, a capitalist construction known as the nonprofit sector. Museum and park visitors were improved by the charitable efforts of nonprofit boards, who in turn distinguished their efforts in this arena from their efforts in the market and themselves from their rival peers, who could be regarded as overly self-interested and greedy. Such distinctions categorized people based on their assumed inherent qualities as persons: good people serve the community, not just themselves. These categories also found expression in the professionalization of occupations. In order to establish expertise, professional societies increasingly required formalized levels of training and the acquisition of scholarly degrees to ensure that those who spoke on behalf of a given profession had sufficient credentials. Professional societies were also nonprofit ventures, once again ensuring that the common good was maintained alongside private interests.

The nonprofit basis for determining expertise ensured that matters of public culture, despite the exclusivity of Cultural authority, appeared to be for the common good. Based in scholarly work and objective, empirical observations, proclamations by the Cultural elite carried a great deal of weight among those who would enact public policy as well as those affected by it. The point here is that this was an entirely new kind of cultural order, one that sought out empirically verifiable knowledge-making practices to bolster its authority. It was in this setting that professional archaeology emerged.

Epitomizing the nonprofit pursuit, archaeology became a science of discovering and identifying the world's hidden historical resources. These resources came in two sorts: One set consisted of the actual archaeological sites that were presented as evidence of the great works of humanity. This approach may be found in American archaeology's stated rationale and its close association with environmental resources protection. For example, the American Antiquities Act of 1906 situated known archaeological sites among natural wonders like Niagara Falls and Devil's Tower and deemed them worthy of protection. The more recent basis for the cultural resource management industry, which came after the National Environmental Protection Act was passed in 1965, similarly identifies archaeological sites as akin to natural resources. A second type of archaeological resource was based in the social Darwinist idea that the diversity of humanity could be explained by the differential evolutionary achievements of the world's many peoples. This was evidence produced by ethnology and verified in the developmental evolutionary sequences revealed in archaeology. With this empirically tested basis in place, a systematic structure for organizing past humanity could be presented to the world in the great museums and World's Fairs. And with the nonprofit stamp applied to the whole process, from the discovery of remains to their public interpretation, the entire project supposedly could be trusted.

An important foundation required to reach this stage of disciplinary security followed: archaeologists were replaced by the discipline of archaeology, and archaeological subjects—past people whose lives were the focus of scholarly interest—were replaced by the archaeological record (Hamilakis 2007). In both cases, an encounter between public personae—those identities demanded of people by urban capitalist public culture—replaced an encounter between actual persons, one that might otherwise allow archaeologists, their supporters, and past persons to meaningfully commune across vast spaces of history and culture.

Archaeologies of Archaeology

I would like now to consider how archaeological research can reveal the emergence of the theoretical principles that underlie the practice of modern archaeology as a capitalist pursuit. Foremost are approaches to knowing and living in the world that rest on empirical foundations of knowledge, and an approach to social relationships that emphasizes their rational and objective construction as essentially stable resources, rather than changing and contested communities. An archaeology of these practices may be found in a study of the field's close relationship with the heritage tourism industry, a relationship that emerged with the objectification of history and culture in the United States in the late nineteenth century. To show how this process may be considered in an archaeological light, I first describe a consideration of modern Las Vegas presented by Martin Hall (2005). I then turn to my own research on the reconstruction of a historical landscape in late-nineteenth-century Annapolis, Maryland (Matthews 2002).

A Decorated Shed, or Heritage Applied

Martin Hall has examined the vast constructions that refer to archaeological heritage built in recent years in Las Vegas, Nevada, as well as in similar casino sites in South Africa (Hall 2005, Hall and Bombardella 2005). Hall considers these casino and entertainment complexes to be as much a part of the heritage industry as proper historic sites. In fact, casinos may be even more important than historic sites when it comes to influencing heritage, given the greater number of people who learn and engage with the past there than at actual historic sites. Additionally, heritage sites, whether historic sites or for-profit replicas, "give form to the public sphere" (Hall and Bombardella 2005: 6). Building on my previous discussion, heritage sites mark out spaces where persons may not only enact their public personae, but may also find resources for fleshing out its meaning through personal connections to past events and ways of life of local, ethnic, and/or national significance. Heritage, that is, complicates the meaning of public cultural spaces by expecting visitors to claim an affinity (or not) with a particular past, and thus membership (or not) in the group whose heritage is on display. For Hall, these are individualized experiences that mirror consumer choice in other market settings, such that people seem to be able to choose whether or not to affiliate with their heritage.

One question is whether heritage sites ought to be constructed in such a way. The answer often presented now, however, is that this is actually *not* a problem, since most visitors recognize the simulation: "heritage destinations are increasingly directed at customers who are fully aware that they are playing a game—that the environment is simulated, or that they are not 'really' in an 'authentic' environment" (Hall and Bombardella 2005: 6). Visitors recognize that they are in a space that has been intentionally differentiated from the norm and thus one that has attractive qualities for offering a unique, even if fabricated, experience. The purpose of heritage here is to offer a backdrop upon which guests can write their own histories and secrets (as evinced in the recent Las Vegas travel slogan: "what happens here stays here" ["Only Vegas" 2008]).

To examine how such simulations and forms of experience have been constructed, Hall focuses on the materiality of architectural space at modern entertainment complexes. A major reconstruction of the Las Vegas strip since the mid-1990s has included the construction of heritage-tourism-themed complexes such as The Luxor, Paris Las Vegas, New York, New York, The Venetian, and Aladdin, which complement the older Caesars Palace (see Figure 8.2). As one promotional Web site describes: "you can travel from Egypt to New York to France to Italy to a pirate ship, all in the space of an afternoon" (*Destination 360* 2008). Underneath this diverse expression of human culture and history there lies a common ground. Hall describes Las Vegas casinos as "decorated sheds. . . . standing in contrast with the idea of architecture as sculpture" (Hall 2005: 263). Rather than a form crafted and cut from solid material into a desired shape, a decorated shed situates "architecture" as a set of elements applied to the exterior like a costume in order to distinguish each essentially interchangeable box from the others. Such external simulations are also found inside casinos in the "extravaganza" of themed decorated and enacted spaces. At Caesars Palace, ancient Rome is encapsulated in "ancient Roman" statues and fountains. Even "a costumed Caesar and Cleopatra, accompanied by two burly legionnaires, wander around to cries of 'Hail, Caesar,' providing photo opportunities for the resort's guests" (Hall 2005: 265). A more "archaeological" experience can be had at The Luxor, where guests may visit a reconstruction of the tomb of King Tutankhamen,

Figure 8.2. Luxor Casino, Las Vegas, Nevada, showing the re-created scene of the Great Pyramid and Sphinx at Giza (photograph by Cornelius Holtorf, after Holtorf 2005: cover).

equipped with an audio tour provided by a simulated Howard Carter, the archaeologist who discovered the tomb in 1922. Hall remarks that "Luxor's claim is to the originality of the idea of Egypt, rather than Egypt itself" (2005: 265). However, the appeal in these cases to ancient pasts and even their archaeological understanding and reconstruction is a component of the very fabricated experience that modern tourists seem so aware they are having. The question is: Why do heritage and archaeology work so well at creating a fake? What is it about archaeology that makes the past so distinctive and appealing that it is worth investing billions of dollars in an archaeologically inspired, fabricated environment?

For one, archaeology and heritage provide excellent raw materials for finishing the decorated shed. These materials consist of the well-known objects, ruins, and surviving structures that can be re-created, such as the Egyptian sphinx and pyramid at The Luxor, the Doge's Palace at The Venetian, or a Parisian shopping street at Paris Las Vegas. More powerfully, the materiality of archaeological heritage also inspires the creation of heritage as an object for display. The Howard Carter tour reconstructs not only his finds, but the acts of his discovery. Samantha Rebovich has identified the same process at "The Dig" exhibition at the Atlantis Hotel in the Bahamas (2007), an exhibit which explains exactly how archaeologists discovered the lost city of Atlantis! In this sense, we may read with Hall how "the entertainment complex, then, is a factory—a set of buildings, systems and support networks dedicated to production. And the products are experiences" (Hall 2005: 274, Holtorf 2007). Especially for recent tourists, this includes the experience of "archaeology" itself, which allows a backstage view of how heritage is made for the sake of further distinguishing one experience from another.

While Hall deconstructs modern Las Vegas using an archaeological perspective, he does not offer any sense of how to practice archaeology in a different way. At best, the implication is that the archaeological fabrications at Las Vegas run parallel to the professional field, rather than representing it as it really is. I question this distinction. For one, it is clear that many more people experience archaeology and archaeological subjects at entertainment sites produced by non-archaeologists than from academically trained professionals. Therefore, more and more people will inevitably know about archaeology only as it is presented as entertainment, and they will likely use these entertainment experiences to approach any experience with "actual" archaeology they might have. Second, the distinction between the theoretical base of professional archaeology and the archaeology at entertainment complexes is slim. Both draw on the objectively presented, empirical aura of surviving objects, artifacts, ruins, and related materials in order to create a connection between people now and those in the past. Moreover, both draw from capitalist constructions that situate people in abstract social terms, even if only the separation between abstract notions of the ancient and the modern. In other words, the wild success of fabrications at Caesars Palace or The Luxor may result from the fact that these sites employ essentially the same processes of abstraction found in standard methods of archaeological social reconstruction. It is just that they use these abstractions for profitable—rather than supposedly nonprofit, politically neutral, and scientific—ends. Turning to my study of the objectification of history in Annapolis, Maryland, I offer a different approach that represents an attempt to shed light on how to practice archaeology with a better sense of its own history, in this way practicing it both within and against capitalism.

Modernizing the Ancient City

As early as 1830, Annapolis, Maryland, identified itself as the Ancient City. The nickname was adopted to balance nearby Baltimore's claim to be the Monumental City because of its association with monuments built in honor of George Washington and the War of 1812. Annapolis had to keep pace with Baltimore because, in the decades after the American Revolution, Baltimore grew to be a major seaport and incipient metropolis, stealing from Annapolis the chance for independent commercial development. Annapolis languished and, as the state capital, was designated the symbolic mantelpiece for modern Maryland, the place where debates about the path of the state's modernization were to be played out. My study of the city explores transformations in Annapolis connected to its struggle to integrate with modern capitalism during the nineteenth century (Matthews 2002: 63–129).

Standard studies of Annapolis published in the beginning of the twentieth century identify the period after the American Revolution until 1845 as the "years between" (Norris 1925), when Annapolis was a "forgotten city" (Stevens 1937). These studies emphasize that Annapolis underwent virtually no change, and thus experienced no history, until the U.S. Naval Academy was installed there. These histories then focus on the building of the Naval Academy and its impact on the city. The result is that history-making in Annapolis began again, but was the result of the nonlocal agency of the Navy. Starting in the 1890s and in response to this, a rash of studies were undertaken to retell the history of Annapolis in local terms, among which the sources cited above may be included. These stories were part of the effort to create a preservation ethos in the city, a process that came to fruition in the 1950s with the creation of the Annapolis Historic District. The fact that there was a colonial-period district in the city to save, however, is a research problem in its own right. The following account shows that there was in fact quite a bit of history in Annapolis in the nineteenth century, just not the sort that usually gets put forward in applications for historic site designation.

In my study, I focused on how people in Annapolis made a living during this "time without history." Building an archaeological biography of Alexander Randall, a leading figure in nineteenth-century Annapolis, and his family, I discovered important transformations of history-making in the city. I provide some of this biography here, highlighting changes to the city that speak about the broader objectification of history within capitalism.

Alexander Randall was a prominent Annapolis native. Born in 1808, he studied law and ran a practice in Annapolis for his entire life, including during the term he served in the U.S. House of Representatives beginning in 1838. Randall was also an advocate for civic improvement. He led the effort to upgrade the city with a water company, a gas works, and several other developments. His efforts in 1868, however, present, in miniature, the struggle to be modern in the Ancient City. Along with other prominent Annapolis men, Randall devised a modernization plan for the city. He proposed running a new lane from Prince George Street to the city harbor, subdividing the lots, and establishing a bathing company. This plan demonstrates that the city harbor had languished to the point that it could be converted into a venue for pleasure rather than commerce. The plan also involved creating the Annapolis Manufacturing Company (AMC), a factory for the manufacture of brick and lime as well as the canning of produce. The AMC bought lots six miles inland for the cannery and another lot in the city for the brick and lime factory. The AMC also proposed construction of a new rail line connecting the cannery, the town site, and a large shipping wharf on Dorsey Creek, which ran along the back of the city opposite from the public harbor.

This plan would have removed the center of commercial production from the heart of downtown Annapolis to the city's western edge, and would have paved the way for an industrial zone along the Dorsey Creek frontage. In place of a harbor half-filled with fishing and oyster boats, downtown could have sported new public baths, a feature highlighting that Annapolis was interested in offering refreshing and healthful activity for residents and visitors alike. The segregation of production from residence, commerce, and pleasure was, as previously discussed, increasingly popular in modern, nineteenth-century cities, where spaces were beginning to be officially zoned for these specific activities. This systematic organization was also interpreted as a sign of modernity.

Randall's plan never materialized. Despite some local support, the majority of the regional politicians rallied against it. As their livelihood was based in the older, extractive industries of agriculture and fishing, opponents saw industrial development as more of a threat than an opportunity. This defeat dampened Randall's enthusiasm, and those who saw an opportunity for developing an extractive versus a productive urban economy came to lead Annapolis in his place. Notably, the new resources these men promoted for Annapolis derived from the city's association with nature and history. Especially after the Civil War and Reconstruction, demand grew for new places of excursion. Noxious industrial development in cities prompted a desire for spaces untainted by pollution, overcrowding, and potential or actual social unrest. Annapolis offered all of this to tourists. It was a small, unassuming city, it presented easily understood historical associations from America's colonial golden age, and it was located on the water, with bathing sites on the Chesapeake Bay nearby. Moreover, none of these tourist-friendly attributes required any substantial capital investment or labor by city officials, only packaging—which is exactly what people in Annapolis embraced as their work.

Cosmetic improvements to the city often made the news, such as this announcement in the *Maryland Republican* from April 1, 1871:

> the spirit of change and goaheadativeness seems to be abroad in our midst, and handsome improvements are being made in different sections of our city. The neat brick addition which Mr. Henry Kaiser is having erected to his establishment, on School Street, is rapidly approaching completion, and when finished, will not only materially enhance the value of his property, but will contribute greatly to the appearance of the particular neighborhood. The Old State House Hill, as if determined not to be behind, and outdone by other sections of the city, has begun to don its spring attire, and, under the orderly hand of Mr. Augustus Gassaway, is commencing to wear its wonted appearance. The handsome ornamental rustic flower baskets and flower stands, which have been constructed during the winter, are being located at appropriate points on the hill, and the general neat and tidy importance of the grounds is very marked.

Under way in the 1870s and later was a transformation of Annapolis into an object of the modern gaze rather than a site for modern production. Improvement was not in labor and economy, but in appearance and beauty, the "look" of progress. The point of these reports was to encourage the development of Annapolis as a tourist destination. Remarking on buildings, fences, and grounds, newspaper editors were promoting a new idea. To improve was to make the town look better, and to look better, especially in Annapolis, was to *be* better, for it enabled the town to extract from its surroundings a saleable commodity: Culture. To hear the following from a Baltimore resident likely bolstered those making this effort:

> I was particularly pleased with a brief visit to your Navy Yard. We of the "Monumental City" would rejoice at having so beautiful a spot to promenade—contiguous as it is—during our summer evenings. The truth is Annapolis, all in all, though antiquated, is a remarkably attractive town in spring and summer, on account of her fine views, her capitol, her antiquities, her Navy Yard, her shade trees, pleasant walks, etc. If all these things were more generally known, I feel confident that many more of our Baltimoreans would unite in pleasure excursions thereto. (Letter to the *Maryland Republican*, May 6, 1871)

Soon after, a proposal was made for the construction of the Baltimore and Annapolis Short Line Railroad. The new rail line would provide quick and direct service between the two cities, bringing to Annapolis the supposedly eager travelers that the above letter predicted and that the new economic program demanded. The lesson learned from all this was that if Annapolis could just look pretty, suitors would arrive to care for her.

Embedded in this letter from Baltimore was a distinction between a negative sense of Annapolis as antiquated and a positive sense of the city as having "antiquities." This was a sign of things to come, as it was soon enough to be the history *in* Annapolis (rather than the history of Annapolis) that would be its most important commodity. Steps in this direction became especially prominent after the nationwide financial collapse in 1893. That same year, Annapolis proceeded with a celebration of two hundred years as the state capital with parades, speeches, and a masquerade ball for which city leaders donned colonial-period clothes. A similar event was held in 1898 to mark the two hundred and fiftieth anniversary of the town. These celebrations were ritualized, daylong events with programs that allowed modern Annapolitans to illustrate the ancient origins of their city while simultaneously showing that they could easily step into and out of the costumes required for the commemorations. Staging the event to show the temporary nature of the costumes ensured that no one would think of Annapolis as being antiquated, but that they would instead appreciate the city for its antiquities. It is the choice to demonstrate an understanding of the value of history as an objective resource, rather than a source of local identity, that shows the effect of modernization on the city.

Material evidence of this way of life may be found in the lot where Alexander Randall lived. In 1895, after the death of Randall and his wife, their children divided the property into smaller segments. Randall's son, architect T. Henry Randall, redesigned a wing of the manor house which had originally been a small office into a two-and-a-half-story house. Henry's design followed the style of the popular seventeenth-century colonial revival then coming into vogue, a style that he himself wrote about in an article on "Colonial Annapolis" published in the first volume of *The Architectural Record* (Randall 1892). It is interesting that an architect intimately aware of not only the city's styles, but the actual history of the house he was working on would choose to build a wing in a style so different from the rest of the house (which was Georgian). The colonial revival, however, fits if we consider that the main house and the wing match in that they both appear to recall the "colonial" era. It mattered more that the site be interesting and current than authentic. Building in the popular colonial-revival style gave Henry the chance to prove his skill and currency without damaging the important historical associations of the property.

A final example shows the extremes to which this practice was taken. In 1899, Naval Academy graduate Winston Churchill published a popular novel titled *Richard Carvel*, which tells of the fictional Carvel's life in Annapolis during the colonial period. Carvel supposedly lived in the William Paca house and was a fashionable member of high society. Though fictional, the use of the city as a setting for a novel aimed at a national audience helped establish Annapolis in the national historical consciousness as a colonial city. The significant local impact of the book is revealed in Walter Norris' scholarly history of Annapolis, written twenty-five years later, which includes multiple clarifications of Churchill's representation of Annapolis:

> as any student of the early history of the city will recognize as he reads the story of Richard Carvel, Churchill had done exactly as he maintained after its publication—drawn a composite and entirely fictitious picture of the geography of the town and used the materials on which any historical story of Colonial Annapolis must rest with an entirely free hand. The atmosphere of the book is ac-

curate and the details mentioned reasonably credible but there is no pretense to anything more. (Norris 1925: 105–6)

One can imagine that, as a local historian, Norris frequently fended off allusions to Churchill's Annapolis, being forced to replace these misconceptions with actual stories, be they more interesting and entertaining or not.

The effect of *Richard Carvel* was also felt at the moment of its publication. While the book seemed to glorify Annapolis for its colonial charm, it juxtaposed that era with the Annapolis of the present. Churchill made the fact of Annapolis' decline clear in the forward to *Richard Carvel*, supposedly penned by Carvel's grandson, Daniel Clapsaddle Carvel, in 1876:

> The lively capital which once reflected the wit and fashion of Europe has fallen into decay. The silent streets no more echo with the rumble of coaches and gay chariots, and grass grows where busy merchants trod. Stately ball-rooms where beauty once reigned are cold and mildewed, and halls where laughter rang are silent. Time was when every wide-throated chimney poured forth its cloud of smoke, when every andiron held a generous log—andirons which are now gone to decorate Mr. Centennial's home in New York or lie with a tag in the window of some curio shop. . . . Mr. Carvel's town house in Annapolis stands to-day, with its neighbours, a mournful relic of a glory that is past. (Churchill 1899: vii)

While this characterization should have angered people in Annapolis, the book's success led them to disregard the critique and embrace the notoriety Annapolis gained. The most powerful evidence of this acceptance was the building of the Carvel Hall Hotel, named after the fictional Richard Carvel, in 1903 (Warren 1990). A large, four-story hotel attached to the back of the William Paca house, this two-hundred-room structure was one of the largest in the city and made an enormous impact on the Annapolis landscape. In particular, it dominated the colonial Paca house and buried one of the last large colonial-era gardens left in the city.

Considering the conception of modernization, the construction of Carvel Hall makes two points. First, the use of Richard Carvel in identifying the hotel shows the juxtaposition of modernization with the ancient character of the city. However, the use of the fictional Richard Carvel instead of the real William Paca makes the historical association expand on the patterns established in Henry Randall's colonial-revival architecture. Because Annapolis relied on its history to spur modernization, the more widely known the history and thus the more recognizable the costume, the better. Simply put, the popular Carvel pushed the increasingly obscure Paca and the rest of Annapolis' actual history aside, because to have *some* history was all that mattered.

The efforts to build recognition for Annapolis within the heritage tourism market greatly impacted the Annapolis landscape. Carvel Hall was the largest structure in the city at the time. The interest in heritage tourism also helped preserve a wide array of homes built in the city during its one true golden age, just before the American Revolution. The fact that there is a historic district with a substantial set of historic houses and an equally significant set of archaeological deposits in Annapolis should itself be seen as an artifact worthy of archaeological research. Considering the transformation of history into a marketable commodity, extracted from the Annapolis landscape and produced for sale and meaningful affiliation, provides some insight into how to approach the problem of archaeology and preservation within capitalism. It was not an antimodern, let alone anticapitalist, interest that drove the rush to history in Annapolis. It was the fact that the city could generate nothing else of its own to support those who sought to lead it. The past *was* Annapolis, and Annapolis, like virtually all small American communities by the late nineteenth century, was for sale. In fact, those who adopted a nonprofit interest in the preservation of Annapolis only came to support the city from elsewhere after Annapolis itself demonstrated its historical significance in these outsiders' terms. Adopting such nonlocal values and non-locally defined, yet still marketable, identities is how the abstractions of capitalism infect everyday practice in archaeology and the everyday experience of history. I turn now to look at some efforts to conceptualize archaeology in a different and perhaps anticapitalist way.

Identity as History: Ethics in Public Archaeology

Kerwin Klein writes that "memory can come to the fore in an age of historiographic crisis precisely because it figures as a therapeutic alternative to historical discourse" (2000: 145). Citing this observation, Erika Doss has analyzed how commemorative memorials constructed at the site of the

Figure 8.3. Ground Zero memorials. *Left:* Official but elaborated memorial to New York's Bravest. *Right:* Unofficial flyer posted adjacent to the firefighter's memorial (photographs by Christopher Matthews).

Oklahoma City bombing and the Columbine High School rampage, to which we must now add Ground Zero in New York City (see Figure 8.3), reflect a changing relationship with death in American society (2002). Doss describes a new American engagement with the meaning of death, in which the search for meaning is disconnected from the events that caused the death. From roadside memorials erected at deadly automobile crash sites to spontaneous shrines constructed at Columbine and Ground Zero to the official memorials built at these and other sites later in time, there is a consistent effect of dissociating the death from the history that caused it. The purpose of the memorial, then, is to allow for individual and communal grieving, but not for investigation and reflection on how these feelings speak about forces in social life, nor how this grief might be managed by social institutions. As Doss states, "a superficial focus on psychic closure—on healing and surviving—skirts the causal, historical dimensions of these visibly public deaths" (2002: 71). Memorial sites are developed for remembering and the construction of identity at the expense of history.

I suggest we consider impromptu and even official memorials to violent and seemingly inexplicable death as novel components of public culture. Yet, we should recognize that these are still made in the same way—and demand the same behavior and public persona—as Central Park, the major museums, and other modern high Cultural sites. The distinction is that site memorials are spaces appropriate for expressions of grief at the loss of life and loved ones, but not for reflection on the causes of, nor especially the continuing structural failures that may be related to, the deaths. Rather, memorials provide a place for feeling.

> Often insulated from death and disaster, and generally discouraged from public displays of grief, people go to these sites to see and touch real-life tragedy, to weep and mourn and *feel* in socially acceptable situations. As shrines to trauma, these sites memorialize the horrible events that occurred there, and also the grief of relatives, survivors, and complete strangers who feel kinship with those who died. (Doss 2002: 70)

Thus, the trauma is made available at memorials for everyone to experience, so that even strangers may feel a kinship with the dead and their families. The result is that contrived, "fictive" emotions are validated in influential public settings.

Why would strangers seek to feel the trauma of others? What would drive someone to become attached to an event that is only tangentially connected to them? The answer may come from reflections on Max Weber's observation that death has no place in modern society, which I mentioned in chapter 1. Weber believed moderns regard death only as the end of life, that it has lost its meaning as the stage where life shifts to afterlife. Memorial sites permit moderns to experience death without challenging this foundational separation of life and death. Memorials essentially sponsor the experience of feelings of loss, fear, and anger, but they are aimed at bringing about resolution through the construct of memory. In other words, what is lost (as well as what is frightening and conducive of anger) can be found, or, more accurately, remembered—if not resurrected—through the experience of feelings at memorial sites.

However, it is also Weber's point that this sense of loss is commonly shared by persons in capitalism as a result of alienation. Experiencing and managing our separations from community caused by the commodification of labor, individualism, and bureaucratic control sustains a state of personal crisis. Thus, the feelings experienced at memorials seem valid since the largely unfulfilled desire to express them is an important constituent of capitalist society. However, the demands of public culture that force a separation between public and private spheres do not allow for grief to support an integration of the two. Even family members have little room for turning grief into action, for fear of politicizing their loved one's death at the expense of the general demand that we instead memorialize it, a process of denying their death in favor of allowing us to reexperience it ourselves.

This approach to memorial sites also applies to understanding archaeology, which may be seen as an industry that produces sites of death for public consumption. While the majority of archaeological sites do not garner a great deal of public attention, the recent and rapid development of heritage tourism and the growing experiential economy have led some to consider archaeology as a mechanism for essentially bringing death to life and perhaps also to the market (Holtorf 2007). An alternative with some efficacy is to conceive of an archaeology that invalidates the separation of life and death. This is often the stated purpose of community and activist archaeologies, but these new subfields encounter and expose as many difficulties as successes in bringing about new forms of practice or consciousness (McDavid 2008, Matthews 2005). Still, some community archaeology projects in the United States show that the potential for constructing histories within and against capitalism can in fact derive from archaeology itself.

The New York African Burial Ground

The New York African Burial Ground (ABG), located at 290 Broadway in the heart of Lower Manhattan, is among the most well-known recently discovered archaeological sites in the United States. Its renown is as much based in the findings made there as in the political entanglements that the site's discovery, excavation, and commemoration have brought about (LaRoche and Blakey 1997, Mack and Blakey 2004). The site also encapsulates the issues involved in community archaeology and the connection between communities, the past, and capitalism. The ABG was the principal cemetery for persons of African descent in New York between 1700 and 1796. It was rediscovered in 1991 during the construction of a Federal Government Services Agency (GSA) office skyscraper. While a preliminary archaeological compliance study identified the site as the location of the burial ground based on historic maps, it was believed to have been significantly disturbed by later urban development. However, construction revealed that the ground surface in the area was raised by as much as twenty-five feet of fill that buried and preserved the bodies of as many as fifteen thousand persons under the streets and buildings of modern New York City. Because the original archaeological study did not require substantial mitigation involving a detailed excavation or preservation plan, the construction project was halted for only a short period while the remains of 424 bodies were removed for analysis (Blakey and Rankin-Hill 2004, Perry et al. 2006).

It was only after intense community pressure had been exerted that these excavations were halted. The descendent New York African American community then took control of the project and saw that the study of the exhumed remains was undertaken by an African-American-led research team based at Howard University, a leading historically black institution (LaRoche and Blakey 1997). After their study, the remains were reburied at the site in October 2003, and the site was designated a U.S. National Monument in February 2006. As part of the creation of the monument, a call was issued for a memorial to be built at the site. The winning design was selected in April 2005, and the memorial was completed and dedicated in October 2007 (see Figure 8.4).

Drawing a comparison between Doss's study of memorial sites associated with violent events in American history and the new memorial at the ABG is instructive.[1] At the presentation of the winning design, Stephen Perry, a GSA spokesperson, stated that "The story of this site, and the story of the people who are here at this site, will never, ever be forgotten. ... I think we can say what a different world we live in today, versus the world that existed at the point in time when these human beings were relegated to this site" (Confessore 2005). Similarly, Rodney Leon, designer of the winning proposal, said, "No longer should one walk past the site or throughout downtown and not be provided the opportunity to note, understand, and acknowledge with respect that history" (Confessore 2005). In response both to the proposed design and to the attitude toward

---

1 The following discussion is adapted from Matthews 2008.

Figure 8.4. Design for the New York African Burial Ground Memorial (rendering by Rodney Leon, Courtesy Rodney Leon Architects).

history found in these statements, New York City Councilman Charles Barron declared, "They disrespected our ancestors when they excavated our bones, they disrespected us when they took them out of the ground, and now they're disrespecting us by turning our grave site into some kind of a museum" (Confessore 2005).

These three statements reveal the various sides of the debate surrounding the public memorial of the ABG site that were presented in the provocatively titled *New York Times* article "Design Is Picked for African Burial Ground, and the Heckling Begins" (Confessore 2005). Obviously, the *Times* was establishing an understanding of the contentious history that has surrounded the ABG since its rediscovery in 1991. Yet by identifying Barron's statements as heckling, the article established that some opinions are more relevant than others, as embodied by whose work was built at the site (that is, Leon's and the GSA's). Despite this slight, we can learn a great deal from Barron's perspective, since he calls for us to reject the memorialization of the site and its consecration as "public" space. Rather than embracing the ABG as a collectively American legacy, Barron thinks that we should respect it as an African American cemetery. Barron thinks that Leon's memorial separates the struggles of the captive

Africans whose remains were discovered at the site from the struggles of those African Americans who now lay claim to the site as descendents, and whose social action changed its meaning.

This is a powerful point. If we consciously allow memorialization to be a social act of change rather than the creation of a space for constructed memories, we provide an opportunity for the history that brought about the need for claiming and creating heritage and sites of commemoration to be a part of the body of experience at the site. The history that more than two million African American New Yorkers live with now as a result of a tradition of exclusion and oppression including enslavement, structural racism, and generational impoverishment is already an aspect of this site's presence in its association with African American history. An understanding of this history should, therefore, be part of what we take from it, or else it should not be memorialized at all.

This approach counters recent trends in site memorialization defined by Doss by suggesting that the context and form of the memorial be integrated with social histories that call out for recognition at such sites in the first place. Following Gerald Sider (1994), we should see identity not as a heritage or a legacy, but as *history*. To construct identities through memory, commemoration or the experience of feelings at particular sites produces merely an applied exterior over an otherwise undistinguished and generalized human shed. Unless sites articulate communities by telling the histories that formed them, they will only be what Dean MacCannell calls "empty meeting grounds" (1992).

What Makes It Archaeological?

While we clearly can see issues of history and identity emerge in the memorialization of sites when it is based on existing and conflicted interpretations, this is a more difficult process when research is beginning and sites have yet to be excavated and understood. Yet, given events at the ABG and comparable episodes involving Native Americans (McDonald et al. 1991, Watkins 2000, Killion 2007), it is necessary that histories of oppression and exclusion be pronounced from the very start of a project if the research is to be articulated, relevant, and useful for promoting understanding and change. This is an ethical issue, and I think that archaeology is uniquely situated to approach history in this way. The continuing existence of archaeological remains despite their abandonment, ruin, burial, and forgetting provokes the very questions we need to ask to include history at the start of our research: What made the site archaeological? Why do people not know about it? Why was it forgotten? (Matthews 2008, Epperson 2004). While archaeological sites inhabit the contemporary world, until they are investigated, their story is unknown and so, effectively, they do not exist. Yet rarely do such absences lack an association with the politics and processes of history, silence, and commemoration (Trouillot 1995, Sider and Smith 1997). We hear this from Councilman Barron, who demands that we ask why the ABG was forgotten and buried. In one sense, we all know the answer, yet unless we take the opportunity that archaeology presents for putting the question forward, we will not be reminded that forgetting about the African Burial Ground is a process that started in 1796 and—despite its excavation and memorialization—continues largely unabated today.

An approach that asks why something is archaeological also asks: Why do archaeology? Obviously, the world is moving forward without the stories that are still buried in the ground today. Do we really need archaeology to address our major social problems? In some cases, burying and forgetting the past was an intentional act to dispose of evidence of wrongdoing (Gonzalez-Ruibal 2008, Bernbeck and Pollack 2008). To bring to light the events revealed by such sites undoes these injustices, even if only by virtue of giving contemporary people the chance to know more about the histories of who they are and what they are ethically responsible for. In other cases, buried and forgotten things should be respected and sites left untouched. For all our desire for knowledge, a desire we certainly share with an abundance of modern people, archaeological research can at times be a dangerous pursuit (Zimmerman 2007). Certainly, one could argue that archaeology has gained quite a bit from the research and the lessons about community engagement related to the project at the New York African Burial Ground. Despite being taught these lessons, I think we still have to wonder whether such a project would proceed any differently now. Community and collaborative archaeology projects are certainly growing in number, as are community advisory boards for research projects (Colwell-Chanthaphonh and Ferguson 2007, Little and Shackel 2007, Derry and Malloy 2003). This is indeed encouraging, but at what point will these movements shift from devising better ways of practicing and protecting archaeology to actually serving and building communities, as our ethical statements imply that we should (see Perry and Blakey 1997, McGuire 2008)? Sacrificing our privilege by supporting the desire to not dig sites and adopting a willingness "to give up a little after having benefited from so much" (Shepard 2007: 112) still seems to be the exception to the rule. To move in this direction, we need to shed our professional public persona and consider seriously, and perhaps for the first time, why we want to be archaeologists, and if we do not know or like our answers, work to find out what we can actually do to change who *we* are.

An Anticapitalist Archaeology: Archaeologists and Communities

Therefore, I propose for archaeology to develop an ethical framework defined in opposition to the expectation that we embrace "archaeology" by ignoring our own histories and dissolving our personal interests when we come to define the relevance of our work. Such a commitment to professionalization places the abstract public value of archaeology above that of its agents, whether these are archaeologists or interested community members. It forces archaeologists into predefined roles, rather than trusting them to handle the multiple demands placed on them in public requiring their attentiveness and flexibility as modern persons. Moreover, professional commitments bind archaeologists to the market for their labor, and thus put them in the service of an archaeology largely defined by capitalism.

To break from a complicity with capitalism, archaeologists can rethink what defines our resource base. We need to shift our focus from preserving control of the archaeological record to better understanding and building the many relationships we gain by the good fortune of being persons who happen to be archaeologists. Moreover, if we really consider and then decide to change why we do archaeology, I predict that we will change who we are as archaeologists and become instead active members of our communities, not just one individuated resident among many. Integration of our roles as archaeologists, historians, and storytellers with our roles as parents, neighbors, and coworkers is the only way our work will have an impact, because we—as fully formed people who happen to be archaeologists—are the ones who have agency, not the discipline, let alone the mute objects awaiting excavation and analysis. Enacting this integration provides an immediate view of the farce that capitalism and its cultural institutions perpetrate in their commitment to value things alienated from those who give them meaning.

Conclusion

The Materialization of Capitalism

> In the river, a short distance from the shore, lying quietly at anchor, with her small boat dancing at her stern, was a large sloop—the *Sally Lloyd*; called by the name in honor of a favorite daughter of the colonel. The sloop and the mill were wondrous things, full of thoughts and ideas. A child cannot well look at such objects without *thinking*.
>
> Frederick Douglass, *My Bondage and My Freedom*

> Capitalism survives by forcing the majority, whom it exploits, to define their own interests as narrowly as possible.
>
> John Berger, *Ways of Seeing*

The tension so eloquently articulated in these statements by John Berger and Frederick Douglass is woven through the diverse examples of American historical archaeology presented in this book. This is the tension between severe restriction and limitless possibility within American capitalism. Put in the hands of individuals, capitalism blossomed in the American context, continuing from colonial origins in the seventeenth century to the present day. American capitalism expanded on inherited European systems of production and socially constructed conceptions of space, identity, and personhood. It re-created markets and shifted the meaning of intersubjective relations toward a focus on private gain. The success of capitalism may be measured in the way that objects were transformed into enriching commodities and, through this very same process, how objects themselves were created essentially out of thin air. It is this process of *materialization* in capitalism that has been the primary focus of this book, and the making of the modern individual has been the most potent and yet complicated example.

John Berger explores the capitalistic process of materializing objects in the commodification of nature and craft through what we now call "landscape" and "fine art." His statement above reflects on one aspect of this transformation: that the possibility of materialization is inherently narrow for those laboring within the capitalist system. Slaves, servants, workers, bureaucrats, and middle-class managers failed to acquire and accumulate, let alone maintain, the principal force that enables the promise of capitalism, which is, of course, capital, a resource for the most part restricted to the labor they could dispense in the market. Having "no other commodity for sale" (Marx 1967: 169), working- and middle-class Americans lacked the resources to build alternatives to the systems of their oppression. Moreover, with their imaginations also restricted, they believed that their self-interest was best served by investing their labor and limited resources in the hegemonic system itself. It is a material record of this widespread, active participation in capitalism that I have presented in this book and which American historical archaeology is poised to recover and interpret through theoretical and methodological approaches unavailable to scholars in other disciplines. From individual Creamware place settings to wampum drills to a personalized cup from a New York City tenement, from rubbish-filled lots to clean yards to the re-creation of the discovery of King Tut's tomb at The Luxor Casino, archaeological evidence of capitalism illuminates the materialization of autonomous individuals and individualized experiences throughout American history. This evidence demonstrates that the making of individuals was guided by the capitalist system, but it also highlights that it was persons themselves who framed and finished the process.

This tension between the domination of a capitalist ideology and the potential of individual agency is captured in the above quote by former slave Frederick Douglass. As he describes, the spectacle of capitalism lies in its material products, for Douglass the Lloyd's plantation mill and sloop. These objects presented to Douglass a view on the seizure of human achievement for private gain in capitalism, the scope of which we know now has no parallel in human history. However, Douglass not only wonders at the objects that enrich his master, but identifies exactly what makes them wonderful: that they reflect the substance of the human mind and in turn inspire one to think. For Douglass, these wonders of the capitalist system symbolized simultaneously his slavery and his freedom. He knew as a child that the sloop, like himself, was his master's property, and he only knew his master as a ruthless tyrant whose every deed expressed a hatred for the enslaved. So, in one sense the sloop established and emphasized the boundaries and violence of slavery. Still, in recalling the mill and the sloop as not only objects, but impressive achievements, Douglass teased out the imagination that went into their planning and the action of the human mind that made them work. While the laboring imagination in capitalism may be appropriated and severely restricted, its ideas remain palpable within objects and thus available for reappropriation by a thinking mind, which by virtue of these thoughts could imagine being free.

Douglass believed that the problem abolitionists faced was a paucity of thinking minds. The enslaved were silenced by the racist violence of their everyday lives, and free laborers were worn down by the burdens of maintaining their status and autonomy in a competitive labor market. Society's leaders, moreover, had little compassion for this suffering, since to them the poor and enslaved seemed simply incapable of helping themselves. Thinking became an expense in capitalism, which, if not compensated, was better not done at all.

This book has recorded several different sorts of compensation for thinking minds. The formal Georgian garden centered the owner as a natural expert; the industrial planners at Lowell imagined themselves as social reformers; Central Park provided a public space for demonstrating one's social legitimacy; and archaeology, as a distinct and disciplined practice, materializes a heritage of human achievement for moderns to appreciate. In these instances, compensation came not only as wealth, authority, and power, but also as credentials and individual distinction. My discussion of resistance embodied in the effort to create communities outside of capitalism showed the limits to acquiring distinction for the oppressed. Nineteenth-century factory workers, middle-class women, and utopian communalists all attempted to extract themselves, but few brought about substantial change, and most failed outright to position themselves beyond the reach of capitalist culture. However, some African Americans did achieve a solidarity that supported a potent criticism of their oppression. The appropriation of objects for ritual, from colonoware pots to root cellars to crystals and coins, helped keep their minds free to think up and practice an African spirituality in America. This thinking not only actively separated Africans from others on their own terms, but challenged an unthinking acceptance of commodification embraced by the majority that disallowed enchantment and rejected object meanings beyond market values.

This book, therefore, has illustrated that the success of American capitalism resides in materialization. This is evident in the way that objects stand in for human relationships, such as the babbitt-mended ball bearing at Paradise, Nevada, but equally and simultaneously in the way capitalism itself *produces* things by changing the immaterial to the material, as in the objectification and commodification of the past. I have claimed that all of American history may be conceived of as an engagement with capitalism, which necessarily includes the labor and products of the historical archaeologists studying it now. The question is: Can we appropriate and share our own materialization as archaeologists to produce new objects and opportunities for thinking about archaeology and engaging past peoples, or will we continue our extensive engagement with individualism and its narrow vision of what the archaeological record is actually good for?

Bibliography

Agnew, Jean-Christophe. 1986. *Worlds Apart: The Market and the Theater in Anglo-American Thought, 1550–1750*. Cambridge University Press, Cambridge.
Althusser, Louis. 1971. "Ideology and Ideological State Apparatuses." In *Lenin and Philosophy and Other Essays*. New Left Books, London.
Anderson, Jeffrey. 2005. *Conjure in African American Society*. Louisiana State University Press, Baton Rouge.
Asad, Talal. 1973. *Anthropology and the Colonial Encounter*. Ithaca Press, London.
Axtell, James. 1975. "The White Indians of Colonial America." *William and Mary Quarterly, 3rd series*, 32 (1): 55–88.
Baker, Lee A. 1998. *From Savage to Negro: Anthropology and the Construction of Race, 1896–1954*. University of California Press, Berkeley.
Baker, Nancy. 1986. "Annapolis, Maryland 1695–1730." *Maryland Historical Magazine* 81: 191–209.
Bakhtin, M. M. 1981. *The Dialogic Imagination: Four Essays*. University of Texas Press, Austin.
Barnett, Stephen, and Michael G. Silverman. 1979. *Ideology and Everyday Life*. University of Michigan Press, Ann Arbor.
Baxter, Jane Eva. 2005. *The Archaeology of Childhood: Children, Gender, and Material Culture*. AltaMira, Walnut Creek.
Beaudry, Mary C., Lauren J. Cook, and Stephen A. Mrozowski. 1991. "Artifacts and Active Voices: Material Culture as Social Discourse." In *The Archaeology of Inequality*, Randall H. McGuire and Robert Paynter, eds., pp. 150–91. Basil Blackwell, Oxford.
Bender, Thomas. 2002. *The Unfinished City: New York and the Metropolitan Idea*. The New Press, New York.
Bennett, Tony. 1995. *The Birth of the Museum: History, Theory, Politics*. Routledge, London.
Berger, John. 1972. *Ways of Seeing*. Penguin Books, New York.
Berkhofer, Robert F. 1979. *The White Man's Indian: Images of the American Indian from Columbus to the Present*. Vintage Books, New York.
Berman, Marshall. 1970. *The Politics of Authenticity: Radical Individualism and the Emergence of Modern Society*. Atheneum, New York.
———. 1982. *All That Is Solid Melts Into Air: The Experience of Modernity*. Simon and Schuster, New York.

Bernbeck, Reinhard, and Susan Pollack. 2008. "'Grabe, Wo Du Shest!' An Archaeology of the Perpetrators." In *Archaeology and Capitalism: From Ethics to Politics*, Yannis Hamilakis and Philip Duke, eds., pp. 217–34. Left Coast Press, Walnut Creek.

Blakey, Michael L. and Lesley M. Rankin-Hill, eds. 2004. *The New York African Burial Ground Skeletal Biology Final Report*. Prepared by Howard University for the United States General Services Administration Northeast and Caribbean Region, New York.

Bledstein, Burton J. and Robert D. Johnston. 2001. *The Middling Sorts: Explorations in the History of the American Middle Class*. Routledge, New York.

Blumin, Stuart M. 1989. *The Emergence of the Middle Class: Social Experience in the American City, 1760–1900*. Cambridge University Press, New York.

Bodley, John H. 2008. *Victims of Progress*, 5th ed. AltaMira Press, Lanham.

Bodnar, John E. 1985. *The Transplanted: A History of Immigrants in Urban America*. Indiana University Press, Bloomington.

Bourdieu, Pierre. 1977. *Outline of a Theory of Practice*. Cambridge University Press, Cambridge.

———. 1984. *Distinction: A Social Critique of the Judgment of Taste*. Routledge and Keegan Paul, London.

Bourgois, Phillipe. 1995. *In Search of Respect: Selling Crack in El Barrio*. Cambridge University Press, London.

Boyer, Paul. 1978. *Urban Masses and Moral Order in America, 1820–1920*. Harvard University Press, Cambridge.

Braudel, Fernand. 1979. *Civilization and Capitalism, 15th–18th Century*. University of California Press, Berkeley.

Brenner, Elise M. 1988. "Sociopolitical Implications of Mortuary Ritual Remains in 17th-Century Native Southern New England." In *The Recovery of Meaning: Historical Archaeology in the Eastern United States*, Mark P. Leone and Parker B. Potter Jr., eds., pp. 147–81. Smithsonian Institution Press, Washington.

Brighton, Stephan A. 2001. "Prices That Suit the Times: Shopping for Ceramics at Five Points." *Historical Archaeology* 35 (3): 16–30.

Brown, John B., and Paul A. Robinson. 2006. "'The 368 Years' War': The Conditions of Discourse in Narragansett Country." In *Cross-Cultural Collaboration: Native Peoples and Archaeology in the Northeastern United States*, Jordan E. Kerber, ed., pp. 59–75. University of Nebraska Press, Lincoln.

Brown, Kenneth L. 1994. "Material Culture and Community Structure: The Slave and Tenant Community at Levi Jordan's Plantation, 1848–1892." In *Working Toward Freedom: Slave Society and Domestic Economy in the American South*, Larry E. Hudson Jr., ed., pp. 95–118. University of Rochester Press, Rochester.

———. 2001. "Interwoven Traditions: Archaeology of the Conjurers Cabins and the African American Cemetery at the Jordan and Frogmore Manor Plantations." In *Places of Cultural Memory: African Reflections on the American Landscape*, pp. 99–114. Conference Proceedings. U.S. Department of the Interior, National Park Service.

Brown, Kenneth L., and Doreen C. Cooper. 1990. "Structural Continuity in an African American Slave and Tenant Community." *Historical Archaeology* 24 (4): 7–19.

Brumfiel, Elizabeth M., and Timothy Earle, eds. 1987. *Specialization, Exchange and Complex Societies*. Cambridge University Press, Cambridge.

Buchli, Victor, and Gavin Lucas, eds. 2001. *Archaeologies of the Contemporary Past*. Routledge, London.

Bushman, Richard L. 1998. "Markets and Composite Farms in Early America." *William and Mary Quarterly, 3rd Series*, 55 (3): 351–74.

Cantwell, Anne-Marie, and Diana diZerega Wall. 2001. *Unearthing Gotham: The Archaeology of New York City*. Yale University Press, New Haven.

Carson, Cary, Norman Barka, William Kelso, George W. Stone, and Dell Upton. 1981. "Impermanent Architecture on the Southern American Colonies." *Winterthur Portfolio* 16: 135–96.

Castañeda, Quetzil E. 1996. *In the Museum of Maya Culture: Touring Chichen Itza*. University of Minnesota Press, Minneapolis.

Castañeda, Quetzil E., and Christopher N. Matthews, eds. 2008. *Ethnographic Archaeologies: Reflections on Stakeholders and Archaeological Practices*. AltaMira Press, Walnut Creek.

Chakrabarty, Dipesh. 2000. *Provincializing Europe: Postcolonial Thought and Historical Difference*. Princeton University Press, Princeton.

Chan, Alexandra. 2007. *Slavery in the Age of Reason: Archaeology at a New England Farm*. University of Tennessee Press, Knoxville.

Childe, V. Gordon. 2003. *Man Makes Himself*. Spokesman, Nottingham.

Churchill, Winston. 1899. *Richard Carvel*. The Macmillan Company, New York.

Clark, John E. and Michael Blake. 1994. "The Power of Prestige: Competitive Generosity and the Emergence of Rank in Lowland Mesoamerica." In *Factional Competition and Political Development in the New World*, Elizabeth M. Brumfiel and Jon W. Fox, eds., pp. 17–30. Cambridge University Press, Cambridge.

Colwell-Chanthaphonh, Chip, and T. J. Ferguson, eds. 2007. *Collaboration in Archaeological Practice: Engaging Descendant Communities*. AltaMira Press, Walnut Creek.

Confessore, Nicholas. 2005. "Design Is Picked for African Burial Ground, and the Heckling Begins." *New York Times*, April 30, 2005, Section B; Column 2; Metropolitan Desk; p. 1.

Cooper, Frederick, and Anne Laura Stoler, eds. 1997. *Tensions of Empire: Colonial Cultures in a Bourgeois World*. University of California Press, Berkeley.

Coplin, Jennifer Wallace, and Christopher N. Matthews. 2007. "The Archaeology of Captivity and Freedom at Joseph Lloyd Manor." *African Diaspora Archaeology Newsletter*, December 2007. http://www.diaspora.uiuc.edu/newsl207/newsl207.html#3.

Corrigan, Philip, and Derek Sayer. 1991. *The Great Arch: English State Formation as Cultural Revolution*. Blackwell, Oxford.

Crane, Brian D. 2000. "Filth, Garbage, and Rubbish: Refuse Disposal, Sanitary Reform, and Nineteenth-Century Yard Deposits in Washington, D.C." *Historical Archaeology* 34 (3): 20–38.

Cronon, William. 1983. *Changes in the Land: Indians, Colonists, and the Ecology of New England*. Hill and Wang, New York.

Dain, Bruce R. 2002. *"A Hideous Monster of the Mind": American Race Theory in the Early Republic*. Harvard University Press, Cambridge.

Davis, David Brion. 1966. *The Problem of Slavery in Western Culture*. Cornell University Press, Ithaca.

———. 2006. *Inhuman Bondage: The Rise and Fall of Slavery in the New World*. Oxford University Press, New York.

Deetz, James F. 1977. *In Small Things Forgotten: Archaeology and Early American Life*. Anchor Books, New York.

———. 1994. *Flowerdew Hundred: The Archaeology of a Virginia Plantation, 1619–1864*. University Press of Virginia, Charlottesville.

———. 1996. *In Small Things Forgotten: Archaeology and Early American Life, Revised and Expanded Edition*. Anchor Books, New York.

Deetz, Patricia Scott, James F. Deetz, and Christopher Fennell. 1998. *The Plymouth Colony Archive Project*, available at http://www.histarch.uiuc.edu/plymouth/index.html. Last accessed November 14, 2008.

Derry, Linda, and Maureen Malloy. 2003. *Archaeologists and Local Communities: Partners in Exploring the Past*. Society for American Archaeology, Washington, D.C.

Destination 360. 2008. Las Vegas Strip Hotels. http://www.destination360.com/north-america/us/nevada/las-vegas/strip-hotels.php. Last accessed November 26, 2008.

Diamond, Stanley. 1974. *In Search of the Primitive: A Critique of Civilization*. Transaction Books, New Brunswick.

Dombrowski, Kirk. 2001. *Against Culture, Development, Politics, and Religion in Indian Alaska*. University of Nebraska Press, Lincoln.

Doss, Erika. 2002. "Death, Art and Memory in the Public Sphere: The Visual and Material Culture of Grief in Contemporary America." *Mortality* 7 (1): 63–82.

Douglass, Frederick. 1969. *My Bondage and My Freedom*. Dover Publications, Mineola.

Douglass, William A. 1998. "The Mining Camp as Community." In *Social Approaches to an Industrial Past*, A. Bernard Knapp, Vincent C. Piggot, and Eugenia W. Herbert, eds., pp. 97–108. Routledge, London.

Drake, James. 1999. *King Philip's War: Civil War in New England, 1675–76*. University of Massachusetts Press, Amherst.

Drinnon, Robert. 1980. *Facing West: The Metaphysics of Indian-Hating and Empire-Building*. University of Minnesota Press, Minneapolis.

DuBois, W.E.B. 1994 (1903). *The Souls of Black Folk*. Dover, Garden City, New York.

Dubosky, M. 1985. *Industrialism and the American Worker, 1865–1920, 2nd Ed*. Harlan Davidson, Arlington Heights.

Eagleton, Terry. 1991. *Ideology: An Introduction*. Verso, New York.

Edwards, Ywone. 1998. "'Trash' Revisited: A Comparative Approach to Historical Descriptions and Archaeological Analysis of Slave Houses and Yards." In *Keep Your Head to the Sky: Interpreting African American Home Ground*, Grey Gundaker, ed., pp. 245–72. University of Virginia Press, Charlottesville.

Emerson, Matthew. 1999. "African Inspirations in a New World Art and Artifact: Decorated Pipes from the Chesapeake." In *I, Too, Am America: Archaeological Studies of*

African-American Life, Theresa A. Singleton, ed., pp. 47–74. University of Virginia Press, Charlottesville.

Emmons, David M. 1994. "Constructed Province: History and the Making of the Last American West." *Western Historical Quarterly* 25 (4): 437–59.

Epperson, Terrence W. 1990. "Race and the Discipline of the Plantation." *Historical Archaeology* 24 (4): 29–36.

———. 1999. "Constructing Difference: The Social and Spatial Order of the Chesapeake Plantation." In *I, Too, Am America: Archaeological Studies of African-American Life*, Theresa A. Singleton, ed., pp. 159–72. University Press of Virginia, Charlottesville.

———. 1999. "The Contested Commons: Archaeologies of Race, Repression and Resistance in New York City." In *Historical Archaeologies of Capitalism*, Mark P. Leone and Parker B. Potter, eds., pp. 81–110. Kluwer Academic/Plenum Press, New York.

———. 2001. "'A Separate House for the Christians Slaves, One for the Negro Slaves': The Archaeology of Race and Identity in Late 17th-Century Virginia." In *Race and the Archaeology of Identity*, Charles E. Orser Jr., ed., pp. 54–70. University of Utah Press, Salt Lake City.

———. 2004. "Critical Race Theory and the Archaeology of the African Diaspora." *Historical Archaeology* 38 (1): 101–108.

Fagan, Brian. 2005. *A Brief History of Archaeology: Classical Times to the Twenty-First Century*. Pearson Prentice-Hall, Upper Saddle River.

Falk, Lisa, ed. 1991. *Historical Archaeology in Global Perspective*. Smithsonian Institution Press, Washington, D.C.

Feder, Kenneth L. 2007. *Frauds, Myths, and Mysteries: Science and Pseudoscience in Archaeology, 6th Edition*. McGraw-Hill Higher Education, New York.

Fennel, Christopher C. 2007. *Crossroads and Cosmologies: Diasporas and Ethnogenesis in the New World*. University Press of Florida, Gainesville.

Ferguson, Leland. 1980. "Looking for the Afro in Colono-Indian Pottery." In *Archaeological Perspectives on Ethnicity in America*, Robert Schuyler, ed., pp. 14–28. Baywood Publishing, Farmingdale, New York.

———. 1992. *Uncommon Ground: Archaeology and Early African America, 1650–1800*. Smithsonian Institution Press, Washington, D.C.

———. 1999. "'The Cross Is a Magic Sign': Marks on Eighteenth-Century Bowls from South Carolina. In *I, Too, Am America: Archaeological Studies of African-American Life*, Theresa A. Singleton, ed., pp. 116–31. University Press of Virginia, Charlottesville.

Fields, Barbara J. 1990. "Slavery and Ideology in the United States of America." *New Left Review* 181: 95–118.

Fitts, Robert K. 1999. "The Archaeology of Middle-Class Domesticity and Gentility in Victorian Brooklyn." *Historical Archaeology* 33 (1): 39–62.

———. 2001. "The Rhetoric of Reform: The Five Points Missions and the Cult of Domesticity." *Historical Archaeology* 35(3): 115–32.

Ford, Richard Thomas. 2008. *The Race Card: How Bluffing About Bias Makes Race Relations Worse*. Farrar, Strauss, and Giroux, New York.

Foucault, Michel. 1977. *Discipline and Punish: The Birth of the Prison.* Pantheon Books, New York.
Frank, Andre G. 1978. *Dependent Accumulation and Underdevelopment.* MacMillan, New York.
Franklin, Maria. 2001. "A Black Feminist Inspired Archaeology?" *Journal of Social Archaeology* 1: 108–25.
Franklin, Maria, and Larry McKee, eds. 2004. "Transcending Boundaries, Transforming the Discipline: African Diaspora Archaeologies in the New Millennium." Special issue of *Historical Archaeology* 38 (1).
Frederickson, George M. 1987. *The Black Image in the White Mind: The Debate on Afro-American Character and Destiny, 1817–1914.* Wesleyan Press, New York.
French, David, and Elena French. 1975. *Working Communally: Patterns and Possibilities.* Russell Sage Foundation, New York.
Fried, Morton H. 1975. *The Notion of the Tribe.* Cummings Publications, Menlo Park.
Gaffney, Elizabeth. 2006. *Metropolis: A Novel.* Random House, New York.
Gardener, J. S. 1992. *The Company Town: Architecture and Society in the Early Industrial Age.* Oxford University Press, New York.
Garman, James C. 2005. *Detention Castles of Stone and Steel: Landscape, Labor and the Urban Penitentiary.* University of Tennessee Press, Knoxville.
Geertz, Clifford. 1973. *The Interpretation of Cultures: Selected Essays.* Basic Books, New York.
Geismar, Joan H. 1982. *The Archaeology of Social Disintegration in Skunk Hollow: A Nineteenth-Century Rural Black Community.* Academic Press, New York.
Gillespie, William B., and Mary M. Farrell. 2002. "Work Camp Settlement Patterns: Landscape-Scale Comparisons of Two Mining Camps in Southeastern Arizona." *Historical Archaeology* 36 (3): 59–68.
Ginsberg, Elaine K., ed. 1996. *Passing and the Fictions of Identity.* Duke University Press, Durham, North Carolina.
Glassie, Henry. 1975. *Folk Housing in Middle Virginia: A Structural Analysis of Historical Artifacts.* University of Tennessee Press, Knoxville.
Goddard, Richard A. 2002. "Nothing but Tar Paper Shacks." *Historical Archaeology* 36 (3): 85–93.
González-Ruibal, Alfredo. 2008. "Time to Destroy: An Archaeology of Supermodernity." *Current Anthropology* 49 (2): 247–79.
Goode, Judith, and Jeff Maskovsky, eds. 2001. *The New Poverty Studies: The Ethnography of Power, Politics, and Impoverished People in the United States.* New York University Press, New York.
Gowans, Alan. 1964. *Images of American Living.* J. B. Lippencott, Philadelphia.
Gramsci, Antonio. 1971. *Selections from the Prison Notebooks.* Q. Hoare and G. N. Smith, eds. and trans. International Publishers, New York.
Griggs, Heather J. 1999. "GO gCUIRE DIA RATH BLATH ORT (God Grant That You Prosper and Flourish): Social and Economic Mobility among the Irish in 19th Century New York City." *Historical Archaeology* 33 (1): 81–101.

———. 2001. "'By Virtue of Reason and Nature': Competition and Economic Scaling in the Needletrades at New York's Five Points, 1855–1880." *Historical Archaeology* 35 (3): 76–88.

Grumet, Robert S. 1995. *Historic Contact: Indian People and Colonists in Today's Northeastern United States in the Sixteenth through Eighteenth Centuries.* University of Oklahoma Press, Norman.

Grusky, David B., and Ravi Kanbur, eds. 2006. *Poverty and Inequality.* Stanford University Press, Stanford.

Guglielmo, Thomas C. 2003. *White On Arrival: Italians, Race, Color, and Power in Chicago, 1895–1945.* Oxford University Press, New York.

Guldenzopf, David. 1986. *The Colonial Transformation of Mohawk Iroquois Society.* PhD Dissertation, State University of New York-Albany. University Microfilms Inc., Ann Arbor, Michigan.

Gundaker, Grey, ed. 1998. *Keep Your Head to the Sky: Interpreting African American Home Ground.* University of Virginia Press, Charlottesville.

———. 1998. *Signs of Diaspora/Diaspora of Signs: Literacies, Creolization, and Vernacular Practice in African America.* Oxford University Press, New York.

Hall, Martin. 2005. "The Industrial Archaeology of Entertainment." In *Industrial Archaeology: Future Directions*, Eleanor Conlin Casella and James Symonds, eds., pp. 261–78. Springer Press, New York.

Hall, Martin, and Pia Bombardella. 2005. "Las Vegas in Africa." *Journal of Social Archaeology* 5 (1): 5–24.

Hamilakis, Yannis. 2007. "Introduction: From Ethics to Politics." In *Archaeology and Capitalism: From Ethics to Politics*, Yannis Hamilakis and Philip Duke, eds., pp. 15–40. Left Coast Press, Walnut Creek.

Hamilakis, Yannis, and Philip Duke, eds. 2007. *Archaeology and Capitalism: From Ethics to Politics.* Left Coast Press, Walnut Creek.

Handler, Richard, ed. 2000. *Excluded Ancestors, Inventible Traditions: Essays Toward a More Inclusive History of Anthropology.* University of Wisconsin Press, Madison.

Handsman, Russell G. 1981. "Early Capitalism and the Center Village of Canaan, Connecticut: A Study in Transformations and Separation." *Artifacts* 9 (3): 1–22.

———. 1983. "Historical Archaeology and Capitalism, Subscriptions and Separations: The Production of Individualism." *North American Archaeologist* 4 (1): 63–79.

Handsman, Russell G., and Mark P. Leone. 1989. "Living History and Critical Archaeology in the Reconstruction of the Past." In *Critical Traditions in Contemporary Archaeology*, Valerie Pinsky and Allison Wylie, eds., pp. 117–35. Cambridge University Press, Cambridge.

Hardesty, Donald. 1998. "Power and the Industrial Mining Community in the American West." In *Social Approaches to an Industrial Past*, A. Bernard Knapp, Vincent C. Piggot, and Eugenia W. Herbert, eds., pp. 81–96. Routledge, London.

Hawes, James. 2000. *Dead Long Enough.* Random House, New York.

Hayden, Delores. 1976. *Seven American Utopias: The Architecture of Communitarian Socialism, 1790–1975.* MIT Press, Cambridge.

Hobbes, Thomas. 1996. *Leviathan*. Cambridge University Press, Cambridge.

Hodder, Ian. 1986. *Reading the Past: Current Approaches to Interpretation in Archaeology*. Cambridge University Press, New York.

Holland, Dorothy, William Lachicotte, Debra Skinner, and Carole Cain. 1998. *Identity and Agency in Cultural Worlds*. Harvard University Press, Cambridge.

Holloway, Joseph E., ed. 1990. *Africanisms in American Culture*. Indiana University Press, Bloomington.

Holloway, Mark. 1966. *Heavens on Earth: Utopian Communities in America, 1680–1880*, 2nd Edition. Dover Publications, New York.

Holt, Thomas C. 2000. *The Problem of Race in the Twenty-First Century*. Harvard University Press, Cambridge.

Holtorf, Cornelius. 2005. *From Stonehenge to Las Vegas: Archaeology as Popular Culture*. AltaMira Press, Walnut Creek.

———. 2007. *Archaeology Is a Brand: The Meaning of Archaeology in Contemporary Popular Culture*. Left Coast Press, Walnut Creek.

Horkheimer, Max, and Theodor W. Adorno. 2002. *Dialectic of Enlightenment: Philosophical Fragments*, Gunzelin Schmid Noerr, ed., Edmund Jephcott, trans. Stanford University Press, Stanford.

Howson, Jean E. 1990. "Social Relations and Material Culture: A Critique of the Archaeology of Plantation Slavery." *Historical Archaeology* 24 (4): 78–91.

Hyde, Lewis. 1983. *The Gift: Imagination and the Erotic Life of Property*. Vintage Books, New York.

Ignatiev, Noel. 1995. *How the Irish Became White*. Routledge, New York.

Isaac, Rhys. 1982. *The Transformation of Virginia, 1740–1790*. W. W. Norton & Company, New York.

Jacobsen, Matthew Frye. 1998. *Whiteness of a Different Color: European Immigrants and the Alchemy of Race*. Harvard University Press, Cambridge.

———. 2006. *Roots Too: White Ethnic Revival in Post-Civil Rights America*. Harvard University Press, Cambridge.

Johnson, Matthew. 1996. *An Archaeology of Capitalism*. Blackwell Publishers, Oxford.

Jones, Lynn D. 2000. *Archaeological Investigation at Slayton House, 18AP74, Annapolis, Maryland*. Report on file, Historic Annapolis Foundation and University of Maryland, College Park.

Jones, Sian. 1997. *Archaeology and Ethnicity: Constructing Identities in the Past and Present*. Routledge, London.

Jordan, David W. 1979. "Political Stability and the Emergence of a Native Elite in Maryland." In *The Chesapeake in the Seventeenth Century: Essays in Anglo-American Society*, Thad W. Tate and David L. Ammerman, eds., pp. 243–73. University of North Carolina Press, Chapel Hill.

Jordan, Kurt A. 2009. "Regional Diversity and Colonialism in Eighteenth Century Iroquoia." In *Iroquoian Archaeology and Analytic Scale*, Laurie E. Miroff and Timothy D. Knapp, eds. University of Tennessee Press, Knoxville.

Jordan, Winthrop. 1968. *White Over Black: American Attitudes Toward the Negro, 1550–1812*. University of North Carolina Press, Chapel Hill.

Kasson, John. 1990. *Rudeness and Civilization: Manners in Nineteenth-Century Urban America*. Hill and Wang, New York.

Katz, Michael B. 1990. *The Undeserving Poor: From the War on Poverty to the War on Welfare*. Pantheon Books, New York.

Kehoe, Alice Beck. 1998. *The Land of Prehistory: A Critical History of American Archaeology*. Routledge, New York.

Killion, Thomas W., ed. 2007. *Opening Archaeology: Repatriation's Impact on Contemporary Research and Practice*. SAR Press, Santa Fe.

Klein, Kerwin. 2000. "On the Emergence of Memory in Historical Discourse." *Representations* 69: 127–50.

Kulikoff, Allan. 1986. *Tobacco and Slaves: The Development of the Southern Cultures in the Chesapeake, 1680–1800*. University of North Carolina Press, Chapel Hill.

———. 1989. "The Transition to Capitalism in Rural America." *William and Mary Quarterly, 3rd Series*, 46 (1): 120–44.

Langley, Batty. 1726. *New Principles of Gardening*. A. Bettesworth and J. Bately, London.

LaRoche, Cheryl J. 2004. *On the Edge of Freedom: Free Black Communities, Archaeology, and the Underground Railroad*. PhD Dissertation, University of Maryland, College Park. University Microfilms Inc., Ann Arbor, Michigan.

LaRoche, Cheryl J., and Michael L. Blakey. 1997. "Seizing Intellectual Power: The Dialogue at the New York African Burial Ground." *Historical Archaeology* 31 (3): 84–106.

Latour, Bruno. 1993. *We Have Never Been Modern*. Harvard University Press, Cambridge.

LeFebvre, Henri. 1991. *Critique of Everyday Life*. Verso, London.

Leone, Mark P. 1984. "Interpreting Ideology in Historical Archaeology: Using the Rules of Perspective in the William Paca Garden in Annapolis, Maryland." In *Ideology, Power, and Prehistory*, Daniel Miller and Christopher Tilley, eds., pp. 25–35. Cambridge University Press, Cambridge.

———. 1988. "The Georgian Order as the Order of Merchant Capitalism." In *The Recovery of Meaning: Historical Archaeology in the Eastern United States*, Mark P. Leone and Parker B. Potter Jr., eds., pp. 235–61. Smithsonian Institution Press, Washington, D.C.

———. 1995. "A Historical Archaeology of Capitalism." *American Anthropologist* 97 (2): 251–68.

———. 1999. "Ceramics from Annapolis, Maryland: A Measure of Time Routines and Work Disciplines." In *Historical Archaeologies of Capitalism*, Mark P. Leone and Parker B. Potter Jr., eds., pp. 195–216. Kluwer Academic/Plenum Press, New York.

———. 2005. *The Archaeology of Liberty in an American Capital: Excavations in Annapolis*. University of California Press, Berkeley.

Leone, Mark P., and Gladys-Marie Fry. 1999. "Conjuring in the Big House Kitchen: An Interpretation of African American Belief Systems Based on the Uses of Archaeology and Folklore Sources." *Journal of American Folklore* 112 (445): 372–403.

Leone, Mark P., Cheryl Janifer LaRoche, and Jennifer Barbiarz. 2005. "The Archaeology of Black Americans in Recent Times." *Annual Review of Anthropology* 34: 575–98.

Leone, Mark P., and Parker B. Potter Jr. 1988. "Issues in Historical Archaeology." In *The

Recovery of Meaning: Historical Archaeology in the Eastern United States, Mark P. Leone and Parker B. Potter Jr., eds., pp. 1–22. Smithsonian Institution Press, Washington, D.C.

Leone, Mark P., Parker B. Potter Jr., and Paul A. Shackle. 1987. "Towards a Critical Archaeology." *Current Anthropology* 28 (3): 283–302.

Leone, Mark P., and Paul A. Shackel. 1987. "Forks, Clocks, and Power." In *Mirror and Metaphor*, Daniel Ingersoll and Gordon Brontisky, eds., pp. 45–61. University Press of America, Lanham.

——. 1990. "Plane and Solid Geometry in Colonial Gardens in Annapolis, Maryland." In *Earth Patterns: Essays in Landscape Archaeology*, William Kelso and Rachel Most, eds., pp. 153–67. University of Virginia Press, Charlottesville.

Leone, Mark P., Paul R. Mullins, Marion C. Creveling, L. Hurst, Barbara Jackson-Nash, Lynn D. Jones, Hannah J. Kaiser, George C. Logan, and Mark S. Warner. 1995. "Can an African-American Historical Archaeology Be an Alternative Voice?" In *Interpreting Archaeology: Finding Meaning in the Past*, Ian Hodder, Alexandra Alexandri, Victor Buchli, John Carman, J. Last, and Gavin Lucas, eds., pp. 110–24. Routledge, New York.

Levine, Lawrence W. 1988. *Highbrow Lowbrow: The Emergence of Cultural Hierarchy in America*. Harvard University Press, Cambridge.

Little, Barbara J., and Paul A. Shackel, eds. 2007. *Archaeology as a Tool of Civic Engagement*. AltaMira, Walnut Creek.

Logan, George C., Marion Creveling, Lynn D. Jones, and Thomas Bodor. 1992. *1991 Archaeological Excavations at the Charles Carroll House in Annapolis, Maryland, 18 AP 45*. Report on file, Historic Annapolis Foundation and University of Maryland, College Park.

Loren, Diana diPaolo. 2001. "Social Skins: Orthodoxies and Practices of Dressing in the Early Colonial Lower Mississippi Valley." *Journal of Social Archaeology* 1 (2): 172–89.

MacCannell, Dean. 1992. *Empty Meeting Grounds: The Tourist Papers*. Routledge, New York.

Mack, Mark E., and Michael L. Blakey. 2004. "The New York African Burial Ground Project: Past Biases, Current Dilemmas, and Future Research Opportunities." *Historical Archaeology* 38 (1): 10–17.

MacPherson, Crawford Brough. 1962. *The Political Theory of Possessive Individualism: Hobbes to Locke*. Clarendon Books, Oxford.

Maniery, Mary L. 2002. "Health, Sanitation, and Diet in a Twentieth-Century Dam Construction Camp: A View from Butt Valley, California." *Historical Archaeology* 36 (3): 69–84.

Marcus, George E. 1998. *Ethnography through Thick and Thin*. Princeton University Press, Princeton.

Marx, Karl. 1865. *Value, Price, and Profit*. Speech by Marx to the First International Working Men's Association, June 1865. http://www.marx.org/archive/marx/works/1865/value-price-profit/index.htm. Last accessed December 5, 2008.

——. 1964. *The Eighteenth Brumaire of Louis Bonaparte*. International Publishers, New York.

———. 1967. *Capital: A Critique of Political Economy.* International Publishers, New York.

———. 1973. *Grundrisse. Foundations of the Critique of Political Economy.* Vintage, New York.

Marx, Karl, and Frederich Engels. 1967a. *The Communist Manifesto.* Pantheon, New York.

———. 1967b. *The German Ideology.* International Publishers, New York.

Matthews, Christopher N. 1998. *Annapolis and the Making of the Modern Landscape: An Archaeology of History and Tradition.* PhD Dissertation, Department of Anthropology, Columbia University. University Microfilms Inc., Ann Arbor, Michigan.

———. 1998. "Part of a 'Polished Society': Style and Ideology in Annapolis's Georgian Architecture." In *Annapolis Pasts: Historical Archaeology in Annapolis, Maryland,* Paul A. Shackel, Paul R. Mullins, and Mark S. Warner, eds., pp. 244–67. University of Tennessee Press, Knoxville.

———. 2001. "Political Economy and Race: Comparative Archaeologies of Annapolis and New Orleans in the 18th Century." In *Race and the Archaeology of Identity,* Charles E. Orser Jr., ed., pp. 71–87. University of Utah Press, Salt Lake City.

———. 2002. *An Archaeology of History and Tradition: Moments of Danger in the Annapolis Landscape.* Kluwer Academic/Plenum Publishers, New York.

———. 2005. "Public Dialectics: Marxist Reflection in Archaeology." *Historical Archaeology* 39 (4): 18–36.

———. 2008. "The Location of Archaeology." In *Ethnographic Archaeologies: Reflections on Stakeholders and Archaeological Practices,* Quetzil E. Castañeda and Christopher N. Matthews, eds., pp. 157–82. AltaMira Press, Walnut Creek.

Matthews, Christopher N., Mark P. Leone, and Kurt A. Jordan. 2002. "The Political Economy of Archaeological Cultures: Marxism and American Historical Archaeology." *Journal of Social Archaeology* 2 (1): 109–34.

Mauss, Marcel. 2002. *The Gift: The Form and Reason of Exchange in Archaic Societies.* Routledge, London.

Mayne, Alan, and Tim Murray. 2001. "The Archaeology of Urban Landscapes: Explorations in Slumland." In *The Archaeology of Urban Landscapes: Explorations in Slumland,* Alan Mayne and Tim Murray, eds., pp. 1–10. Cambridge University Press, Cambridge.

McAtackney, Laura, Matthew Palus, and Angela Piccini, eds. 2007. *Contemporary and Historical Archaeology In Theory: Papers from the 2003 and 2004 CHAT Conferences.* Archaeopress, Oxford.

McBride, Kim A. 2005. "Lessons from Two Shaker Smoking Pipe Fragments." Contribution to *Unlocking the Past,* http://www.sha.org/unlockingthepast/sidebars/sidebar13.htm. Last accessed November 24, 2008.

McCracken, Grant D. 1990. *Culture and Consumption: New Approaches to the Symbolic Character of Consumer Goods and Activities.* Indiana University Press, Bloomington.

McDavid, Carol. 1997. "Descendants, Decisions, and Power: The Public Interpretation of the Archaeology of the Levi Jordan Plantation." *Historical Archaeology* 31 (3): 114–31.

———. 2008. "Archaeologies That Hurt; Descendents That Matter: A Pragmatic Approach to Collaboration in the Public Interpretation of African-American Heritage." In *The Heritage Reader*, Graham Fairclough, Rodney Harrison, John H. Jameson Jr., and John Schofield, eds., pp. 514–24. Routledge, London.

McDonald, J. Douglas, Larry J. Zimmerman, A. L. McDonald, William Tall Bull, and Ted Rising Sun. 1991. "The Northern Cheyenne Outbreak of 1879: Using Oral History and Archaeology as Tools of Resistance." In *The Archaeology of Inequality*, Randall H. McGuire and Robert Paynter, eds., pp. 64–78. Blackwell, New York.

McGill Ghost Town. 2008. *McGill Ghost Town Web site*. http://www.ghosttowns.com/states/nv/mcgill.html. Last accessed November 24, 2008.

McGuire, Randall H. 1992. *A Marxist Archaeology*. University of Arizona Press, Tucson.

———. 2008. *Archaeology as Political Action*. University of California Press, Berkeley.

McGuire, Randall H., and Paul A. Reckner. 2002. "The Unromantic West: Labor, Capital, Struggle." *Historical Archaeology* 36 (3): 44–58.

McKee, Larry. 1992. "The Ideals and Realities behind the Design and Use of 19th-Century Virginia Slave Cabins." In *The Art and Mystery of Historical Archaeology: Essays in Honor of James Deetz*, Anne E. Yentsch and Mary C. Beaudry, eds., pp. 195–213. CRC Press, Boca Raton.

Melosi, Martin V. 2000. *The Sanitary City: Urban Infrastructure in America from Colonial Times to the Present*. Johns Hopkins University Press, Baltimore.

Miller, Christopher L., and George R. Hamell. 1986. "A New Perspective on Indian-White Contact: Cultural Symbols and Colonial Trade." *Journal of American History* 73 (2): 311–28.

Miller, Daniel. 1987. *Material Culture and Mass Consumption*. Blackwell, New York.

Miller, George. 1991. "A Revised Set of Index Values for Classification and Economic Scaling of English Ceramics from 1878 to 1880." *Historical Archaeology* 25: 1–25.

Mintz, Sydney W., and Richard Price. 1992. *The Birth of African-American Culture: An Anthropological Perspective*. Beacon Press, Boston.

Morgan, Edmund S. 1975. *American Slavery, American Freedom: The Ordeal of Colonial Virginia*. W. W. Norton & Company, New York.

Morton, J. C. 1964. *Stephen Bordley of Colonial Annapolis*. PhD Dissertation, University of Maryland, College Park. University Microfilms Inc., Ann Arbor, Michigan.

Mouer, L. Daniel, Mary Ellen N. Hodges, Stephen R. Potter, Susan L. Henry Reaud, Ivor Noel Hume, Dennis J. Pogue, Martha W. McCartney, and Thomas E. Davidson. 1999. "Colonoware Pottery, Chesapeake Pipes, and 'Uncritical Assumptions.'" In *I, Too, Am America: Archaeological Studies of African-American Life*, Theresa A. Singleton, ed., pp. 83–115. Charlottesville: University Press of Virginia.

Mrozowski, Stephen A. 2006. *The Archaeology of Class in Urban America*. Cambridge University Press, Cambridge.

———. 2007. "The Possession and Dispossession of Responsibility: Lessons from Lowell's Industrial History." Paper presented at the 2007 Annual Meetings of the American Anthropological Association, Washington, D.C.

Mrozowski, Stephen A., Grace H. Ziesing, and Mary C. Beaudry. 1996. *Living on the Boott: Historical Archaeology at the Boott Mills Boardinghouses, Lowell, Massachusetts.* University of Massachusetts Press, Amherst.

Mullins, Paul R. 1999. *Race and Affluence: An Archaeology of African America and Consumer Culture.* Plenum Press, New York.

———. 2008. "Excavating America's Metaphor: Race, Diaspora, and Vindicationist Archaeologies." *Historical Archaeology* 42 (2): 104–22.

Nassaney, Michael S. 1989. "An Epistemological Enquiry into Some Archaeological and Historical Interpretations of 17th Century Native American-European Relations." In *Archaeological Approaches to Cultural Identity*, Stephen J. Shennan, ed., pp. 76–93. Unwin Hyman, London.

———, ed. 2000. *Interpretations of Native North American Life: Material Contributions to Ethnohistory.* University Press of Florida, Gainesville.

Nassaney, Michael S., and Marjorie R. Abel. 1993. "The Political and Social Contexts of Cutlery Production in the Connecticut Valley." *Dialectical Anthropology* 18: 247–89.

———. 2000. "Urban Spaces, Labor Organization, and Social Control: Lessons from New England's Nineteenth-Century Cutlery Industry." In *Lines That Divide: Historical Archaeologies of Race, Class, and Gender*, James A. Delle, Stephen A. Mrozowski, and Robert Paynter, eds., pp. 239–75. University of Tennessee Press, Knoxville.

Newton, Isaac. 1999. *The Principia: Mathematical Principles of Natural Philosophy.* I. Bernard Cohen, Anne Whitman, and Julia Budenz, trans. University of California Press, Berkeley.

Noel-Hume, Ivor. 1962. "An Indian Ware of the Colonial Period." *Quarterly Bulletin of the Archaeological Society of Virginia* 17 (1): 2–12.

Norris, Walter B. 1925. *Annapolis, Its Colonial and Naval Story.* Thomas Y. Crowell Company, New York.

O'Neale, Sondra A. 1993. *Jupiter Hammon and the Biblical Beginnings of African-American Literature.* The American Theological Library and The Scarecrow Press, Inc., Metuchen, New Jersey.

Only Vegas. 2008. *Official Las Vegas Tourism Web Site.* http://www.visitlasvegas.com/vegas/index.jsp. Last accessed November 26, 2008.

Orser, Charles E., Jr. 1994. "The Archaeology of Slave Religion." *Archaeological Review from Cambridge* 4 (1): 33–45.

———. 1996. *A Historical Archaeology of the Modern World.* Plenum Publishers, New York.

———. 1998. "The Archaeology of African Diaspora." *Annual Review of Anthropology* 27: 63–82.

———. 2007. *The Archaeology of Race and Racialization in Historic America.* University Press of Florida, Gainesville.

Parmenter, Jon William. 1999. *At the Wood's Edge: Iroquois Foreign Relations, 1727–1768.* PhD dissertation, University of Michigan, Ann Arbor. University Microfilms Inc., Ann Arbor, Michigan.

Patterson, Orlando. 1982. *Slavery and Social Death: A Comparative Study.* Harvard University Press, Cambridge.

Patterson, Thomas C. 1995. *Towards a Social History of Archaeology in the United States.* Harcourt Brace, Fort Worth.

———. 1997. *Inventing Western Civilization.* Monthly Review Press, New York.

Pauketat, Timothy R., ed. 2001. *The Archaeology of Traditions: Agency and History Before and After Columbus.* University Press of Florida, Gainesville.

Paynter, Robert. 1982. *Models of Spatial Inequality: Settlement Patterns in Historical Archaeology.* Academic Press, New York.

———. 1988. "Steps to an Archaeology of Capitalism: Material Change and Class Analysis." In *The Recovery of Meaning: Historical Archaeology in the Eastern United States,* Mark P. Leone and Parker B. Potter Jr., eds., pp. 407–33. Smithsonian Institution Press, Washington, D.C.

Perry, Warren, and Michael L. Blakey. 1997. "Archaeology as Community Service: The African Burial Ground Project in New York City." *North American Dialogue* 2 (1): 1–5.

Perry, Warren, and Robert Paynter. 1999. "Artifacts, Ethnicity and the Archaeology of African Americans." In *I, Too, Am America: Archaeological Studies of African-American Life,* Theresa A. Singleton, ed., pp. 299–310. University Press of Virginia, Charlottesville.

Perry, Warren R., Jean Howson, and Barbara A. Bianco, eds. 2006. *New York African Burial Ground Archaeology Final Report, Volume 1.* Prepared by Howard University for the United States General Services Administration, New York.

Pinksy, Valerie, and Allison Wylie, eds. 1989. *Critical Traditions in Contemporary Archaeology.* Cambridge University Press, Cambridge.

Pitts, Reginald H. 2001. "'Suckers, Soap-Locks, Irishmen, and Plug-Uglies': Block 160, Municipal Politics, and Local Control." *Historical Archaeology* 35 (3): 89–102.

Powell, Eric. 2000. "Shakers Behaving Badly." *Discover* 21 (5): 20–24.

Purser, Margaret. 1991. "'Several Paradise Ladies Are Coming to Town': Gender Strategies in the Early Industrial West." *Historical Archaeology* 25 (4): 6–16.

———. 1999. "Ex Occident Lux? An Archaeology of Later Capitalism in the Nineteenth-Century West." In *Historical Archaeologies of Capitalism,* Mark P. Leone and Parker B. Potter Jr., eds., pp. 115–41. Kluwer Academic/Plenum Press, New York.

Raboteau, Albert J. 1995. *A Fire in the Bones: Reflections on African American Religious History.* Beacon Press, Boston.

Randall, T. Henry. 1892. "Colonial Annapolis." *The Architectural Record* 1 (3): 309–44.

Ransom, Stanley A., ed. 1970. *America's First Negro Poet: The Complete Works of Jupiter Hammon of Long Island.* Kennikat Press, Port Washington.

Rawls, John. 1971. *A Theory of Justice.* Harvard University Press, Cambridge.

Rebovich, Samantha. 2007. "Mythological Pasts in an Archaeological Present: The Dig at Atlantis." Paper presented at the 2007 Annual Meetings of the Society for Historical Archaeology, Williamsburg, Virginia.

Reckner, Paul E. 2001. "Negotiating Patriotism at the Five Points: Clay Tobacco Pipes and Patriotic Imagery among Trade Unionists and Nativists in a 19th-Century New York Neighborhood." *Historical Archaeology* 35 (3):103–14.

Reckner, Paul E., and Stephen A. Brighton. 1999. "'Free From All Vicious Habits': Archaeological Perspectives on Class Conflict and the Rhetoric of Temperance." *Historical Archaeology* 33 (1): 63–86.

Robinson, Paul A. 1990. *The Struggle Within: The Indian Debate in Seventeenth-Century Narragansett Country*. PhD Dissertation, State University of New York-Binghamton. University Microfilms Inc., Ann Arbor, Michigan.

Robinson, Paul A., M. A. Kelly, and Patricia E. Rubertone. 1985. "Preliminary Biocultural Interpretations from a Seventeenth-Century Narragansett Indian Cemetery." In *Cultures in Contact: The Impact of European Contacts on Native American Cultural Institutions, A.D. 1000–1800*, William W. Fitzhugh, ed., pp. 107–30. Smithsonian Institution Press, Washington, D.C.

Roediger, David R. 1991. *The Wages of Whiteness: Race and the Making of the American Working Class*. Verso, New York.

———. 2005. *Working Towards Whiteness, How America's Immigrants Became White: The Strange Journey from Ellis Island to the Suburbs*. Basic Books, New York.

Roseberry, William. 1989. *Anthropologies and Histories: Essays in Culture, History, and Political Economy*. Rutgers University Press, New Brunswick.

Rosenberg, Carroll Smith. 1971. *Religion and the Rise of the American City: The New York Mission Movement, 1812–1830*. Cornell University Press, Ithaca.

Rosenzweig, Roy, and Elizabeth Blackmar. 1992. *The Park and the People: A History of Central Park*. Cornell University Press, Ithaca.

Rubertone, Patricia E. 1989. "Archaeology, Colonialism and Seventeenth-Century Native America: Towards an Alternative Interpretation." In *Conflict in the Archaeology of Living Traditions*, Robert Layton, ed., pp. 32–45. Routledge, London.

———. 1994. "Grave Remembrances: Enduring Traditions Among the Narragansett." *Connecticut History* 35 (1): 22–45.

———. 2001. *Grave Undertakings: An Archaeology of Roger Williams and the Narragansett Indians*. Smithsonian Institution Press, Washington, D.C.

Russell, Aaron E. 1997. "Material Culture and African–American Spirituality at the Hermitage." *Historical Archaeology* 31 (2): 63–80.

Saitta, Dean J. 2007. *The Archaeology of Collective Action*. University Press of Florida, Gainesville.

Samford, Patricia M. 2007. *Subfloor Pits and the Archaeology of Slavery in Colonial Virginia*. University of Alabama Press, Tuscaloosa.

Sayer, Derek. 1987. *The Violence Of Abstraction: The Analytic Foundations Of Historical Materialism*. Blackwell, New York.

———. 1991. *Capitalism and Modernity: An Excursus on Marx and Weber*. Routledge, New York.

Schmidt, Peter R., and Thomas C. Patterson, eds. 1995. *Making Alternative Histories: The Practice of Archaeology and History in Non-Western Settings*. SAR Press, Santa Fe.

Scott, James. 1990. *Domination and the Arts of Resistance: Hidden Transcripts*. Yale University Press, New Haven.

Shackel, Paul A. 1993. *Personal Discipline and Material Culture: An Archaeology of Annapolis, Maryland, 1695–1870*. University of Tennessee Press, Knoxville.

———. 1994. "Town Plans and Material Culture: An Archaeology of Social Relations in Colonial Maryland's Capital Cities." In *Historical Archaeology of the Chesapeake*, Paul A. Shackel and Barbara J. Little, eds., pp. 85–96. Smithsonian Institution Press, Washington, D.C.

———. 1998. "Maintenance Relations in Early Colonial Annapolis." In *Annapolis Pasts: Historical Archaeology in Annapolis, Maryland*, Paul A. Shackel, Paul R. Mullins, and Mark S. Warner, eds., pp. 97–118. University of Tennessee Press, Knoxville.

———. 2000. *Archaeology and Created Memory: Public History in a National Park*. Kluwer Academic/Plenum Press, New York.

———. 2003. *Memory in Black and White: Race, Commemoration and the Post-Bellum Landscape*. AltaMira Press, Walnut Creek.

Shanks, Michael. 1996. *Classical Archaeology of Greece: Experiences of the Discipline*. Routledge, London.

Shanks, Michael, and Christopher Tilley. 1987. *Re-Constructing Archaeology: Theory and Practice*. Routledge, London.

Shepard, Nick. 2007. "What Does It Mean 'To Give the Past Back to the People'? Archaeology and Ethics in the Postcolony." In *Archaeology and Capitalism: From Ethics to Politics*, Yannis Hamilakis and Philip Duke, eds., pp. 99–114. Left Coast Press, Walnut Creek.

Sider, Gerald M. 1987. "When Parrots Learn to Talk, and Why They Can't: Domination, Deception, and Self-Deception in Indian-White Relations." *Comparative Studies in Society and History* 29: 3–23.

———. 1994. "Identity as History: Ethnohistory, Ethnogenesis, and Ethnocide in the Southeastern United States." *Identities* 1 (1): 109–22.

Sider, Gerald M., and Gavin Smith, eds. 1997. *Between History and Histories: The Making of Silences and Commemorations*. University of Toronto Press, Toronto.

Simmel, Georg. 1969. "The Metropolis and Mental Life." In *Classic Essays in the Culture of Cities*, Richard Sennett, ed. Appleton-Century-Crofts, New York.

Simmons, Alexy. 1998. "Bedroom Politics: Ladies of the Night and Men of the Day." In *Social Approaches to an Industrial Past*, A. Bernard Knapp, Vincent C. Piggot, and Eugenia W. Herbert, eds., pp. 59–80. Routledge, London.

Singleton, Theresa A. 1991. "The Archaeology of Slave Life." In *Before Freedom Came: African-American Life in the Antebellum South*, E. Campbell, III and K. S. Rice, eds., pp. 155–75. University of Virginia Press, Charlottesville.

———. 1995. "The Archaeology of Slavery in North America." *Annual Review of Anthropology* 24: 119-40.

Singleton, Theresa A., and Marc Bograd. 1995. *The Archaeology of the African Diaspora in the Americas. Guides to the Archaeological Literature of the Immigrant Experience in America, Vol. 2*. Society for Historical Archaeology.

Smith, Adam. 2003. *An Inquiry into the Causes of The Wealth of Nations*. Bantam Classic, New York.

Snow, Dean. 2006. *Indian Castle Catalog Guide*. New York State Museum, Albany.

Sobel, Mechel. 1987. *The World They Made Together: Black and White Values in Eighteenth-Century Virginia*. Princeton University Press, Princeton.

Spencer-Wood, Suzanne M. 1996. "Feminist Historical Archaeology and the Transformation of American Culture by Domestic Reform Movements, 1840–1924." In *Historical Archaeology and the Study of American Culture*, Lu Ann de Cunzo and Bernard L. Herman, eds., pp. 397–445. University of Tennessee Press, Knoxville.

———. 1999. "The World Their Household: Changing Meanings of the Domestic Sphere in the Nineteenth Century." In *The Archaeology of Household Activities: Gender Ideologies, Domestic Spaces and Material Culture*, Penelope M. Allison, ed., pp. 162–89. Routledge, London.

———. 2004. "A Historic Pay-for-Housework Community Household: The Cambridge Cooperative Housekeeping Society." In *Household Chores and Household Choices: Theorizing the Domestic Sphere in Historical Archaeology*, Kerri S. Barrile and Jamie C. Brandon, eds., pp. 138–58. University of Alabama Press, Tuscaloosa.

St. George, Robert Blair. 1983. "Maintenance Relationships and the Erotics of Property in Historical Thought." Paper presented at the American Historical Association Meetings, Philadelphia.

Stansell, Christine. 1987. *City of Women: Sex and Class in New York, 1789–1860*. University of Illinois Press, Urbana.

Starbuck, David R. 2004. *Neither Plain Nor Simple: New Perspective on the Canterbury Shakers*. University Press of New England, Hanover, New Hampshire.

———. 2005. "The Archaeology of Rural Industry." Contribution to *Unlocking the Past*, http://www.sha.org/unlockingthepast/archaeology_of_work/starbuck.htm. Last accessed November 24, 2008.

Stevens, William O. 1937. *Annapolis: Anne Arundel's Town*. Dodd, Mead, and Co., New York.

Stine, Linda F., Melanie A. Cabak, and Mark. D. Groover. 1996. "Blue Beads as African-American Cultural Symbol." *Historical Archaeology* 30 (3): 44–75.

Stocking, George W. 1992. *The Ethnographer's Magic and Other Essays in the History of Anthropology*. University of Wisconsin Press, Madison.

Strong, John A. 2001. *The Mountakett Indians of Eastern Long Island*. Syracuse University Press, Syracuse.

Symonds, James. 2005. "Experiencing Industry: Beyond Machines and the History of Technology." In *Industrial Archaeology: Future Directions*, Eleanor Conlin Casella and James Symonds, eds., pp. 33–57. Springer, New York.

Tarlow, Sarah. 2007. *The Archaeology of Improvement in Britain, 1750–1850*. Cambridge University Press, Cambridge.

Thomas, Peter. 1981. "The Fur Trade, Indian Land, and the Need to Define Adequate 'Environmental' Parameters." *Ethnohistory* 28 (4): 359–79.

———. 1985. "Cultural Change on the Southern New England Frontier, 1630–55." In *Cultures in Contact: The Impact of European Contacts on Native American Cultural Institutions, A.D. 1000–1800*, William W. Fitzhugh, ed., pp. 131–61. Smithsonian Institution Press, Washington, D.C.

Thompson, E. P. 1993. *Customs in Common*. Penguin, New York.

Thompson, Robert Farris. 1983. *Flash of the Spirit: African and Afro-American Art and Philosophy*. Random House, New York.

Trigger, Bruce G. 1989. *A History of Archaeological Thought*. Cambridge University Press, Cambridge.

Trouillot, Michel-Rolph. 1995. *Silencing the Past: Power and the Production of History*. Beacon, Boston.

Turnbaugh, William A. 1993. "Assessing the Significance of European Goods in Seventeenth-Century Narragansett Society." In *Ethnohistory and Archaeology: Approaches to Post Contact Change in the Americas*, J. Daniel Rogers and Samuel M. Wilson, eds., pp. 133–60. Plenum Press, New York.

Upton, Dell. 1988. "White and Black Landscapes in Eighteenth Century Virginia." In *Material Life in America, 1600–1860*, Robert B. St. George, ed., pp. 357–70. Northeastern University Press, Boston.

———. 1990. "Imagining the Early Virginia Landscape." In *Earth Patterns: Essays in Landscape Archaeology*, William M. Kelso and Rachel Most, eds., pp. 71–86. University Press of Virginia, Charlottesville.

———. 1997. *Holy Things and Profane: Anglican Parish Churches in Colonial Virginia*. Yale University Press, New Haven.

Van Bueren, Thad M. 2002. "Struggling with Class Relations at a Los Angeles Aqueduct Construction Camp." *Historical Archaeology* 36 (3): 28–43.

———, ed. 2006. "Daring Experiments: Issues and Insights about Utopian Communities." Special issue of *Historical Archaeology* 40 (1).

Voss, Barbara L. 2008. *The Archaeology of Ethnogenesis: Race and Sexuality in Colonial San Francisco*. University of California Press, Berkeley.

Wall, Diana diZerega. 1991. "Sacred Dinners and Secular Teas: Constructing Domesticity in mid-19th Century New York." *Historical Archaeology* 25 (4): 69–81.

———. 1994. *The Archaeology of Gender: Separating the Spheres in Early America*. Plenum Press, New York.

———. 1999. "Examining Gender, Class, and Ethnicity in 19th Century New York City." *Historical Archaeology* 33 (1): 102–17.

———. 2001. "Family Meals and Evening Parties: Constructing Domesticity in Nineteenth-Century Middle-Class New York." In *Lines that Divide: Historical Archaeologies of Race, Class, and Gender*, James A. Delle, Stephen A. Mrozwoski, and Robert Paynter, eds., pp. 109–41. University of Tennessee Press, Knoxville.

Wallerstein, Immanuel M. 1974. *The Modern World-System*. Academic Press, New York.

Walters, Ronald. 1978. *American Reformers, 1815–1860*. Hill and Wang, New York.

Warren, Mame. 1990. *Then Again . . . : Annapolis, 1900–1965*. Time Exposures Limited, Annapolis.

Watkins, Joe. 2000. *Indigenous Archaeology: American Indian Values and Scientific Practice*. AltaMira Press, Walnut Creek.

Weber, Max. 1969. "The Nature of the City." In *Classic Essays in the Culture of Cities*, Richard Sennett, ed. Appleton-Century-Crofts, New York.

———. 1970. *From Max Weber*. H. Gerth and C. Wright Mills, eds. Routledge, London.

———. 1981. *General Economic History*. Transaction Books, New Brunswick, New Jersey.

———. 2003. *The Protestant Ethic and the Spirit of Capitalism*. Dover Publications, Garden City, New York.

Weik, Terrance. 2004. "Archaeology of the African Diaspora in Latin America." *Historical Archaeology* 38 (1): 32–49.

———. 2007. "Allies, Adversaries and Kin in the African Seminole Communities of Florida: Archaeology at Pilaklikaha." In *Archaeology of Atlantic Africa and the African Diaspora*, Akinwumi Ogundiran and Toyin Falola, eds., pp. 311–31. Indiana University Press, Bloomington.

White, Richard. 1983. *The Roots of Dependency: Subsistence, Environment, and Social Change Among the Choctaws, Pawnees, and Navajos*. University of Nebraska Press, Lincoln.

———. 1991a. *Its Your Misfortune and None of My Own: A New History of the American West*. University of Oklahoma Press, Norman.

———. 1991b. *The Middle Ground: Indians, Empires, and Republics in the Great Lakes Region, 1650–1815*. Cambridge University Press, Cambridge.

Wilentz, Sean. 1984. *Chants Democratic: New York City and the Rise of the American Working Class, 1788–1850*. Oxford University Press, Oxford.

Wilkie, Laurie A. 1995. "Magic and Empowerment on the Plantation: An Archaeological Consideration of African-American Worldview." *Southeastern Archaeology* 14 (2): 136–48.

———. 1996. "Glass-knapping at a Louisiana Plantation: African-American Tools?" *Historical Archaeology* 30 (4): 37–49.

———. 1997. "Secret and Sacred: Contextualizing Artifacts of African-American Magic and Religion." *Historical Archaeology* 31 (4): 81–106.

———. 2000. "Culture Bought: Evidence of Creolization in the Consumer Goods of an Enslaved Bahamian Family." *Historical Archaeology* 34 (3): 10–26.

———. 2000. *Creating Freedom: Material Culture and African American Identity at Oakley Plantation, Louisiana, 1840–1950*. Louisiana State University Press, Baton Rouge.

Wilkie, Laurie, and Kevin Bartoy. 2000. "A Critical Archaeology Revisited." *CURRENT ANTHROPOLOGY* 41 (5): 747–77.

Willey, Gordon R., and Jeremy A. Sabloff. 1993. *A History of American Archaeology, 3rd Ed*. W. H. Freeman, New York.

Williams, Raymond. 1973. "The Country and the City." Oxford University Press, New York.

———. 1976. *Keywords: A Vocabulary of Culture and Society*. Oxford University Press, New York.

Wise, Tim J. 2008. *White Like Me: Reflections on Race from a Privileged Son*. Soft Skull, Brooklyn.

Wittkower, Rudolf. 1971. *Architectural Principles in the Age of Humanism*. W. W. Norton, New York.

Wolf, Eric R. 1982. *Europe and the People Without History*. University of California Press, Berkeley.

———. 1984. "Culture: Panacea or Problem?" *American Antiquity* 49 (2):393–400.
Woodruff, Janet, Gerald F. Sawyer, and Warren R. Perry. 2007. "How Archaeology Exposes the Nature of African Captivity and Freedom in Eighteenth and Nineteenth Century Connecticut." *Connecticut History* 46 (2): 155–83.
Wurst, Lou Ann, and Randall H. McGuire. 1999. "Immaculate Consumption: A Critique of the 'Shop Till You Drop' School of Human Behavior." *International Journal of Historical Archaeology* 3 (3): 191–99.
Yamin, Rebecca. 2001a. "Alternative Narratives: Respectability at New York's Five Points." In *The Archaeology of Urban Landscapes: Explorations in Slumland*, Alan Mayne and Tim Murray, eds., pp. 154–70. Cambridge University Press, Cambridge.
———. 2001b. "From Tanning to Tea: The Evolution of a Neighborhood." *Historical Archaeology* 35 (3): 6–15.
Yentsch, Anne E. 1991. "The Symbolic Dimensions of Pottery: Sex-related Attributes of English and Anglo-American Household Pots." In *The Archaeology of Inequality*, Randall H. McGuire and Robert Paynter, eds., pp. 192–220. Basil Blackwell, Oxford.
———. 1992. "Gudgeons, Mullet, and Proud Pigs: Historicity, Black Fishing, and Southern Myth." In *The Art and Mystery of Historical Archaeology: Essays in Honor of James Deetz*, Anne E. Yentsch and Mary C. Beaudry, eds., pp. 253–315. CRC Press, Boca Raton.
———. 1994. *A Chesapeake Family and Their Slaves: A Study in Historical Archaeology*. Cambridge University Press, Cambridge.
Young, Amy L. 1997. "Risk Management Among African-American Slaves at Locust Grove Plantation." *International Journal of Historical Archaeology* 1 (1): 5–38.
Zimmerman, Larry J. 2007. "Multivocality, Descendent Communities and Some Epistemological Shifts Forced by Repatriation." In *Opening Archaeology: Repatriation's Impact on Contemporary Research and Practice*, Thomas W. Killion, ed., pp. 91–107. SAR Press, Santa Fe.

Index

Abel, Marjorie, 5, 151–53, 155–58
Abstraction, 7, 15–16, 19, 25, 49, 70, 76, 80, 83, 125, 201, 211, 218. *See also* Abstraction of labor
Abstraction of labor, 16, 18, 20–22, 104, 111, 114, 117, 121
African American religion, 182, 188
African Americans, 6–7, 32, 84, 101–2, 123, 151, 177–93, 213–14. *See also* African Diaspora; African Diaspora archaeology; Africans; *Minkisi*
African Burial Ground National Monument, 7, 221–24
African Diaspora, 6, 151, 178–79, 182, 187
African Diaspora archaeology, 178–79, 182
Africans, 84, 178–83, 187–89, 224, 229
Alabama Gates camp, 135, 137
Albany, New York, 29, 47
America, 27–30, 61–63, 71, 84–86, 151, 157, 176, 180, 193–94, 203, 205. *See also* Colonial America
American West, 116, 131–34, 139–41, 143
The American Women's Home (Beecher and Stowe), 163, 165
Annapolis, Maryland, 4, 7, 65–70, 80–82, 197, 208, 211–18. *See also* Bordley, Thomas; Bordley-Randall house; Carroll, Charles; Chase-Lloyd house; Churchill, Winston; Leone, Mark P.; Paca, William; *Richard Carvel*; U.S. Naval Academy; William Paca Garden
Anticultural, 150–51, 203
Archaeology, 1–3, 6, 7, 9–11, 15, 22, 26, 28, 57–58, 61, 85, 86, 87–101, 105, 108, 116, 121–22, 131, 142 –43, 149, 151, 152, 153, 155, 166, 169, 173, 175–76, 177–79, 182, 193, 195–202, 206–8, 210–11, 218, 221, 224–26, 227–30. *See also* African Diaspora archae-

ology; Burials; Cemetery archaeology; Critical archaeology; Historical archaeology; History of archaeology; Landscape; Materialization
Arizona, 5, 132, 136
Authenticity, 2, 9, 11–14, 22

Babbitt, 117–18, 121, 141, 144–48, 230
Baldwin, James, 177, 193–94
Barnum, P. T., 205–6
Barron, Charles, 222–23, 225
Battle, Frank, 129
Beaver pelts, 29, 34
Belmont, Nevada, 133
Bender, Thomas, 85, 202–5
Berger, John, 227–28
Boards of Health, 120, 123, 129
Boott Mills, 123, 128–29
Bordley, Thomas, 4, 65, 67–69, 82, 86, 109
Bordley-Randall house, 65–66
Boston Associates, 124, 128
Brant, Joseph, 52, 54–55
Brant, Molly, 52, 54–55
Brighton, Stephen, 112
Brothels, 139–40
Buckingham, Frederick Charles, Sr., 141
Buckland, William, 80
Bureaucracy, 22, 119–21, 123, 147, 201
Burials, 1, 34–35, 38, 42–44
Butler, Jim, 134–35

California, 5, 132–33, 135, 164
Calvinism, 21
Cambridge Cooperative Housekeeping Society, 164
Canterbury Shakers, 6, 168, 171, 174

Capitalism, 1–26, 27–29, 44, 55, 61, 70, 72, 74, 76–78, 84, 85–91, 94, 96–98, 100–102, 104, 106, 111–15, 116–18, 120–21, 125, 131–32, 142–43, 147, 149–52, 156, 161–62, 167–69, 172–73, 176, 177, 187, 195–98, 201–3, 211–13, 218, 221, 226, 227–30. *See also* Abstraction of labor; Commodification; Commodity; Commodity fetishism; Competition; Culture of capitalism; Exchange-value; Industrial capitalism; Merchants; Private property; Spirit of capitalism; Victorious capitalism
Carroll, Charles, 82
Carter, Howard, 210
Carvel Hall Hotel, 217
Cemetery archaeology, 32–34, 38, 43, 45–47, 221–25
Central Park (New York City), 203–6, 220, 229
Ceramics, 1, 4, 52, 71–76, 78, 96–99, 111–12, 144, 159, 166, 175, 185
Chakrabarty, Dipesh, 201
Chase-Lloyd house, 80–81
Chesapeake, 67–69, 179–80, 214
Childe, V. Gordon, 86–87
Children, 38, 42–44, 65, 77, 94, 100–101, 107, 113–15
Children of capitalism, 100–101
Christianity, 7, 166, 188–89, 193
Churchill, Winston, 216
Clay tobacco pipes, 49, 173
Clinton, DeWitt, 88, 205
Colonial America, 27–56, 57–84
Colonoware, 179–81, 184–85, 229
Commodification, 2, 4, 11–14, 19, 23, 25, 96, 118–19, 149, 156, 187, 196, 221, 228, 230
Commodity, 12, 16, 19, 23, 32, 55, 104, 111, 113, 116–18, 192, 215, 228
Commodity exchange, 27, 30, 57, 116
Commodity fetishism, 3
Communities outside of capitalism, 5, 132, 152, 166
Community, 2, 5–6, 10, 14–15, 17, 19–20, 23, 24, 26, 28, 35, 57–58, 61–62, 64, 65, 68, 69–71, 76, 82, 95, 97, 99, 101, 105, 113, 117–18, 124–26, 129, 132–34, 140, 142–47, 149–50, 152, 158–59, 161–62, 167–70, 173, 176, 180, 183, 187, 191–92, 196, 206, 221–22, 225, 226. *See also* Communities outside of capitalism

Company towns, 5, 135–41
Competition, 18–19, 20, 35, 43, 50–52, 57, 74, 76–77, 88, 101, 102–4, 113, 118, 123, 158, 172
Consumption, 1, 5, 13, 86, 101, 107–11, 117–21, 141–43, 147–48, 161, 221
Contracts, 70–71
Conversion, 16, 188–92
Cooperative housekeeping, 158, 162–63
Corporate paternalism, 124
Country Party, 70
Crane, Brian, 119–23, 147
Creamware, 52, 72–74, 228
Critical archaeology, 25–26, 195
Culture of capitalism, 1, 5–7, 22, 96, 100, 152, 172–73, 196

Dead Long Enough (Hawes), 9, 11, 13, 14
Decorated shed, 208–10
Dedham, Massachusetts, 63
Deetz, James, 4, 58–64, 67, 71–73, 77, 79, 180–82
Deskilling, 152
Dickens, Charles, 104
Disease, 34, 43, 54, 119–20, 123
Domestic sphere, 85, 88, 94, 162
Doss, Erika, 218–20, 222, 224
Douglass, Frederick, 227–29
Downing, Andrew Jackson, 97
DuBois, W.E.B., 177, 191–93
Dutch, 29, 34, 36, 47

Enlightenment, 58, 79, 167, 199–200
Ethnicity, 5, 86, 102–10, 111, 123, 132, 138, 140, 197
Ethnogenesis, 24, 30
Etiquette, 74, 77, 95, 110–11
Exchange-value, 3, 186–87
Expert authority, 202

Fagan, Brian, 198–99
Farrell, Mary, 136
Feminism, 24
Ferguson, Leland, 179–81, 184
Fitts, Robert, 99–100, 108–12
Five Points (New York City), 5, 74, 86, 93, 97, 100–114, 120, 162–63
Fort Hunter, 47–51
Fort Orange, 47–48

Fourier, Charles, 167–68
Freedom, 1, 11–12, 14–15, 16, 18, 19, 23, 70, 114–15, 164, 178, 191–92, 229
Freeman, Sylvia, 189
Fur trade, 27–36, 43–48, 55, 61, 116

Gardens, 4, 58, 71, 79, 81–83, 163, 172, 217. *See also* Landscape
Gender, 18, 86–87, 150, 158, 162, 197, 202
General Trades Union, 89
Georgian architecture, 72, 75, 79–82
Georgian Order, 59, 61, 64, 67, 71–72, 79–80, 85, 116. *See also* Georgian architecture
Gillespie, William, 136
Glassie, Henry, 58, 62, 64
Gothic Revival, 96–98
Gowans, Alan, 59, 79
Great Awakening, 82
Greek Revival, 91
Griggs, Heather, 106–9, 114
Grumet, Robert, 47, 51–52, 54
Guldenzopf, David, 49–50, 52

Hall, Martin, 108–11
Hammon, Jupiter, 189–92
Hancock, Massachusetts, 169, 172
Hartford, Connecticut, 36–37, 165, 189
Hawes, James, 9–14, 25–26
Hayden, Delores, 167–73
Hidden transcripts, 150, 152, 157
Historical archaeology, 1, 2, 7, 10, 24–25, 28, 58, 65, 84, 100, 197, 202, 227–28
History of archaeology, 6, 7, 196, 198–202
Houses, 10, 49–50, 57–58, 61–71, 79, 81–83, 96, 93, 101–4, 120, 122, 135, 145, 164, 169, 180, 183, 218
Howard University, 222

Ideology, 6, 10–12, 18–21, 55–57, 61, 71, 78, 79, 80, 83, 91
Immigrants, 5, 101–2, 106, 109–10, 144, 157
Inclusion and exclusion, 4, 29, 54, 98
Individualism, 1, 11–12, 15, 18–19, 56, 58, 73, 116, 149, 151, 158, 172, 192, 221, 230. *See also* Possessive individualism
Industrial capitalism, 85, 142, 147, 149, 156
Industrial cowboys, 134
Industrial Revolution, 157

Irish, 5, 102, 105–12, 177
Iroquois Six Nations, 29

Johnson, William, 52–54
Jonathan Fairbanks house, 63
Jordan, Kurt, 49–51

Kanienke, 47–51

Landscape, 57, 65, 67, 81, 90, 102, 104, 126, 128, 136, 139, 158, 163, 168–69, 172, 183, 208, 217–18. *See also* Gardens; Georgian architecture; Houses
Las Vegas, 7, 197, 208–11
Lawrence Company, 128
Leon, Rodney, 222–23
Leone, Mark P., 4, 58–59, 71, 78, 81–83, 185
Lewis, Sinclair, 117
Long Island, 36–37, 189, 191
Lowell, Massachusetts, 5, 120, 123, 152
Lowell Offering (newspaper), 123–24
The Luxor, 209–11
Lynch, Timothy, 109

MacCannell, Dean, 224
MacPherson, C. B., 1, 18, 59, 78
Maintenance relations, 64, 69–70, 145
Manners, 58, 78
Marx, Karl, 1–3, 9, 11, 14–26, 87, 94, 98, 121, 147, 228
Marxist anthropology, 14
Massachusetts, 5, 34, 36, 62–63, 75, 120, 123, 126, 152–53, 163, 169
Matched sets, 73–79, 107, 111
Materialization, 227–30
Mayne, Alan, 105
McGill, Nevada, 135, 138, 147
McGuire, Randall, 9, 13, 79, 132, 141, 152, 196, 225
Memorials, 218–21
Mendiola family, 144–46
Merchant, Ida, 143
Merchant, John, 143
Merchants, 4, 69, 82, 88, 90, 112, 131, 133, 142–44, 217
Miantonomi, 36–37, 47, 54–55
Middle class, 87, 100, 105, 109–11, 123, 146, 200–201, 232

Miller, George, 73, 76, 112
Mining camps, 5, 136, 147
Minkisi, 185–86
Modernity, 23, 59–64, 94, 213
Mohawks, 4, 32, 47–55
Mohegans, 36–37
Mott farmhouse, 67–68
Mrozowski, Stephen, 123–25, 128, 131, 147, 156
Murray, Tim, 105

Narragansetts, 4, 32–38, 42–47, 51, 54–55. *See also* RI-1000
Nassaney, Michael, 5, 29, 34, 152–58
Native American, 4, 24, 28–34, 36, 46, 55, 57, 177, 180–81, 224
Natural law, 58, 79, 196
Nevada, 5, 117, 133, 135, 138, 141, 144, 197, 208, 210, 230
New England, 28, 34, 46–47, 63, 124, 151, 164
New England Public Kitchen, 164
New Hampshire, 168–70, 173
New Harmony, Indiana, 167
New Orleans, 188
New York City, 4, 74, 85–115, 189, 219–23, 228. *See also* African Burial Ground National Monument; Central Park; Five Points; Trinity Church
North American Phalanx, 168
North Kingstown, Rhode Island, 34

Oakley Plantation, 189
Olmstead, Frederick Law, 94, 203
Owen, Robert, 177

Paca, William, 81–82, 84, 88, 216–18
Palatine German, 50
Paradise, Nevada, 117, 141–47, 230
Paynter, Robert, 23, 179
Pearlware, 73–75
Pequot War, 36
Pierce, Melusina Fay, 163–66
Pleasant Hill, Kentucky, 174
Plymouth, Massachusetts, 34
Portsmouth, Rhode Island, 68–69
Possessive individualism, 1, 78–79
Prestige, 35, 53
Private property, 18–19, 22, 25, 51, 116, 117

Privy, 114, 138
Probate, 10, 69–73, 142
Profit, 1, 5–6, 14, 16, 20–21, 68, 83, 87, 99, 124–25, 130–31, 147, 149, 208
Public culture, 22, 202–3, 207, 220–21
Purser, Margaret, 116–17, 141–46

Raboteau, Albert, 183, 191–94
Race, 18, 124, 151, 170, 176–80, 197
Racism, 151, 178, 182, 185, 187–89, 192, 224
Randall, Alexander, 212–13, 214
Reckner, Paul, 100, 108–10, 132, 141
Red Bank, New Jersey, 178
Reinhart Ranch, 144, 146
Reipetown, 138–40, 147
Resistance, 5–7, 24, 32, 45, 116–17, 131–32, 149–76, 177–94, 229
Revolution, 19, 23, 26, 58, 59, 61, 85, 86–87, 150
Rhode Island State Prison, 156
RI-1000 (Narragansett cemetery site), 32–33, 38, 43–44, 46–47, 51, 54. *See also* Narragansetts
Richard Carvel (Churchill), 216–17
Ridout, John, 82
Robson, Eliza, 159
Rubertone, Patricia, 34, 37–38, 43–46
Russell Cutlery Factory, 5, 153, 155

Saloon, 108–9, 136, 138–40
Sanitation, 5, 118–23, 128–29
Sayer, Derek, 16–18, 21, 26, 30, 201
Schulyer, Peter, 52
Sedgwick, Catherine, 94
Shackel, Paul, 25, 57–58, 68, 77, 81, 150, 152, 197, 225
Shaker myth, 173, 176
Shakers, 6, 168–70, 173–76
Sider, Gerald, 14, 30–31
Snow, Dean, 52–53
The Souls of Black Folk, 191–92
Specialization, 86–88, 94, 104, 121
Spencer-Wood, Suzanne, 151, 158, 162–63
Spirit of capitalism, 19–20, 114, 152
Starbuck, David, 6, 151, 168–76
Steptoe City, 138–39, 147
St. George, Robert Blair, 64–65
Symonds, James, 147

Tammany Hall, 109
Tarlow, Sarah, 125
Teàware, 52, 95–96, 112, 159, 161
Thomas, Peter, 35
Thomas, Rev. Abel, 123
Tiononderoge, 48
Tonopah, Nevada, 133–34
Toys, 114–15
Trigger, Bruce, 196, 198–200
Trinity Church (New York City), 98

Uncas, 37
United States, 5–7, 10, 24, 91, 100, 104, 124–25, 150, 162, 164–66, 178, 188–89, 192, 208, 211, 232, 235–40, 243–44, 246
Upper Castle site, 48, 52
Upton, Dell, 183
Urban revolution, 86–87, 94
Use-value, 3, 15–16, 96, 111
U.S. Naval Academy, 212
Utopian societies, 59, 151

Van Bueren, Thad, 137
Vernacular, 62–63, 79
Victorious capitalism, 4, 115–48
Virginia, 180–81, 183
Vodou, 188–89

Wall, Diana diZerega, 89, 94, 158–59
Wampum, 35–36, 43–45, 228
Washington, D.C., 122, 147
Weber, Max, 11, 15, 20, 121, 201
White, Richard, 143
William Paca Garden, 81
Winnemucca, Nevada, 142
Wolf, Eric, 1, 9, 14, 27–29, 34
Women, 6, 44, 46, 54, 86, 88, 94, 96, 98–99, 106, 139–40, 144, 150, 151, 158–66, 168, 172, 229
Working class, 100–101, 104–5, 108, 201

Yamin, Rebecca, 5, 74, 86, 97, 100–105, 107

Christopher N. Matthews is professor of anthropology at Montclair State University. He is the author of *An Archaeology of History and Tradition: Moments of Danger in the Annapolis Landscape* and coeditor of *Ethnographic Archaeologies: Reflections on Stakeholders and Archaeological Practices*.

The American Experience in Archaeological Perspective
Michael S. Nassaney, Founding Editor
Krysta Ryzewski, Co-editor

The American Experience in Archaeological Perspective series was established by the University Press of Florida and founding editor Michael S. Nassaney in 2004. This prestigious historical archaeology series focuses attention on a range of significant themes in the development of the modern world from an Americanist perspective. Each volume explores an event, process, setting, institution, or geographic region that played a formative role in the making of the United States of America as a political, social, and cultural entity. These comprehensive overviews underscore the theoretical, methodological, and substantive contributions that archaeology has made to the study of American history and culture. Rather than subscribing to American exceptionalism, the authors aim to illuminate the distinctive character of the American experience in time and space. While these studies focus on historical archaeology in the United States, they are also broadly applicable to historical and anthropological inquiries in other parts of the world. To date the series has produced more than two dozen titles. Prospective authors are encouraged to contact the Series Editors to learn more

The Archaeology of Collective Action, by Dean J. Saitta (2007)
The Archaeology of Institutional Confinement, by Eleanor Conlin Casella (2007)
The Archaeology of Race and Racialization in Historic America, by Charles E. Orser Jr. (2007)
The Archaeology of North American Farmsteads, by Mark D. Groover (2008)
The Archaeology of Alcohol and Drinking, by Frederick H. Smith (2008)
The Archaeology of American Labor and Working-Class Life, by Paul A. Shackel (2009; first paperback edition, 2011)
The Archaeology of Clothing and Bodily Adornment in Colonial America, by Diana DiPaolo Loren (2010; first paperback edition, 2011)
The Archaeology of American Capitalism, by Christopher N. Matthews (2010; first paperback edition, 2012)
The Archaeology of Forts and Battlefields, by David R. Starbuck (2011; first paperback edition, 2012)
The Archaeology of Consumer Culture, by Paul R. Mullins (2011; first paperback edition, 2012)
The Archaeology of Antislavery Resistance, by Terrance M. Weik (2012; first paperback edition, 2013)
The Archaeology of Citizenship, by Stacey Lynn Camp (2013; first paperback edition, 2019)
The Archaeology of American Cities, by Nan A. Rothschild and Diana diZerega Wall (2014; first paperback edition, 2015)
The Archaeology of American Cemeteries and Gravemarkers, by Sherene Baugher and Richard F. Veit (2014; first paperback edition, 2015)
The Archaeology of Smoking and Tobacco, by Georgia L. Fox (2015; first paperback edition, 2016)

The Archaeology of Gender in Historic America, by Deborah L. Rotman (2015; first paperback edition, 2018)

The Archaeology of the North American Fur Trade, by Michael S. Nassaney (2015; first paperback edition, 2017)

The Archaeology of the Cold War, by Todd A. Hanson (2016; first paperback edition, 2019)

The Archaeology of American Mining, by Paul J. White (2017; first paperback edition, 2020)

The Archaeology of Utopian and Intentional Communities, by Stacy C. Kozakavich (2017; first paperback edition, 2023)

The Archaeology of American Childhood and Adolescence, by Jane Eva Baxter (2019)

The Archaeology of Northern Slavery and Freedom, by James A. Delle (2019)

The Archaeology of Prostitution and Clandestine Pursuits, by Rebecca Yamin and Donna J. Seifert (2019; first paperback edition, 2023)

The Archaeology of Southeastern Native American Landscapes of the Colonial Era, by Charles R. Cobb (2019)

The Archaeology of the Logging Industry, by John G. Franzen (2020)

The Archaeology of Craft and Industry, by Christopher C. Fennell (2021)

The Archaeology of the Homed and the Unhomed, by Daniel O. Sayers (2023)

The Archaeology of Contemporary America, by William R. Caraher (2024)

The Historical Archaeology of the Pacific Northwest, by Douglas C. Wilson (2024)

The Archaeology of American Medicine and Healthcare, by Meredith Reifschneider (2025)

The Archaeology of American Protests, by April M. Beisaw and Dania Jordan-Talley (2025)

The Historical Archaeology of Michigan, by Dean L. Anderson, Michael S. Nassaney, and Krysta Ryzewski (2025)

The Historical Archaeology of Massachusetts, Joseph Bagley and Holly Herbster (2026)

www.ingramcontent.com/pod-product-compliance
Lightning Source LLC
LaVergne TN
LVHW040614250326
834688LV00035B/556